100

Oklahoma Outlaws, Gangsters, and Lawmen

100
Oklahoma Outlaws, Gangsters, and Lawmen
1839-1939

DAN ANDERSON WITH LAURENCE YADON

EDITED BY ROBERT BARR SMITH

PELICAN PUBLISHING COMPANY
GRETNA 2010

First printing, April 2007
Second printing, September 2007
Third printing, December 2010

Library of Congress Cataloging-in-Publication Data

Anderson, Dan, 1950-
100 Oklahoma outlaws, gangsters, and lawmen : 1839-1939 / Dan
Anderson with Laurence Yadon ; edited By Robert Barr Smith.
    p. cm.
Includes bibliographical references and index.
ISBN 978-1-58980-384-8 (pbk. : alk. paper)
1. Crime—Oklahoma—History—Case studies. 2. Outlaws—Oklahoma—
Biography. 3. Gangsters—Oklahoma—Biography. 4. Law enforcement—
Oklahoma—History. 5. Peace officers—Oklahoma—Biography. 6.
Oklahoma—History. I. Yadon, Laurence J., 1948- II. Smith, Robert B.
(Robert Barr), 1933- III. Title. IV. Title: One hundred Oklahoma outlaws,
gangsters, and lawmen.
    HV6793.O5A63 2007
    364.1092'2766—dc22
                                                    2007003531

Printed in the United States of America

Published by Pelican Publishing Company, Inc.
1000 Burmaster Street, Gretna, Louisiana 70053

Contents

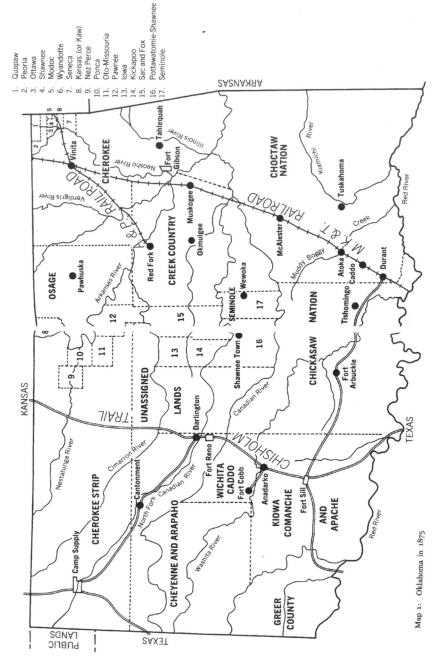

Map 1: Oklahoma in 1875

(Courtesy of University of Oklahoma Press)

1. Quapaw
2. Peoria
3. Ottawa
4. Shawnee
5. Modoc
6. Wyandotte
7. Seneca
8. Kansas (or Kaw)
9. Nez Perce
10. Ponca
11. Oto-Missouria
12. Pawnee
13. Iowa
14. Kickapoo
15. Sac and Fox
16. Pottawatomie-Shawnee
17. Seminole

Preface

Our goal in this project has been to present a fresh if unconventional examination of the entire story of Oklahoma outlawry from the earliest days of Indian Territory to the death of the last criminally active member of the Barker gang in 1939. We have covered one hundred years in all, in a series of biographical essays and profiles of individuals who are significant to this story.

In essence, we have explored criminal history within Oklahoma, as well as famous crimes committed elsewhere by Oklahomans, such as the Barker gang, Pretty Boy Floyd, and Machine Gun Kelly, relying upon the well-researched books and articles of established writers who focus on the West. Perhaps the most enjoyable part of developing this book was exploring the remarkable, yet little known Oklahoma connections of legendary figures such as Wyatt Earp, Billy the Kid, John Dillinger, and Baby Face Nelson.

The knowledgeable reader will find that we have often relied upon familiar, predictable sources and traditional versions of events. However, in some instances we have rejected traditional narratives or at least have also related alternative versions of events, relying upon recent scholarship or often neglected sources that appeared credible to us. Since this is intended to be a work of popular history rather than of serious scholarship, in those instances where traditional tales appeared questionable to us we have usually said so, without necessarily exploring our reasoning.

Our efforts have been thoughtfully guided by our consulting editor, noted author Robert Barr Smith (*Daltons!* and *Last Hurrah of the James-Younger Gang*) who has been of great assistance. Nevertheless, the judgments we have made regarding the relative credibility of competing sources and in sifting fact from mythology have been our own.

Dan Anderson, Katy, Texas
Laurence Yadon, Tulsa, Oklahoma
January 2006

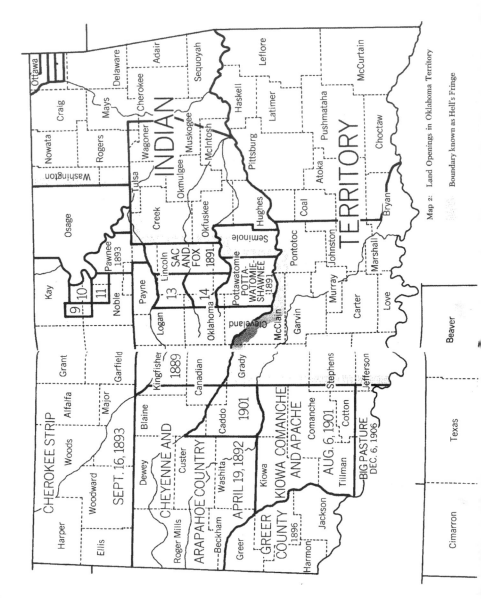

Map 2: Land Openings in Oklahoma Territory

Boundary known as Hell's Fringe

Introduction

Texas Jack had reinvented himself on the dusty paths that passed for streets in frontier Tulsa, only to be blown off his feet in a gunfight with Marshal Tom Stufflebeam. The deadly feud had started casually enough, when Stufflebeam insulted the horse that Texas Jack rode in on. Mortally wounded and carried to a nearby house, he refused to reveal his true identity even at the very end, preserving that measure of independence as his last possession.

Oklahomans of all backgrounds still value that sense of independence, opportunity, and freedom offered by this almost new state. November 16, 2007 will mark one hundred years of statehood for this land, which was created from the marriage of the Indian and Oklahoma Territories.

From the beginning, outlaws mercilessly exploited that very freedom and independence for ill purposes. In the early years there was very little legal infrastructure at all in the two territories. The brave deputy U.S. marshals and lighthorse and Indian police that constituted law enforcement were virtually on their own from day to day. A significant number of deputy U.S. marshals who left Fort Smith, Arkansas, to pursue outlaws in the territories met violent ends.

Outlawry of course existed long before the Twin Territories were even thought of. The term "outlaw" did not originate in the American West, but in the north of England, Scotland, and Ireland, as an apt description of those who opposed the Crown and sometimes, as was said at the time, "died with their boots on." It is fair to say however, that the outlaw tradition was perpetuated in Oklahoma.

This work examines those individuals who carried on the outlaw tradition in the early territories, those who transitioned into the age of the automobile and telephones, and the gangsters who operated in the Depression years. The lawmen who pursued them, to whom this book is dedicated, are also profiled here.

We begin then with the story of the first recorded gang of serial rapists in the American West and perhaps America. These were the despicable adolescents known as the Rufus Buck gang.

Chapter 1

Rufus Buck:
A Man Too Bad for Hollywood

Indian Territory was a kind of "land of the second chance" for the many Native Americans who, by treaty, treachery, or both, wound up there. They were determined to start anew with homesteads, farms, and mercantile operations comparable to those they had been forced to abandon in the Southeast as a result of the Indian Removal Act of the late 1830s. In the new territory they formed governments that closely resembled that of the United States. They set up courts, justices, councils, and even their own police forces called the lighthorse. The tribes hoped they would be alone to govern themselves without the influence or interference of the white man.

Greed and the lust for power proved to be harmful to the tribes. Little more than sixty years after being granted their new lands, to include sovereign governance, white settlers would flood the territories. The Indian nations, as they were called, would once again be forced to bow in submission. Perhaps it was in dread of this event that some in Indian Territory resisted the white incursions, mostly through legal means.

Against this background one young Indian, Rufus Buck, vowed to teach the white man a lesson and dissuade him from wanting to step into Indian Territory ever again. What he couldn't have imagined was that his actions and the actions of the four who rode with him would bring about a call for his lynching even by his Native American brothers.

Believing he saw a pattern of entrepreneurial and political aggression oppressive to his fellow countrymen, Buck's anger rose to a monumental rage. Only too short a time earlier, he had learned through tribal lore that his people had been forced from land they had held for hundreds of years until the whites came and took it from them. Apparently Buck vowed that he would not stand idly by and watch that happen again.

Rufus Buck has been described as both a full-blood Euchee Indian and as a mixed-breed who was also part black.[1] The Euchee tribe had allied itself with the Creeks before the forced removal to Indian Territory. He was born on the family farm some distance southeast of Tulsa near present-day Leonard. He grew to be a stocky young man who sported a plumage of black hair and hot, black eyes. For a time young Rufus attended the white-run mission school at Wealaka, established in 1881, one year after the town itself was founded. Wealaka town was situated about two miles northwest of Leonard near the tributary of the Arkansas River made up of the joined Duck and Snake Creeks. Wealaka is a Creek word meaning, "rising water."[2]

Like many schools in the territory, Wealaka Mission insisted that its student body, comprised mainly of Indians, speak English only. No Native American language was allowed either in the classroom or on the playground. Adult monitors usually enforced the English-only rule, and consequences for violators were swift and memorable. The mission was run by Superintendent S. P. Callahan whose son, Benton, ran the U-Bar Ranch southeast of Okmulgee. Old man Callahan was a strict disciplinarian. Rufus was a constant if not blatant violator of the Callahan-instituted rule of language at the mission, to the point that he was branded a "mean boy" and summarily expelled by Callahan. Little could the old schoolmaster have known what smoldering hatred he had fanned.

Not really an experienced criminal at that point in his life, Buck nonetheless found company with two who were: Lewis Davis and Luckey Davis, not related, except by deed. The trio got along famously, stealing hogs and horses and going on wild drinking binges, getting so sloppily drunk that strangers came across various articles of clothing and even the lads' gun belts. Despite the gang's stupidity in carrying out thievery, Buck avoided charges until deputy United States marshals served him with a warrant for introducing liquor into Indian Territory. Buck was tried, convicted, and sentenced. He served ninety days in jail at Fort Smith, Arkansas, where he earned trusty status by displaying "exemplary" behavior, something he apparently couldn't do at Wealaka Mission.

While serving his sentence at the Fort Smith jail Buck's passion for making his mark on the territories as a patriot (in his mind), but more precisely as a criminal, were fed by a cellmate of known evil repute. Nineteen-year-old Crawford Goldsby, otherwise known as

Cherokee Bill, was awaiting his own hanging for the shooting death of an innocent bystander during a robbery at Lenapah.

Buck had perhaps long heard of and was deeply impressed by the predations of Cherokee Bill and his cohorts, the Bill Cook gang. Buck listened with rapt attention as Cherokee Bill shared details of his and the gang's many exploits. Buck proved to be a most ardent student.

Buck wasn't out of jail long when he evidently applied some of what he had learned from his idol and was quickly arrested by Deputy Marshal Mark Moore. The charge, Moore told Buck, was that he was suspected of "being mixed up in some cattle stealing" near Okmulgee.[3]

Posseman Zeke Wilson was left with Buck in custody while Moore went off in search of Buck's alleged accomplices in the cattle-stealing business. Wilson proved not very good in matters custodial and while walking his prisoner one fine day came face to face with the business end of his own pistol. Buck had grabbed Wilson's fine, semiautomatic pistol, turned it on the posseman, and boldly strode to freedom. Buck didn't have to be on the "scout" (run) much during his early criminal escapades because his father, John, was only too accommodating with him and his cohorts, allowing them harbor at the family farm, no questions asked. Rufus Buck later recruited two others, making the gang a quintet. They were, as mentioned, Luckey and Lewis Davis and the two new recruits: Sam Sampson and Maomi "Maoma" July, both full-blood Creeks who hailed from the Cussetah tribal town of Tulsey (Tulsa).[4] Buck declared himself leader of the pack. Emboldened by their number, this pride of jackals set out to wreak the havoc that Buck justified as revenge on the white interlopers.

His clan, however, could not have cared less about Buck's apparent passion to rid the Indian Territory of whites.

The gang members swore to an early oath that no matter what the crime, if one committed it they all would commit it. To disobey this solemn promise meant death to the offender at the hands of each of the other gang members.[5]

The band started their collective brigandry with petty grocery store holdups as well as stealing horses and cows from nearby ranches. Buck made sure that his bunch only took from whites or those who sympathized with whites. However, mere thievery wasn't quenching his thirst for reprisal. Soon things turned very ugly.

None of the other gang members seemed to share Buck's outrage at white settlers and those who did business with them. Instead they were more interested in causing pain and outrage to people merely as a form of adolescent fun. Then too, July, Sampson, and the Davises had a tendency to perversions against women.

First, however, the gang robbed and burned several businesses late in the night of July 28, 1895, in the town of Checotah, about thirty miles southeast of Muskogee. Citizens were roused from sleep with gunshots and shouts of "Fire!" The work was later tied to the Buck gang. The next day the entire gang was rumored to be in Okmulgee visiting "Big Nellie's place," where they hung out for a few hours while Buck planned their next move. Before they could put that plan into action, the town marshal, a freedman who also held the position of deputy U.S. marshal and a member of the Creek Lighthorse, got wind of the boys' rumored presence. Marshal John Garrett's detective work would prove both correct and fatal.[6]

Buck's mother was on the back porch of Parkinson's dry goods store when Marshal Garrett came to inquire as to the whereabouts of her son. Just as he approached Buck's mother the young suspect stepped from a barn door and fired several times at the lawman. Garrett was only a few feet from Buck's mother when her son opened fire. Evidently Buck had resolute confidence in his marksmanship. That Garrett should die at the hand of a deranged brat was itself an outrage, but his quick death could be said to have been far better than the fate of the women the gang forced themselves upon.

The next time Buck and his jackals appeared was on August 3. Buck had a longstanding grudge against Dave and Jesse Pigeon, two Indians whom Buck claimed were white sympathizers. The gang set fire to the homes and other buildings on both men's property. Little did they know that a posse was on their heels.

The gang turned northward from the Saturday night rampage and found themselves with time to kill around the small community of Natura, in Okmulgee County, on Sunday, August 4. Buck and Luckey Davis watched as a wagon drew near. At the reins was old man Ayers. His daughter sat beside him. Buck knew the Ayers to be a white family living in the Seminole Nation, "invaders" in his demented mind. Springing on the unsuspecting pair Buck and Davis ordered the girl off the wagon at gunpoint. Despite the old man's desperate pleadings the girl was forced to the side of the road where she was raped. Her father was held at gunpoint during the assault. When the rape was concluded she was told she could rejoin her father at the wagon. That freedom was short lived however as just then the remaining three members of the gang rode up and in keeping with their previous oath "one for all and all for one" each took his turn at the girl. Only then did they allow the girl to retake her seat on the wagon with her father. According to an article published in the *Muskogee Phoenix*, Ayers' daughter would be the first woman to die as a result of the abuse suffered from the Buck gang.[7]

The gang later happened on one Jim Shafey who was riding along a trail that followed Berryhill Creek, not more than eight miles from Muskogee. Shafey was a white timber dealer in Indian Territory. Buck saw him and others of his kind as interlopers and was quick to show his disgust.

As the mounted gang sauntered up next to Shafey he was knocked from his saddle by a ferocious blow from the butt of Buck's Winchester. After nearly an hour of all manner of abuse at the hands of the hyenas, a vote was taken as to whether or not to kill Shafey. Remarkably, a three-to-two vote against murdering Shafey spared his life. However Shafey lost his horse, saddle, bridle, fifty dollars, and a gold watch to the brigands before being allowed to flee on foot.

Robberies and attempted robberies were the order of the day for the Buck gang. They rode toward Sapulpa from Berryhill Creek and came to the ranch of Gus Chambers. There they intended to help themselves to some fresh horses without, of course, negotiating a deal with Chambers. After a brief firefight in which Chambers staunchly defended his property, the gang came away with only one horse. No one was wounded during that late-night gun battle even though the walls of Chambers' house were riddled.[8]

At some point during the gang's visit to Sapulpa that week, all five forcibly raped a Native American girl. If an article in the *Muskogee Phoenix* is to be believed, she would become the second woman to die from the pack's attack.

The territorial terror continued, as travelers were being accosted, robbed, taunted, and abused. One man, Benton Callahan, the son of Wealaka Mission superintendent S. P. Callahan who had expelled Buck from that school, was targeted for abuse. Bent Callahan and a young black cowhand named Sam Houston, were driving a small herd back to the U-Bar Ranch. The plan was to pen the cattle and prepare them for shipping to auction. Suddenly Callahan, Houston, and the cattle were startled with the whoops and gunshots of a fast-riding bunch coming straight for them. Houston's horse was hit and crumpled to the ground beneath him, dead. Houston made a run for it, but a slug in the shoulder ended his escape. Believing he was dead the gang paid no more attention to him.

Callahan was hit too when a bullet ripped off a piece of his ear. Surrounding the bleeding rancher and assuming they had killed Houston, Buck growled, "Your ol' man kicked me out of school. I ought to have the boys kill you too." Houston did in fact recover from his wound.[9]

This time after a vote was suggested on whether or not to murder Callahan, none was taken. Instead he was robbed of money, horse and tack, his boots and hat, and his clothes. He was told to "git!" and he did so under the added incentive of the gang firing at him as he fled, naked, into the brush.[10]

The Buck gang's activities had captured the attention of just about every person in the territory, and even the Creeks grew hostile with the gang's practices. Buck and his bunch were considered the worst scourge Indian Territory had ever seen—bar none.

Posses began forming all over the territory. More than a hundred outraged citizens of the Creek Nation took up arms in search of the marauders. The Creek Lighthorse, led by Capt. Edmund Harry, was closing the distance to the homicidal rapists. Noted Deputy U.S. Marshals Paden Tolbert and Bud Ledbetter were hot on the trail as well. With them were deputies Zeke Wilson, whose semiautomatic pistol Buck now carried, and William Frank Jones.

Today, at 225 1/2 N. Rosedale, in Tulsa, near where West Edison Street forms a perfectly straight border between Tulsa and Osage Counties, is the former home of Deputy Marshal Jones. Jones published his memoirs of the event from his Tulsa home on April 19, 1937.[11]

At age sixty-five when he was interviewed, Jones's memory may have begun to fail. He is quoted as saying the Buck gang consisted of seven men. Jones did state with clarity that the gang raped a farmer's wife who lived just four miles southeast of old man Buck's place, about ten miles from Okmulgee. The woman, a Mrs. Smith, was on horseback, Jones states, on her way to Okmulgee when "she was seized by the outlaws and raped." Jones hid out on the Buck ranch for three days hoping to capture the Buck boy, but he never made an appearance, Jones said.[12]

Buck and his collection of brigands continued to commit atrocities of the worst kind with wild abandon, but their days were numbered. Respectable citizens of the Creek Nation took up arms and mounted horses, mules, and wagons in pursuit of them. The Buck gang didn't yet know it but their fate was perilously close to ending in a harsh form of frontier justice: mob rule.

For all the dastardly crimes the quintet of degenerates committed, no singular aggression toward another human being more galvanized the community against the thugs than the rape of Rosetta Hassan.

From the dense brush-covered bottoms along Snake Creek somewhat north of Okmulgee, Henry Hassan carved a modest farm. He spent many long, back-breaking days clearing a spot of scrub oak and thorn-laden wild berry bushes. Upon this plot of land he would build a comfortable log house. Living with him in that house was his wife, Rosetta, their three tots, and Rosetta's aging mother. Adjacent to the house Henry had constructed an arbor, the perfect place for a hard-working frontiersman to catch a little summertime midday shut-eye while the wife and mother-in-law put up fruit for the winter ahead.

On a hot day in August, the family was so engaged when their attention turned to five horsemen who passed through Hassan's gate and headed up to the house. Court records would show that the attack on the Hassan family occurred on the fifth. As the riders drew near, Henry Hassan first recognized Luckey Davis. He and Davis had exchanged words sometime during a recent encounter. The family man became alarmed and whispered for Rosetta to take her mother and the children inside the house. Rosetta instantly obeyed, hustling the brood and the elderly woman inside.

The riders stopped at the nearby well. Henry couldn't help but recall an earlier incident in which he and the unpredictable Buck also had a disagreement. Buck had spewed his usual venomous remarks about white invaders and how the Creek tribal laws were of little help in dealing with them.[13] Hassan had dismissed the remarks, but now he was beginning to question the wisdom of disagreeing with either of the two young men.

Hassan stood up from the cot he was napping on under the arbor and greeted his "company" courteously. Buck responded only by saying he wanted a drink of water. As Hassan neared the well to fetch a pail for the gang, he was aware that several of the gang had quietly dismounted and surrounded him. Henry evaluated the situation and realizing his predicament began backing toward a corner of the house. If he could get there he could dart inside and grab his Winchester.

Henry did reach the corner of the house where he bolted for the door and the relief of his waiting Winchester. Just as Henry started through the door, Maomi July appeared, blocking his path. July brushed Henry's face with the coveted rifle. Apparently Maomi had slipped from his horse and entered the Hassan home unnoticed through another door.

Henry turned, and there stood Sampson holding a six-gun on him. Henry backed away from the house door, and Buck rode up and announced, "I'm Cherokee Bill's brother. We want your money."[14]

Were it only money the gang wanted Henry would have likely been only too happy to give them all he could muster. Henry was ordered at gunpoint to sit in a corner of the room where they could keep an eye on him. Fearing for his family, he obeyed. Next, Rosetta and her mother were told in terms vile and despicable to stir up some grub. They too complied with the outlaws' demands. Busying themselves with thrashing about in the house on the hunt for loot, the gang managed to confiscate a whopping $5.95. Not satisfied with the paltry sum collected, the criminals decided to take a suit of men's clothing, some baby dresses, and anything else they thought useful. Luckey Davis, who kept his gun trained on Henry all this time, was eventually given his turn at the table after the rest of the group had finished eating.

Rosetta had hoped that by unquestioningly and promptly serving the outlaws a meal of eggs, meat, and coffee, she and her family would suffer no harm. She too was miles apart from the truth that would be her everlasting terror.

Later, when the incident was recounted at trial, the courtroom of Judge Isaac Parker in Fort Smith would be packed with curious citizens. Henry Hassan had just completed his sworn testimony on that twenty-third day of September, 1895, when a sudden quiet fell over the crowd. Rosetta replaced her husband on the witness stand. Every eye was upon her, every neck stretched to get a glimpse of her, and the silence that followed her was deafening. Rosetta Hassan was about to suffer the public indignation of reliving the most humiliating event of her young life. She would tell all present of her merciless assault and persistent fear of being killed with her husband and children if she failed to comply with the rapists' demands. Facing those five mean little men who took such great pleasure in her torment a second time would be no less horrific than her first time.

Her head lowered, she spoke in a soft, disturbed manner. The edginess she bore was felt by the entire courtroom. Through quiet sobs she told, as her husband had done before her, of seeing the riders come up to the house, the asking for water, the hurriedly prepared meal, and her constant fear for the safety of her husband and children. In order to convict, the jury needed to hear her tell of the multiple rapes in her own words. She was gently urged to do so. Thus she began to relive the event one more unbearable time.

She said that after all the riders had eaten, and with her husband still under guard by at least three of the five men at all times, Luckey Davis said to her, "You have to go with me." She told of how she frantically pleaded with Davis not to take her away from her "babies"; how he retorted with, "We'll throw the god dam brats in the creek"; how he told her to get up on his horse and ride off with him; and how she convinced him she couldn't ride—anything to delay the inevitable.

Davis then commanded her to walk "a little ways" with him. She hesitated, but believing death for her family would result from her refusal, Rosetta allowed herself to be taken from the sight of them. She told of how Davis kept the muzzle of the rifle at the back of her head as the two marched off some two hundred feet from the house.

She said that when they reached a barn at that distance he forced her to the back of it. Then she told of how Davis laid the rifle down, pulled a pistol from his belt, and, "told me to lie down."[15]

Then Rosetta completely fell apart. Her sobbing became uncontrollable. S. W. Harman, who witnessed the trial and wrote about it in his book, *Hell on the Border,* said that "her frame shook with convulsions and she sobbed like a child, yet as a child could not."[16]

There were not many women in the courtroom that day, but those who were there were overcome with compassion and grief for the witness. Harman also wrote that even the old "hanging judge" himself, Judge Isaac C. Parker, pulled off his glasses and "while suspicious moisture twinkled upon his glasses, drew a handkerchief from his pocket, wiped the lenses, then spoke a few words of gentle encouragement to the witness."[17]

Rosetta continued and told how when Davis had satisfied his lust the others came each one at a time to ravish her. All the while at least three of the waiting monsters surrounded Henry Hassan with rifles leveled at his skull, threatening to blow his brains out if he so much as whimpered.[18]

The jury didn't even deliberate. They chose a foreman, John N. Furgeson, and he signed the unanimous decision, which was then read in open court. His voice was the only sound heard after Rosetta's testimony. "We, the jury, find the defendants, Rufus Buck, Lewis Davis, Luckey Davis, Sam Sampson, and Maoma July guilty of rape, as charged in within indictment," Furgeson pronounced.[19]

The gang had been captured on or about August 10 after a massive manhunt took place involving the entire force of the Creek Lighthorse police, United States deputy marshals, county sheriffs, and hundreds of armed, fighting-mad citizens of the Creek Nation. Rufus Buck and the gang never appeared more confident than on the day they were captured.

They had just robbed two stores northwest of Okmulgee. They rode to a place called Flat Rock, nothing more than a knoll overlooking the countryside about a mile and half southwest of Preston. There they let their horses graze while they split up the loot. They did so with much squabbling, even after Buck reminded them that he was the leader and would therefore decide how the spoils were to be divided.

While the five outlaws were boisterously arguing their claims, three posses rode up on them. One of the posses was the lighthorse, led by Capt. Edmund Harry. A second posse included Deputy U.S. Marshals Bud Ledbetter, Paden Tolbert, and W. F. Jones. The third party was made up of a hundred or so outraged private citizens, led by C. G. Sloan.[20]

Having failed to post a lookout, the boys were surprised and scattered when the first gunshot sounded. While running to take cover atop Flat Rock with its many trees, one of the outlaws fired a round that passed through the hat of Captain Harry, grazing his head. The concussion knocked Harry from his horse, but he sustained no real injury and took up the good fight.

The gang was surrounded. They had plenty of ammunition, acquired earlier the same day at the unwilling generosity of Mr. Knobbles' dry goods store near Okmulgee. The roaring gun battle lasted seven hours. It probably could have lasted much longer except for the actions of one Indian elder who had had enough. Glenn Shirley in his book, *Thirteen Days of Terror,* says the wily fighter's name was "Shansey." Shirley writes that Shansey boldly rose from the rock protecting him and declared; "I've had enough of this."

A dynamite cartridge has been described as a rifle cartridge whose lead tip has been drilled just enough for dynamite to be inserted inside it. Once fired, upon striking an object presumably hard enough to cause friction or a spark, the dynamite explodes.

Old Shansey had one of those dynamite cartridges handy. As he stood up, declaring his frustration at the prolonged gun battle, he shoved it into the chamber of his rifle, took quick aim, and squeezed the trigger. It sped straight for a tree behind which Buck took cover. On impact the cartridge exploded. Fragments cut at Buck's gun belt, so shocking the outlaw that he threw down his rifle and ran.

Seeing their frightened leader loping down the hill, the others followed suit. Scampering away from the posse of marshals and lighthorsemen, they ran straight into the waiting arms of C. G. Sloan and his eager citizen possemen. Lewis Davis, the only individual hit, escaped the fray. He was later captured.[21]

So reviled were the gang members, that on more than one occasion and in more than one town the gang was under constant threat of a lynching. In Okmulgee, where the gang was initially jailed, hundreds of outraged men crowded the steps of the courthouse, calling for swift justice by means of a short rope. It was the same everywhere they went. In Okmulgee a seething crowd of armed men, disappointed that they couldn't get to the gang for a real hanging, strung up a dummy on an electric light pole, temporarily satisfying their blood thirst. Finally, in the dead of night, deputies managed to whisk their charges to Fort Smith. Even there, mob rule was gaining popularity.

Marshal Samuel Rutherford and his chief deputy, a man named McDonald, kept cool heads in the midst of the citizens' call for the prisoners to be turned over to the mob. Rutherford finally dispersed the crowd by declaring convincingly, "If you rush the jail, some of you will die."

Judge Parker sentenced the gang to die by hanging on October 31, 1895. An appeal to the United States Supreme Court was a wasted effort. That court at once refused to intervene. Part of their time awaiting execution was given over to devotions and instructions from Father Pius, a pastor of the German Catholic Church. The entire Buck gang was later baptized.[22]

The hanging was not a public affair as were most at Fort Smith. Only relatives of the condemned, relatives of the victims, and lawmen, reporters, and Father Pius were allowed inside the compound. The sisters of Luckey Davis and Sam Sampson were there, but they left the enclosure at the moment black caps were placed over the condemned men's heads. Luckey Davis asked Father Pius to pray for him, and he did. Rufus's father was stumbling drunk and attempted to ascend the steps of the gallows but was ushered from the area. No one else made a commotion.

As was common among these brigands, even the hour at which they should be hanged was argued over. Luckey Davis insisted that he be hanged at ten thirty in the morning so his corpse could make the eleven-thirty train. Rufus objected, saying that would postpone his carcass's train ride home by several hours. As was their custom, they conducted a vote, and it was decided four to one to allow Marshal George W. Crump to decide the hour. Crump chose one o'clock. Then Davis said he didn't want to be hanged as part of the group, choosing instead to be executed alone. The marshal explained that the court's decision was the final decision, and he could not alter it.

At 1:28 on the afternoon of July 1, 1896, as all five stood with nooses fitted to their necks and black hoods covering their faces, the trap door gave way. Sam Sampson and Maoma July died instantly as their necks broke. Rufus Buck and Luckey Davis died of strangulation. It took three minutes for Lewis Davis to die.[23]

There is a family cemetery on the grounds of the old Buck place not far from Wealaka, but Rufus Buck's body does not lie there. Evidently, while hauling the body from Fort Smith, the family couldn't take the stench of the deceased once the heat of the day began to work on the corpse. They got as far as Fort Gibson where they chose to inter the lad.[24]

Chapter 2

Oklahoma Assassins

Political rivalries are certainly nothing new, but when rivals kill each other, politics takes on a new and disquieting personality.

Recorded political murder in Indian Territory began among its native people as early as 1839. In 1835, a group of Cherokees led by Maj. John Ridge offered to sell their lands to the white man's government for around $20 million, apparently figuring that if they didn't agree to the sale they would likely fall victim to a forced exodus. Eventually Ridge realized that his asking price had fallen on deaf ears and settled for considerably less money. Rather than wait the three years the treaty allowed all Cherokees to evacuate their lands in the eastern states, Ridge and a party of followers left for Indian Territory almost immediately.[1] They encountered a group of Cherokees already ensconced in Arkansas and Indian Territory who, because they had settled those areas prior to the arrival of Ridge and the Treaty Party members, were called "Old Settlers." Each group lived peaceably while maintaining a comfortable existence in the land they now called home. The Treaty and Old Settler factions eventually merged into one.

Only a few short years separated the arrivals of the two factions of Cherokeess in the new lands west of civilization. They in turn were followed to Indian Territory by a third group known as the John Ross faction. Any kindred spirit these three bands had coming to the new territory would soon give way to vile hatred and bloodshed of a raging turf war.

Ridge, his sons and a nephew, Elias Boudinot, wasted no time in networking their way into the Old Settlers' hierarchy and became quite prominent within its ranks. For the politically bent Ridges and Boudinots it was a clever move and one that happened none too soon. For John Ross, principal chief of the Eastern Cherokees, who loathed Ridge's signing of the New Echota Treaty, soon arrived in Indian Territory to survey his tribe's situation.

Having survived the Trail of Tears, the name dispersed Cherokees gave to their forced march from their homelands in Georgia, Alabama, and Tennessee, Ross felt that fate had provided this new territory in which new native lands would be established, and he would lead his people. The only thing standing in the way of Ross's reassuming power was the reluctance of Ridge to move aside. Despite efforts by Ross and Ridge the two factions soon became political enemies whose contentious relationship led to a civil war within the tribe. It wasn't long before the hard feelings erupted, and a bitterly fought rivalry for control of the tribe began with the murders of the three Treaty Party leaders: John Ridge, his son John, and Elias Boudinot. The deaths might have appeared to have been the work of rogue bandits, except that all three were killed miles apart on the same day, June 22, 1839. Clearly these were political assassinations.[2]

Two other members of the party were targeted for assassination but somehow received word of the plan and escaped. John Starr and Stand Watie learned of the conspiracy and made their way to Fort Gibson, the only government outpost in Indian Territory at that time. Watie would later become an officer in the Confederate army, rising to the rank of brigadier general.[3] James Starr, a forebear of Henry Starr and Belle Starr's husband, Sam, didn't ignore the violence gripping the Cherokees in the years following the 1839 murders of his party members. Instead he chose public office as his way of trumping his murderous political enemies. His brother, Ezekiel Starr, did likewise, and in 1841 the Starr brothers held considerable sway over tribal affairs as members of its legislature.

Ezekiel won a seat representing the Flint District, while James served from the Goingsnake District. But it was the election of James Starr, a known advocate of Cherokee removal in the New Echota Treaty of 1835 and a perceived political opportunist, that rankled the faithful Ross supporters. Those stung by what they saw as the treachery of the original Treaty Party, which Ridge formed, now sought Treaty men's blood. As a result many men died, and the carnage went on unabated for two years. This was the Cherokee Civil War, which pitted the Trail of Tears survivors against the Treaty men not murdered earlier.[4]

Thomas Starr had had enough. James, his father, had been the target of an assassination attempt, and Thomas was poised to take action against those who wanted his father dead. Thomas Starr is credited with the slaughter, if the accounts are true, of a trader named Benjamin Vore, his family, and a visiting traveler at the Vore home near Dwight Mission on September 15, 1843.[5] None of the victims of these so-called political assassinations had any dealings with the Treaty Party, nor were they known supporters. This fact openly embarrassed the Ross Party faction, who up until that time had been acting from a stance of righteous indignation, however loosely justified. Chief John Ross realized that unless he brought in the cavalry, literally, the revenge killings would continue and at an ever increasing rate.

Finally Ross asked Gen. Zachary Taylor of Fort Smith, Arkansas, to aid in the investigation of the Vore murders and the capture of the likely perpetrators. Ross probably saw an opportunity to wash his hands of the whole affair if the white man, and not he, brought the Vore murderers to justice.

To expedite the capture of Tom Starr and his alleged accomplices a bounty of $3,000 was placed on their heads; it was an enormous sum in late-nineteenth century dollars, equaling $75,000 by today's measure.[6] But to Ross and General Taylor's dismay, even that was not enough to coax information from the locals as to the whereabouts of the suspected killers. They were never apprehended.

The murders of Vore and the visiting unnamed traveler remain unsolved to this day. Worse yet for the Cherokees, the killings continued at a daunting pace, costing the lives of nearly thirty supporters of both factions until, in 1846, a truce was called.

A last-ditch effort to seize control through intimidation and fear before the truce was orchestrated by Tom Starr. Presumably retaliating for the assassination of his father, James, and his younger brother, Buck, a twelve-year-old cripple, Tom Starr went on a killing rampage. Western mythology has it that he doggedly stalked each of the thirty-two men he deemed responsible for the murders, killing every last one who had not died of sickness or old age before he got to them.[7]

Legend also has it that Tom Starr would show discontent if one of his prey met a demise not committed by him. And death at the hands of Tom Starr was nothing short of brutal. One account has

Starr dragging a man from the bedroom of his house and stabbing him fifty-three times while the victim's wife looked on in absolute horror. Finally this violent chapter in Cherokee history came to a close. Yet even the closing of that chapter was met with some discontent. During the very meeting at which the truce was publicly announced with all leaders of both factions present, Ross was threatened and nearly attacked by those opposed to the truce. The faction most unhappy with the terms of the new agreement was reportedly the very group rumored to have done in James and Buck Starr.

The truce penned into tribal law in summer of 1846 between Chief John Ross and members of the Treaty Party, read in part; "all offenses and crimes committed by a citizen of the Cherokee Nation . . . are hereby pardoned," a provision said to be aimed especially at Tom Starr and his followers.[8] The probability that the pardon was directed at Tom Starr was not lost on the terrorized and beleaguered Cherokees. But better a dubious peace than a deadly protest.

Edward O. Kelly

Edward O. Kelly, the killer of Jesse James' assassin, Robert Ford, was apparently motivated by greed rather than politics. Kelly killed Robert Ford on June 8, 1892, in Creede, Colorado at a tent saloon Ford was operating.[9] Today that site is occupied by an ice cream parlor. Kelly received life imprisonment for that incident but was released from Canon City Penitentiary in 1902.[10] Kelly was born in 1857, the child of North Carolinians. Apparently well educated for the time, Kelly remained a bachelor. Kelly traveled west, making his home in Pueblo, Colorado, in 1882. He fixed himself solidly in local affairs, taking a position as policeman in the city. While Kelly was in the process of arresting a man named Ed Karse, during the summer of 1891, Karse stepped on Kelly's toes. Kelly shot Karse and killed him.

Not long after that Kelly took up residence near Creede, a wild silver mining town in the San Juan Mountain Range of the Rockies, just a few miles away from the headwaters of the Rio Grande River. In its heyday throughout the late 1890s, Creede boasted several thousand residents, prospectors, and prostitutes, a half-dozen hotels, bars, and bathhouses, and at least one motivated and undeterred

Congregational church. Not far as the crow flies, in the neighboring county of Hindale, was an even smaller more lawless community. This was called Bachelors Field.

Here, in a tiny community of wood shacks and high hopes, Kelly found work. Once again he donned the badge and six-shooter of a lawman and took the unenviable job of town marshal, hardly a prestigious position. Kelly breezed his way into a saloon tent Ford had established in Creede following a brief exile for bad behavior.

Kelly was apparently upset by a public humiliation and was determined to even the score. The two men, it seems, had been arguing about a piece of jewelry that Ford accused Kelly of stealing from him. Kelly evidently resented the accusation and, armed with a long knife, strode with evil intent into Ford's saloon. Ford was quicker than Kelly on that occasion and disarmed his acquaintance by conking him across the head with a pistol. Ford summarily tossed Kelly out onto the rocky streets and probably thought that ended the disagreement.

It didn't. Soon Kelly returned and opened up on Ford with a borrowed shotgun. Sentenced for second-degree murder on July 12, 1892, Kelly was received into the state penitentiary at Carson City, Colorado, where he assumed a new identity: #2970.[11] After nine years in prison and numerous attempts at early release, Kelly eventually caught the ear of a sympathetic board of pardons. On June 7, 1901, Kelly's parole was approved, and on October 3, 1902, he was released after serving less than ten years of a life sentence.[12]

Kelly's troubles only multiplied with his release. According to one newspaper account of the time, Kelly returned to Pueblo, Colorado, and was arrested almost immediately. The arresting officer didn't do much to uphold the honor of the Blue Brotherhood however, as he skipped town shortly before Kelly was released from the pokey because Kelly threatened to kill him.

About a year later, in November, Kelly arrived in Oklahoma City, and within a month he found himself an unwilling guest of yet another Iron Bar Inn. The police there had placed Kelly under surveillance because his behavior "indicated that he was a bad man who would resort to almost anything."[13] Just having a reputation as a ruffian could land most people in jail, especially newcomers. Another rumor being bounced around town was that Kelly was a member of a gang suspected of committing several burglaries. Strike two for the stranger in town.

The Oklahoma City Police Department kept pretty close tabs on Kelly. It was not a difficult task, since Kelly hung out at or near establishments known for catering to con men, thieves, prostitutes, and other lowlifes. But Kelly's fate was sealed when one Otto Ewing, who had been in Creede when Kelly shot and killed Ford, recognized him. Kelly was usually prepared for most any kind of situation. He was said to always carry two guns, one in each pocket of an overcoat. Whenever Kelly walked the streets his hands were always tucked inside those pockets. Ewing whispered about town the warning that Kelly was a dangerous man; one to be avoided.[14]

And so it was that Kelly was arrested on what today would be a mighty thin charge, "being a suspicious character." The arresting officer that December day in 1903 was longtime police officer Joe Burnett.[15]

Perhaps partly out of bravado or to save face, upon his release Kelly boasted to all within earshot at his fleabag hotel that he was "gunning for a man." Kelly craftily omitted one minor detail: the name of his target. His dubious constituents were undoubtedly impressed. That didn't last very long. By January, an Officer Bunker saw Kelly out and about and promptly, and without much in the way of evidence, arrested him. Outraged beyond control, Kelly then made his threats directly toward the local police. Kelly made straight for the Lewis Hotel, sneering a warning that no police had better try to arrest him again.

The cops didn't hear Kelly's grousing, nor would they have been likely to take any notice had they known about it. Officer Joe Burnett, Kelly's nemesis, happened upon Kelly, who struck out at the officer. Kelly had a gun in his hand and mockingly told Burnett to come with him, saying, "You come with me. I'll arrest you, you son of a bitch."[16]

Kelly was a towering man standing about six feet five inches, whose red hair and mean gaze gave him a dangerous look. Burnett was in for the fight of his life on that evening of January 13, 1904, and knew it. The two adversaries immediately recognized that their fight was a death struggle from the start.

The men punched, clawed, bit, and kicked one another, and Burnett, sensing things weren't going very well, at least once called for a passerby to come to his aid. "I am a police officer. Help me," he managed to shout at some men passing the brouhaha. They answered in cowardly fashion, "We don't know whether you are a policeman or not," and ran away.[17]

Burnett at least won the fight, in the process suffering two chewed-up ears, burnt gloves, and burnt clothes, apparently as a result of the muzzle blast of Kelly's pistol. As for Edward O. Kelly, he lay dead, shot with his own gun. Kelly's unclaimed body lay at Street and Harper's Furniture Store two solid weeks to enable relatives to claim the body. None did.

Instead, on January 28, 1904, the body of Edward O. Kelly, age forty-six, the man who shot the man who shot Jesse James, was buried in Fairlawn Cemetery in Oklahoma City. The burial was handled by Street and Harper funeral directors at a cost to the taxpayers of $12.50.[18]

Officer Joe Burnett rose through the ranks of the Oklahoma City Police Department, first as captain and later as assistant chief of police. He died in 1917 and was buried in the same cemetery as the remains of Ed Kelly.[19]

James B. "Deacon" Miller

Among the men of heartless disposition in the Old West, Jim Miller was by all accounts near the very top of the heap. Miller held the dubious distinction of being among an elite group of men who killed mostly for personal gain, rather than jealousy, pride, or a good stake at a card game. Born in Van Buren, Arkansas, on October 24, 1866, he moved with his parents to Franklin, Texas, when he was one year old. A few years later both parents died, and Miller moved in with his grandparents in Avant, Texas. When Miller was eight years old both his grandparents were murdered in their home. And while other eight-year-olds were thinking of ways to avoid chores and playing hooky, Miller was being arrested for possibly having murdered his grandparents. He was never convicted, and later was sent to live with his sister and her husband, J. E. Coop, on the couple's family farm in Gatesville, Texas.[20]

Coop and young Miller had a rather contentious relationship and in a few years, at the age of about seventeen, Miller was charged with yet another murder; the ambush of his sister's husband.[21] Jim was acquitted of that crime and soon left Gatesville and headed to McCulloch County where he took a job as a cowhand on the Mannen Clements ranch.[22] Even when engaged in honest work, Miller seemed to be surrounded by mystery and murder. In 1887 his boss, Mannen Clements, was killed. Before long Miller avenged that death by ambushing Clements' suspected killers.[23]

By the time Miller was twenty-five years old he had acquired a wife, Sallie Clements, Mannen's daughter, a badge, and a reputation as both a merciless killer and a devout Methodist. Thus at some point during his formative years as a gunslinger, he was dubbed "Killin' Jim," "Killer Miller," and "Deacon Jim," all at the same time.

Before he married Sallie Clements, Miller wandered almost aimlessly around the Mexico-Texas border country. At one point he operated a saloon in San Saba before pinning a deputy sheriff's badge of Reeves County to his breast pocket and later becoming the town marshal of the county seat, Pecos.[24] His effectiveness as a lawman usually came under scrutiny in light of Miller's questionable killings of Mexicans, claiming they were all "trying to escape." By now Miller may have earned the reputation of "Killer Miller," but none of his nicknames were ever linked to a specific event or date. Even at that, Miller likely appreciated and thus wore with some respect the name "Deacon," given his devout attention to church matters.

Deacon Miller went on killing for hire and soon targeted a fellow law officer. Sheriff G. A. "Bud" Frazer it is said, accused Deacon of stealing a pair of mules, something which greatly affronted the self-anointed man of the Word. In fact the accusation affronted Deacon Miller so much so that he apparently felt the only way to reach satisfaction was to kill the accuser. The two men exchanged gunfire in the streets of Pecos, but neither received a serious injury.

The disagreement was not over as far as the Deacon was concerned. So he simply chose a better time for a better shot and murdered Frazer. Once again Miller was acquitted of any wrongdoing on the rationale that Miller "had done no worse than Frazer."[25] However Miller didn't stop with the assassination of Frazer. And when he caught up to the man who testified against him at trial, Joe Earp, Miller wasted little time in silencing him.[26]

Miller got away with murder—literally—in the ambush of Joe Earp. The Deacon received no punishment. District Attorney Stanley, who prosecuted the case, had better sense than to stay around Pecos once the jury turned Miller loose. Stanley lit out for a small town in Texas called Memphis. Killer Miller got wind of Attorney Stanley's whereabouts, and it wasn't long before Memphis, Texas, became Stanley's eternal residence. Accounts from the time say the departed Stanley died of food poisoning. Most accounts all agree on one thing: arsenic in a plate of stew *is* food poisoning.

Many who knew Jim Miller, or knew of him, thought that it was just a matter of time before the law caught up with him. Instead just the opposite happened. Jim Miller caught up with the law and once again became an extension of that long arm. He joined the renowned, respected, and sometimes feared Texas Rangers. Miller's penchant for indiscriminate killing apparently didn't sit well with the Rangers' code. After a brief stint as resident agent in two different counties, Miller left the Ranger service after killing a man in Collingsworth County.

He and his wife then moved to Fort Worth. There, Sallie opened a rooming house while Deacon Jim added a new dimension to his resume; that of a hired assassin.[27] He killed two men in Midland, but that was just the beginning of his new work. Word on the street—that Killer Miller's services were available for $150 per assassination—was good news to many a profiteer, political foe, or land grabber.

Between assassinations Deacon Miller filled his down time by regularly attending prayer meetings and the like, speaking from the pulpit with the greatest fervor. Miller's long history of murder eventually did catch up with him, but not through the efforts of any lawman.

Ironically, Miller is said to have killed one of the most renowned lawmen of the time, a man who to this day lives on in history as hero or heel, depending on the witnesses. Patrick Floyd Garrett, known simply as Pat Garrett, the man who killed Billy the Kid, was felled either by Miller or an accomplice. Garrett's murder was widely believed to have been a contracted "hit tied to an elaborate plot." Miller, it is thought, may have duped the otherwise savvy former lawman by posing as a cattle buyer. Garrett never laid eyes on Miller before the arranged meeting of the two men and a "cattle broker" in Las Cruces, New Mexico.

The idea was to discuss a grazing lease of Garrett's land for cattle Miller was supposed to drive up from Mexico later that spring. Since Garrett was not as good with finances as he was with a gun, several ventures he had embarked upon ended in financial ruin. Discouraged, Garrett was by that time intent on doing whatever it took to keep his beloved ranch from falling to the wolves at his door. Time was precious, and Garrett's finances were in dire straits. Just about any opportunity probably seemed like potential manna from heaven to the cash-strapped Garrett.

The deal, as proposed by Miller's confidence man, Carl Adamson, was that Garrett would be paid so much per head for grazing until fall, after which the cattle would be moved to Miller's ranch in Oklahoma.[28] The problem was, Miller had neither cattle, nor an Oklahoma ranch, and Adamson was anything but a legitimate businessman.

Garrett's horse-breeding operations failed, leaving him with back taxes and a $3,000 supply bill at the local mercantile.

So, when an offer to graze cattle came along, Garrett agreed. But to his chagrin the lessee, Wayne Brazil, son of Jesse M. Brazil, the very man who had helped Garrett capture Billy the Kid, loaded the pasture not with cattle but with goats, the bane of Western cattlemen.[29] Garrett was incensed, but a deal's a deal; after all, Brazil never said what he was going to graze on Garrett's ranch, and so therefore not much could be done about the situation. Garrett's sheepishness about grazing a herd of goats where most ranchers believed only cattle should roam made him ripe for the sting operation concocted by Miller and Adamson.

Garrett believed Adamson's offer was legitimate, and in mid-February when word spread through Las Cruces that two cattlemen were looking for prime grazing land for a thousand head of cattle, Garrett arranged a meeting. This was the news Garrett needed to bring back dignity to his ranch, Bear Canyon, from the scourge of goats Brazil had foisted on him. The two men posing as cattle barons were none other than Deacon Jim Miller and a man calling himself Carl Adamson.

Miller sent word to Garrett that he would lease the entire ranch, including the goat-infested Bear Canyon pasture, but the goats had to go before a single head of beef cattle would be put on the pasture. Garrett was growing desperate to get Brazil's goats off his land. The price per head to graze cattle was more than the price paid to graze goats. The goats ate everything in sight, leaving little more than brown stubble and dust, raising the possibility of poor or even non-existent grassland for Miller's more profitable cattle should the goats remain much longer.

Miller eventually agreed to buy Brazil's twelve hundred goats and dispose of them in a fitting manner, but before any money changed hands Brazil increased the number of bleaters grazing on Bear Canyon to eighteen hundred head. Miller refused to pay the extra money for the secretly added goats, agreeing only to the original terms: twelve hundred goats. Brazil remained stubborn and declared that he would not get off Garrett's land unless all eighteen hundred goats were purchased by Miller.[30] Garrett in the meantime became distraught at Brazil's chicanery, even to the point of slapping the goat magnate in the face with his open hand. Brazil was quietly outraged. Some have said that the act of a man slapping another man was the lowest possible insult.

Seeing that he was getting nowhere with Brazil, and finding himself in a now-or-never situation with Miller, Garrett was forced into a kind of détente with Miller, Brazil, and Adamson. On the evening of February 28, all four men met at Bear Canyon to discuss and hopefully resolve the whole affair. After hours of contentious wrangling, they agreed on just one point; the matter had to be settled to the benefit of all parties the next day or not at all.[31]

Things were then working in Miller's favor, thanks in great part to the silver-tongued promoter Adamson and the cantankerous leaseholder Brazil. After all, Miller's only reason for going to New Mexico and contriving this entire scheme was to meet and then kill Pat Garrett. Garrett still suspected nothing, and readily agreed to accompany Adamson and Brazil back to Las Cruces where Garrett would finally meet up with Miller and talk business. Over the objections of his wife, Apolinaria Gutierrez, Garrett readied for the trip to Las Cruces and a chance to regain financial control of Bear Canyon Ranch and the family legacy.

Garrett's wife felt uneasy about Adamson, but could not pinpoint the source of her distrust. Garrett dismissed his wife's suspicions as those of a woman who knew not the ways of the world and the men who ran it. The next morning Garrett dressed in his best black broadcloth suit and string tie, announcing to his beloved Apolinaria, "This Miller sounds like somebody important, and I don't want him to think I'm plumb down on my luck." That was the last time Mrs. Garrett ever saw her husband alive.[32]

Soon Brazil turned himself in to Sheriff Felipe Lucero and confessed to killing Garrett. Lucero thought Brazil was joking at first. "What are you trying to do, josh me?" Lucero told a reporter in a 1923 recounting of the incident. But when Brazil insisted he had shot Pat Garrett to death, Lucero took him at his word. "I put his gun in a safe and locked him up in a cell," Lucero told the reporter.[33]

Some of the facts surrounding the murder are undisputed. Garrett and Adamson were riding together in a buggy on their way to meet with Miller. About four miles east of Las Cruces, the two men met the contentious goat herder, Brazil. Brazil wasn't having any luck persuading Miller to purchase the added six hundred goats he had sneaked in on the lands leased from Garrett, and Garrett had already made his feelings known with that sharp crack to Brazil's face. Now the deal seemed to be sliding somewhat in Garrett's favor and away from Brazil. There was one thing left to do.

As Adamson got out of the buggy to relieve himself, Garrett did the same. Adamson later told lawmen at the inquest that he and Garrett had turned their backs to Brazil while beginning to answer the call of nature when two shots shattered the quiet of the peaceful New Mexico countryside. Pat Garrett was dead. Brazil turned himself in and was acquitted of murder. Adamson was only questioned, then released. This was the second time another man confessed to killing one of Miller's victims and then claimed the deed was done in self-defense. Another good man had fallen to a Deacon Jim Miller's assassination plot. Although the law apparently could not put a stop to Killin' Jim's ways, a few fed-up Okies were about to put him out of business.

Miller's involvement in the assassination of Garrett was widely accepted. In fact, Miller's reputation had long been established as a hired killer; he boasted of fifty-one executed "contracts." No wonder then that when a small group of Oklahoma ranchers and whiskey merchants were unable to come to terms with a fellow entrepreneur, they turned to the man known as the Deacon.

Ada, Oklahoma Territory, sat very near the infamous whiskey towns of Indian Territory that openly followed the once-illegal trade of providing whiskey to anybody with coin, cattle, or other stake. Four men, known saloon keepers and whiskey providers, were constantly feuding over "trade infringements." It was no secret that Joe West, Jesse Allen, and B. B. Burrell held disagreeable sentiments from their dealings with Angus A. Bobbitt.[34] So it was, then, that Bobbitt became the next man marked for assassination at the hands of Killer Jim.

Miller chose to handle the Bobbitt job himself. He rode another man's horse to do the job, and that is what eventually led to his arrest. The mare Miller rode to the assassination belonged to a twenty-four-year-old man named John Williamson. The mare's peculiar hoof marks and a farmer witness told a riled posse where to find the mare and its owner. Using interrogation methods that would certainly not pass scrutiny by today's standards, the posse was able to extract the name of the man who rented the mare for thirty dollars the night Bobbitt was gunned down outside his home. Williamson told the posse, who by that time were pretty close to lynching him, that the man who rented the horse was his uncle, Jim Miller. Miller, Allen, Burrell, and West were already jailed in Ada on suspicion that they were involved in the killing of Bobbitt when a lynch mob took matters into their own hands. The townspeople had had all they could stomach of the three conspirators and Miller.

Even though they didn't really care much for Bobbitt, they apparently thought that even he deserved a better death. Had the assassin met Bobbitt in the light of day and out of cover, the whole incident might have been overlooked as just another feud that ended in gunplay. But killing a man just outside his own property with his wife within earshot under cover of darkness was just plain unforgivable.

Shortly after 2:00 a.m., April, 19, 1909, a mob of about forty men overpowered the two guards left to protect the accused men from such a peril.[35] The righteous mob hanged all four in an abandoned livery barn behind the jail but not without hearing a request by the loquacious "Deacon," Jim Miller.

Miller was the last of the four to be hanged. He had but one request of his executioners; that he be hanged with either his long coat or his hat on. One participant is said to have crammed the Deacon's hat on the side of his head. Then "Killin' Jim" had but one last bold statement to leave with the lynch mob, "I'm ready now," Miller laughed. "You couldn't kill me otherwise. Let 'er rip!" And they did.[36]

A Massacre in Missouri

Union Station in Kansas City, Missouri, is a magnificent structure even by today's standards. In 1933, it was an architectural marvel and a railroad hub for Midwestern travelers, and the scene of one of modern-day's most memorable and written-about gangland assassinations.

June 1933 found the Bureau of Investigation, later renamed the Federal Bureau of Investigation, hot on the trail of an Oklahoma man. The culprit had unceremoniously slipped away from the home of the warden of the state penitentiary at the federal prison in Leavenworth, Kansas, and returned to his trade as a bootlegger.[37] The bureau sent Oklahoma City agents Frank C. Smith and F. Joseph Lackey to round up the elusive Frank "Jelly" Nash, who they believed was holed up in Hot Springs, Arkansas. Since Nash had altered his appearance they recruited Otto Reed, an acquaintance of Nash's from the old days of outlawry in Oklahoma. Both Reed and Nash had plied their trades long before the automobile came on the scene.

Smith and Lackey successfully captured their man and hauled him to Kansas City, where a car and other lawmen waited to deliver Nash back to Leavenworth. They arrived at Union Station around 7:15 a.m., with what they thought was a pretty good plan to thwart any attempts to free Nash by his mob cronies. That confidence proved unfounded within a matter of only seconds.

Three brave officers were killed with Nash. One theory is that Nash was the first to die, as the veteran McAlester, Oklahoma, cop, Otto Reed, put a slug in the back of his head the moment he realized trouble was upon them. Then Reed was shot to death while still inside the police car with the dead Nash. Agent Lackey took three shots in the back but pulled through, while his partner, Agent Smith, was unharmed. Two local Kansas City officers, Frank Hermanson and W. J. "Red" Grooms, were killed by machine-gun fire.[38]

The participation of two Oklahoma gangsters in the Kansas City Massacre is contentiously debated to this day. Some authorities rely on interviews with known associates that say Charles Arthur "Pretty Boy" Floyd and Adam Richetti were there, firing away at the officers as part of the ambush. Still others maintain that Floyd and Richetti simply had bad timing and were in Kansas City at the time of the gunplay but not a party to it. Floyd, not known for shying away from the notoriety produced by such activities, denied all his days that he had any involvement in the Kansas City Massacre.

One acquaintance and former getaway driver for Pretty Boy, Elmer Steele, said publicly nearly sixty years after the Kansas City Massacre— or Union Station Massacre—that Floyd was innocent of the alleged crime. "All of us on the scout back then knew at once that he didn't have anything to do with that mess. Others did it, and he took the fall. Choc was never a hired gun."[39] "Choc" was a nickname Floyd's closest associates knew him by. Still others were not as convinced of Floyd's innocence in the whole affair. No one knows for sure to this day.

Chapter 3

Raiders and Guerrillas

Oklahoma's bank- and train-robbing tradition was inspired by raids conducted in Missouri and adjoining states by both regular troops and guerillas during the Civil War. The guerilla tactics of Quantrill's Raiders were particularly significant. William Clarke Quantrill was born in Canal Dover, Ohio, on July 31, 1837, and traveled west to teach school but took to outlawry and gambling instead. Soon he was accused of petty thievery and murder.[1]

When the Civil War broke out, Quantrill masked his lust for stealing and killing by plying his trades under the guise of patriot for the Southern cause. He soon became known among the leadership of the Confederate army as a firebrand who couldn't or wouldn't follow orders.

He used his frequent border skirmishes in Missouri and Kansas to exploit the conflict for his own purposes by robbing and sacking communities with known Union sympathies.[2] Prior to his death in 1865 when he was forever silenced by a well-placed Union slug during a raid in Kentucky, Quantrill tutored a few Missouri boys in the practice of guerilla warfare.

Hatred for the North accounted for the enlistment of Alexander Franklin James. His younger brother, Jesse Woodson James, and friend, Thomas Coleman "Cole" Younger, and his younger sibling, James Younger, likewise joined the fight, becoming Southern irregulars. All four men, teenaged boys really, spent much of their service in the ranks of Missouri raiders throughout the Civil War. Both the Jameses and the Youngers experienced first-hand the atrocities of war. The Younger boys' father was killed by Kansas Jayhawkers in an ambush in 1862. Although the Youngers were slaveholders, they were Union sympathizers up until that time.[3] Frank James took part in the horrific Lawrence, Kansas, massacre, in which 150 to 200 men were shot or burned to death by Quantrill's Raiders. Frank's exact role that heinous day on August 21, 1863, has never been clearly defined. While it is recorded that Cole Younger was there, at least one account actually credits him with saving the lives of at least a dozen innocent citizens at Lawrence.[4]

As brutal as Quantrill's methods of beating the enemy were, they paled beside those of fellow guerrilla, William Anderson, better remembered as Bloody Bill Anderson. "Bloody Bill" kept score of his killings by collecting scalps.[5] Anderson's battlefield strategy included taking no prisoners.

Often he dispatched an enemy soldier by running him down, clubbing him, and for good measure confirming the kill with a lead ball to the back of the head. Anderson, with sadistic efficiency, held true to his mantra of "take no prisoners."

On the other side, the Federals were no batch of robed choirboys. Tortures, hangings, clubbings, molestations of all kinds, barn and house burnings were common sins committed by Union soldiers. The atrocities committed by each side of the war produced one common quality: a detestable lack of regard for humanity and a base need to get even.

Against this backdrop, the James and Younger brothers transformed themselves from teenage farm boys to guerilla raiders. While riding with Quantrill and Anderson, Frank and Jesse James and Cole and Jim Younger made their first appearances in what is now Oklahoma.

It was while riding with those infamous guerrilla units that the Jameses and Youngers were introduced to robbery and villainy of all sorts, in the name of supplying their own troops or denying supplies to the enemy. So it's easy to see just how it was that the boys took to banditry so effortlessly. Between raids, present-day Oklahoma probably seemed a pretty safe hiding place since Federal troops were few and far between there. Even before the Civil War many who chose the outlaw trail found themselves taking up residence there, finding shelter in caves, tents, shacks, or shanties.

Not all the Civil War raids were carried out by Quantrill, Anderson, or other guerillas. One of the most successful raids ever perpetrated by regulars of the Confederate army was carried out by troops at Big Cabin Creek in far northeast Mayes County near present-day Grand Lake. A battleground memorial park still exists there today in a secluded wooded area near present-day Pensacola. A heavily wooded, hilly area sitting about twenty yards above Big Cabin Creek was a perfect spot for Brig. Gen. Stand Watie, a Cherokee Indian with a plan to attack a Union supply convoy.

The attack was under the actual command of Gen. R. M. Gano, a Texas native and look-alike great-grandfather of another Texas scion, billionaire recluse Howard Hughes. Watie, mentioned in Chapter 2, "Oklahoma Assassins," was already acknowledged as a master of cunning guerilla warfare. Watie formed a Cherokee volunteer regiment in 1861. The Cherokee Mounted Rifles soon became recognized by the Confederate government, and Watie was appointed its colonel.[6] In 1864 Watie and Gano captured a Union supply train, just one year after the pair attempted a similar attack from the same spot at Big Cabin Creek. In that first unsuccessful raid of July 1863, Watie and Gano were repelled by the Union forces. The convoy proceeded to its destination at Fort Gibson. But in 1864 the two officers successfully netted loot of more than $1 million in military supplies and other goods.[7]

In addition to the military supplies, food, and clothing, however, another of the spoils was barrels of whiskey, which the celebrating Confederate troops consumed with gusto. Tiring of the drunken revelry, Watie ordered the remainder of the rye dumped into Big Cabin Creek, bringing the revelry to a sobering end.[8]

Watie's other more memorable escapade came that same year, when he and his Cherokee Mounted Rifles captured a Union steamer heading up the Arkansas River to Fort Blunt.

At Pleasant Bluff, Waite and his raiders engaged in naval warfare, the only recorded maritime conflict to reach so far inland. Watie and his men surprised and captured the Union steamer *J. R. Williams,* sending its escort back to Fort Smith in hasty retreat. The captured cargo was estimated to have been worth only about $120,000, a paltry sum compared to the value of the loot from the Big Cabin raid.[9]

Watie, born in Georgia near present-day Rome on December 12, 1806, was the last Confederate general to surrender to the Union forces. The war had been over for a month when he finally gave up his sword to the Union command on June 23, 1865. Watie died in present-day Delaware County, Oklahoma, on September 9, 1871.[10]

This raiding tradition laid the foundation for the Doolin gang and others. This was an ideal environment where the likes of the Daltons,

Jameses, and Youngers, and other not so famous outlaws made Oklahoma and Indian Territories a very bad place to be. Some of those very bad places came to be known as Oklahoma's disreputable and deadly Whiskey Towns.

Chapter 4

Whiskey Towns of Oklahoma: Gunfights, Naked Men, and Debauched Women

Movies such as *Unforgiven* and television programs series such as *Deadwood* have abandoned the wide-eyed, childlike portrayal of Western figures donned in either black or white, and chosen instead to depict a closer characterization of the towns and men from whom producers received inspiration. The old towns of Oklahoma and Indian Territories of the late 1880s portray the factual basis for those two fictional adaptations. These towns, dedicated to the pursuit of happiness through purveying pleasures and debauchery, no matter how decadent, often included among their roughhouse activities gambling, gunfights, prostitution, and murder of all kinds and for all or no reasons.

These towns became home to those on the run from much tamer societies. These inhabitants, who were once merely on the lam and searching for a hideout, sometimes caught the entrepreneurial spirit and chose to better their condition. They did so by establishing saloons and gambling halls and setting up brothels to tend to their kindred spirits.

A number of these hardscrabble, raucous towns, most of which disappeared after statehood in 1907 when prohibition took effect, were known then and are remembered today as the Whiskey Towns of Oklahoma.

Today's floating beer barges, prevalent on area recreational lakes, resemble the floating saloons that were moored to the banks of the Canadian River near the town of Purcell in the late 1890s. There liquor flowed from keg to bottle and bottle to a dry-throated cowhand's glass faster than the Canadian River could take a raft downstream. The community, Sandtown, although never an incorporated town, prospered until prohibition dried up the sale of liquor once Indian Territory became part of the state of Oklahoma.

In fact, the various whiskeys' variety lay more in their naming than in their manufacture. Popular border-town whiskeys then were not much more than grain alcohol with a pinch of sulfuric acid added for increased spirit and either creosote or chewing tobacco added for color.

The selling of liquor to Indians was considered a serious offense of the day. Selling liquor in the territories carried very stiff penalties, which included imprisonment and costly fines. The lure of profit, however, far outweighed the threat of punishment. So strong and prevalent was the enticement to gain quick wealth from the illegal sale of liquor in Indian Territory that even some U.S. deputy marshals were building and operating saloons in the border counties of Indian Territory.

Tucked into a narrow bend in the Arkansas River, the town of Ralston exists today on a stretch of Highway 18 just tipping the western edge of Osage County, once part of the great Osage Nation. Ralston's position along the Arkansas River was important in 1903, even more so than in present times. Because of its location just outside the Osage Nation, Ralston's liquor trade was brisk, and so long as no liquor found its way to the Osage Indians it was legal. Those Osage had little regard for white man's law. They regularly crossed into Ralston, where they garnered a trading preference of sorts. There were seven saloons in Ralston during the period, from around 1896 to 1906. Most were nothing more than hastily erected tents. The Mayflower Saloon and Red Front Saloon were two such canvas-topped liquor and beer halls.[1]

Lawmen sought the source, but their efforts were often thwarted because the drunken patron wasn't talking, or if he did talk it was usually somewhat unintelligible. The bartender or saloon owner adamantly claimed he did not observe liquor being served to an Indian, and he was being at least halfway honest. He didn't see anyone serve any Osage residents because of a rather ingenious method of providing them with liquor while at the same time abiding by the law.

Many operators of frame-built saloons included a secret back room for sales to the lucrative Indian trade, and some added a further creative twist. For a liquor dealer to be able to swear on oath that he had not seen a Native American being served alcohol, dumbwaiters were discretely installed so the only thing the bartender did see was the money he received for the purchase.[2] An important legal point at the time was that he really *didn't* see who tendered the cash. Therefore, under oath, the offending barkeep could answer righteously that he hadn't witnessed any such wrongful doings as selling liquor to Indians.

These half-truths worked, leaving local law enforcement in search of witnesses. There were "15 to 20 intoxicated Indians on the streets . . . at the time," Warren Bennett, chief of police for the Osage Nation, observed in 1905. "Some of whom, almost naked, have bartered their blankets for whiskey." Bennett added that the women didn't behave any better: "Some of the women have become so debauched as to make a practice of bartering their virtue for liquor."[3]

The seemingly harmless carnival atmosphere was sometimes described in the local media as nothing more than casual entertainment, but that was hardly the whole story. Things got pretty rough in those days, for sometimes the only law enforcement was provided by proprietors of a nearby local saloon. The law those businessmen enforced wasn't the law of the courts. Theirs was the unwritten law of the land. New competition in the liquor business was seen as a restriction of trade, and it wasn't tolerated. Men were known to carry on feuds over the right to be the sole provider of liquor in the whiskey towns. Saloon owners used any means available to them to establish their place on the ladder of financial success.

Situated on the north bank of the Canadian River across from the Choctaw Nation was what was probably the first Oklahoma whiskey town: Lexington. Ironically, considering its origins, and probably only coincidentally, Lexington is now the home of the Joseph Harp Correctional Facility for men. However beginning in 1889, after the U.S. Government opened up Indian lands for white settlement in April, Lexington was a raw whiskey town in full bloom.

Before Lexington had a post office or a jail, One-Armed Ed's Saloon was built. Ed's was purportedly the first building of wood-frame construction in the town, whose main business was liquor. Saloons far outnumbered any other businesses in Lexington, and one such establishment cleverly added convenience to commodity.[4] The middle of the Canadian River channel was the legal boundary between Indian Territory (I. T.) and Oklahoma Territory (O. T.). A few miles to the east lay the Chickasaw Nation and the town of Purcell. But because it was located in Indian Territory across the Canadian River from Lexington, no saloons were allowed there.

One saloon owner, showing great ingenuity, circumvented the law when he erected his saloon on a sandbar right in the middle of the river. The Sand Bar Saloon gave rise to similar establishments built along or in the river, prompting visitors and locals alike to dub the area Sandtown. The Sand Bar was one of twenty-one saloons opened in the month of the Oklahoma Land Run in 1889. Purcell was then the second-largest town in the Chickasaw Nation, and it saw its population explode to 2,277 just one year later in 1900.[5] The wild time lasted as long as the whiskey flowed, and local lawmen were content to stand by and watch the goings-on with minimal interference.

Lexington had the added benefit of the Santa Fe Railroad, which built a train station at Purcell, providing thirsty passengers aboard one of eight daily trains an opportunity to wet their whistles. Because Purcell was off-limits to whiskey purveyors, a wooden foot bridge spanned the river from the Sand Bar to the Chickasaw Nation's shoreline and Purcell, providing convenient access to the train's parched patrons. Lore has it that the Sand Bar was built on stilts, and its wooden bridge leading to it gave it an appearance more resembling a houseboat than a saloon—patrons subsequently nicknamed it "the ark."[6]

Before statehood, liquor laws in the territories were unclear at best. Although U.S. marshals arrested six men in March of 1890 who were accused of illegal liquor sales, there were many more who somehow escaped the sharp eye of the law. With the burgeoning of whiskey sales in the territories came all the other known vices. Gambling and prostitution, while sidelines, were nevertheless profitable ones.

In Sandtown, the Riverside, Point Comfort, and a floating saloon constructed from a flat-bottom boat called "The City of Purcell" dotted the Canadian River shoreline across from Purcell. In Lexington itself, early saloons such as the Thomas Farmers' Saloon, Buckhorn, J. H. DeBerry, and French Saloon supplied satisfaction, carnal as well as liquid, as did the Two Brothers and the Dutch Saloon. Each had its own brand of whiskey, music, "dancehall" girls, and gambling nearly every hour of every day.

Unfortunately for Lexington, the surrounding whiskey communities, and the raucous patrons, none of them long escaped the wary eye of the more moralistic.

"You could almost see a pin on the streets from the flashes of their pistols," a settler told the *Lexington Leader* after a particularly disorderly weekend.[7] On another night, November 14, 1891, the *Leader* reported that at least twenty shots filled the town's night air when two constables battled it out with two residents of the Chickasaw Nation who had been drinking in one of the saloons. No official source tells why gunplay was necessary or who won the fight. Such occurrences were not uncommon. "Lexington has a hard name abroad," the *Leader* reported after a particularly rebellious night, "probably harder than it deserves but the rowdyism indulged in here late Saturday evening will not add much to its moral status."[8]

The *Leader* was correct in its assumption about the outside world's assessment of the goings-on in whiskey towns, but Lexington was not alone in its reputation for depraved moral character. Corner, Keokuk Falls, and Violet Springs in Pottawatamie County, as well as Keystone, Tulsey Town (now Tulsa), and Pauls Valley had reputations as places that provided whiskey in open defiance of local and federal regulations. Lexington and Sandtown, along the Canadian River, maintained their legal status by virtue of being situated on the Oklahoma Territory side of the river, where it was legal to sell whiskey.

Cowhands working ranches there and separated by the river were left to pretty desperate devices of their own for entertainment. Competitive games included sharpshooting contests, horse racing, roping and bronc busting, knife-throwing contests, and boxing matches, which were nothing more than loosely organized fist fights. Since the nearest town was miles away, the men were deprived of a good, steady supply of whiskey to quench their dust-coated throats during all that play time on their days off.

That all changed when a man with the outward appearance of a circuit preacher established a place on the river meant to bring about a revival of sorts. In 1891 a tall, quiet man distinguished by his dapper apparel and a long gray beard arrived on the border between the territories and set to work cutting and erecting rough-hewn logs from the river bottom. When the somber, distinguished fellow was finished, the Corner Saloon stood on the banks of the Canadian, ready to welcome all those thirsty cowhands.

This wasn't the Long Branch, and Miss Kitty wasn't the congenial host, nor was the barkeep a mustachioed complacent defender of honor named Sam. The Corner Saloon's proprietor was William "Bill" Conner, a feared former member of Quantrill's Raiders.

Conner hired as his barkeep a hoodlum named George Miller, called "Hookey," because of a hook used to replace a hand shot off as the result of taking on a few U.S. marshals near Lawton in earlier times.[9]

The Corner Saloon's clientele tended to be the toughest of the toughs, not only because of the renown of its owner, Conner, but also in part because of the day-to-day management style of Hookey Miller, said to be as deadly with his steel appendage as he ever was with a pistol. With customers like the Christian brothers and Doc Garrison, a ringleader of a reputed cattle rustling gang working I. T., the Corner Saloon was a regular bandito watering hole. "It was wild country, broken by river bluffs in black jack barrens . . . remote, uncultivated, and uninhabited. There was no store, no blacksmith shop, no dwelling. In a rough, rawhide house was a saloon [Corner Saloon], frequented by gamblers, refugees, robbers, landless resolutes and droughty [sic] cronies."[10] Those men felt safe from the law there, primarily due to its location. It was isolated from any incorporated town and miles away from federal forces. If U.S. marshals came snooping around, it took no time at all to hop a steed and ford the Canadian River to Indian Territory.

None of that deterred many of the cowhands working the nearby Box X Ranch in the Seminole Nation or the ranch hands of W. E. Washington's spread near Roff. Drovers came in droves, and business was good, so good, in fact, that Conner added a smokehouse to his saloon and was soon serving up all manner of beef and pork dishes. Although the ownership of the cattle and swine bartered to the Corner Saloon was sometimes questionable, no one ever proved the saloon was engaged in or encouraged rustling. It was known, however, that a man without money could trade a dressed hog or side of beef for a jug of whiskey with no questions asked.[11]

Corner was the smallest of the pre-land run towns in O. T., but it carried a well-deserved reputation as being the wildest, with a reputation for violence and lawlessness unsurpassed by any place in the territory. One major ingredient fueling regular gunfire was the liquor war that ensued when a second tavern opened its doors in Corner, much to the consternation of Bill Conner and Hookey Miller. Interference with one's trade meant war. Records filed in the Oklahoma territorial capital in 1905 reported that at least fifty murders had been committed in Corner, a hefty number given that the town's entire population never rose above a few hundred. That same year, the Shawnee *Daily Herald* reported that an additional nine murders, sixteen cases of attempted murder, and eighty-one liquor violations occurring throughout Oklahoma were "directly traceable to Corner."[12]

In another Pott County community, one year before its first post office opened its doors in 1892, Keokuk Falls' first saloon was already doing a brisk business. The Black Dog's thriving enterprise, thanks largely to its trade with the Seminoles across the North Canadian River, caught the attention of other entrepreneurs, and soon other saloons began cropping up. That meant competition for the lucrative trade, and that of course meant war.

A Mr. Beatty and his Black Dog were initially the only game in town. However with the advent of a post office the following year and businesses such as a ferry across the North Canadian and other enterprises, Keokuk Falls began to thrive. The population never reached more than three hundred, and according to early records, the number of the town's saloons grew disproportionately to the number of residents, reaching as many as sixty-two saloons by 1900.[13] Early on though, there were seven bars known as "the seven deadly saloons," a moniker received primarily as the result of ongoing feuds among tavern owners.

The Black Dog attracted all manner of characters who frequented the establishment with such regularity as to be mistaken by the casual patron as part of the help. One such character was a physician, Dr. Ñ. Stutsman, a great understudy to the famous Doc Holliday. Stutsman gave more attention to honing his skills in the precision of gambling, gunslinging, and bootlegging than he gave to his medical practice. He was not very different from the character of Doc Holliday that movies and television have created. Stutsman was so at home in the Black Dog gambling hall that even the town's citizenry believed he owned part of it. There is no record to substantiate ownership, but the rumor persisted. In fact, Stutsman did want in on the action and offered to buy into the Black Dog at one point. Beatty was a long-standing acquaintance of Doc Stutsman—after all, the two men saw each other with great regularity. Nevertheless Beatty refused Stutsman's offer.

Stutsman did the only reasonable thing he could do at the time;

he opened a joint of his own, the Red Front Saloon.[14] It was an apt name, as soon both saloons were painted red with the bloody feud that followed. Evidently Beatty didn't care much for Stutsman's capitalistic view that competition was a good thing, so he proceeded to wage war on the Red Front.

Shootouts were commonplace among factions—liquored-up patrons, really—of both saloons. Apparently Beatty had less of a stomach for gunplay than did the good doctor, and during one lead-spewing all-nighter, Beatty sent a messenger to fetch Sheriff Jim Gill from the county seat of Tecumseh. The ride was a twenty-eight-mile journey, but Sheriff Gill and a small posse arrived the following day to arrest twelve of the combatants. Among the shackled were two men who had been wounded in the wild gunplay, and in addition there was one corpse.[15]

The first distillery in Pott County was installed upriver from Keokuk Falls in 1899. Two tavern owners decided to manufacture their own wares locally, thus eliminating the middleman and costly transportation fees. Then Ed Thomlinson and Mike Rooney threw in together to open the distillery. It supplied not only their saloons but also anyone else who sought to do business and keep their own saloons in good supply.

Whiskey was such a vital source of revenue for Keokuk Falls that licensing fees and taxes for distilleries under territorial law were completely waived by the town's trustees. Indeed, more attention was given to supporting and promulgating the liquor trade in Keokuk than was given even to some basic services, as was noted in the town's newspaper. "The whiskey in this town is all right, but the water could be improved upon," said one editorial in the *Keokuk Kall.*[16]

The prevailing attitude that whiskey reigned supreme lent itself to the fight for supremacy in the business. Supremacy meant survival, no matter the cost; even if the cost of doing daily business was measured in human lives, which it often was. The town's first marshal was killed by one of the town's first distillery owners. Ed Thomlinson killed the long-forgotten marshal in a gunfight but was acquitted of a murder charge. Apparently evidence revealed that the marshal had drawn his weapon first.[17] After all, just about anybody foolish enough or brave enough to pin on a badge could be marshal, but only individuals of vision could bring a distillery to town.

Against this backdrop Doc Stutsman brought to a head the feud between himself and his former friend, Beatty. For reasons unknown, Stutsman ordered Black Dog Saloon bartender, Al Cook, to leave town. The details of the gunfight that followed differ somewhat, but all agree that after the encounter Stutsman had been shot twice in the stomach. He later recovered, but Cook lay dead. Some accounts claim Cook and Stutsman encountered one another on the streets of Keokuk Falls after Doc told the bartender to vamoose. Yet another account claims that Cook and Stutsman met each other while riding to Tecumseh. Either way, the results didn't change. Deputy Sheriff Perry Brewer and Deputy Marshal Fate Smith were clearly allied with Stutsman. Upon seeing Cook, Stutsman began a loud-mouthed rampage and attempted to fire his pistol into the air. Forgetting he had emptied the revolver in an earlier display of marksmanship, Stutsman grabbed Brewer's holstered revolver. Fearing being gunned down, Cook pulled his own gun, and the two men fired upon each other simultaneously.[18]

Here Doc Stutsman once again displayed his knack for marksmanship; although both he and Deputy Smith were wounded, Cook slid from the saddle a dead man with two bullet wounds to his stomach.[19] Because Stutsman used Brewer's pistol for the assault, Brewer was terminated from his job as deputy sheriff. Still, Brewer wasn't out of a job; he may have found employment with Stutsman as a hired gun.

Tensions escalated between the two saloon owners and their loyal clientele, culminating in an all-out gunfight in the street. Beatty had had enough. He decided to sell the Black Dog but not to Stutsman. Instead, he sold the place to Aaron Haning, a local hotel proprietor. On the morning of July 2, 1896, Haning was found dead not long after acquiring the tavern by none other than Doc Stutsman.[20] According to later testimony by Stutsman's disgruntled, soon-to-be ex-wife, the good doctor's shot to the back of Haning's head didn't kill him immediately.

When Stutsman went to check on his victim in the pre-dawn hours of July 2, after shooting him the night before, he found Haning unconscious but alive. A fellow named Howard accompanied the good doctor that night, on his "rounds." Howard told Mrs. Stutsman that upon discovering that Haning was still alive, the doctor took a long nail he found nearby and drove it into the skull via the new bullet hole. That was probably the last surgery Dr. Stutsman performed. A trial was held in Oklahoma City, and Stutsman was found guilty of first-degree murder. A later appeal, however, resulted in the ruling being reversed, and Stutsman was eventually acquitted.[21]

Other communities carried similar reputations as wild, wooly places tied to the whiskey business. Stroud, now the halfway point between Tulsa and Oklahoma City, had beginnings innocent enough. Begun in 1898 to accommodate a depot for the St. Louis and San Francisco Railroad, the town grew from humble beginnings. Because it was situated just one and a half miles west of Indian Territory, the town touted itself as "The Gateway between Oklahoma and the Creek Nation."

Originally, Stroud was known for its cotton market, but its close proximity to Indian Territory made it equally well known as a place where whiskey was readily available to those who lived in Indian Territory. Business was brisk, as bootleggers found easy passage for their goods by train into the forbidden market from Stroud. Using false-bottomed trunks, they would stash their wares inside, covering them with wooden planks and stacking linens or clothes on top of the false floor. If the trunks were ever inspected, at first glance they would appear to be nothing more than a man's wardrobe or a chest of clothes.[22]

At that time Stroud even had an Anheuser-Busch beer warehouse. Fire insurance maps covering the years from 1898 to 1904 show as many as seven saloons in Stroud. The town never became the riotous, murderous place that Keokuk Falls or Corner became.

Established before 1836 in the Creek Nation, Tulsa was not much more than a place on a knoll where the Creeks set up residence. Cherokees, Seminoles, Quapaws, Senecas, and Shawnees, forced out of their lands in Alabama, called Tulasi home. Tulasi was a Creek Indian word meaning "old town." White settlers began establishing their own residences there, and in the late 1890s the town's first post office was opened.[23] Whites called the place Tulsey or Tulsey Town, and later the name changed to Tulsa.

Tulsa had humble origins and at first wasn't much more than a wide spot in an otherwise less-traveled, dusty road. But its proximity to Indian Territory gave rise to a burgeoning whiskey trade, and the town's business district grew, thanks in part to several enterprising gents who saw how to take advantage of a thirsty Indian Nation. Even at that, Tulsa was relatively tame by comparison to Keokuk Falls, Corner, and Lexington, whose residents were stepping over slumbering drunks when not ducking flying lead.

Up the Arkansas River, across from the Osage Nation and just a few hundred yards from the Creek Nation boundary, a town called Keystone was born. Even though a post office was opened as late as 1900, Keystone remained a somewhat insignificant Oklahoma territorial town until the advent of the territory's first real estate development, nearby on the shores of the Cimarron River.[24] The Kansas City development company responsible for the venture lured a former county sheriff from Texas, and he built the town's first saloon. Word spread that the new town of Appalachia was a profitable place from which to sell whiskey. Soon as many as seven taverns were doing a vigorous business. Adhering to the law, no liquor sales were conducted in the Creek Nation, but all that separated the saloons from their Native American customers was a river. So, not unlike the creative proprietors of Pott County, bar owners in Appalachia constructed a swinging bridge to span the water as a means of reaching out to those "in need."

The bridge soon was dubbed the Carrie Nation Bridge, in honor of the Kansas temperance leader. Not uncommonly, a staggering patron lost his balance and ended up soaked in the river. Since Keystone held the enviable geographic site on the easternmost point in what was then "wet" Oklahoma Territory, it soon surpassed neighboring Appalachia in the race to win liquor distribution rights.

Whiskey left Keystone bound for all parts of Indian Territory, in all manner of travel transport. Flat-bottomed boats traversing the Arkansas River were a common sight into the early 1900s. Most carried no contraband. However, a boat or two would sometimes make its way downriver with a hidden cache of whiskey on board. One such shipment was discovered after the crew of one of the boats became disoriented in a heavy snowstorm in December of 1906 and got stuck in shallow waters. The river's swift current proved too much for the boat, causing it to overturn. Nearby law enforcement officers confiscated both crew and cargo.[25]

Towns throughout central and northeast Oklahoma Territory

cropped up like weeds from beneath a rock, and often became outposts for liquor sales to the Indian Territory population. Cleveland, for example, settled in 1893, became one of the liveliest whiskey towns in Pawnee County. Once oil was discovered nearby in 1904, the town's population exploded tenfold. As many as eleven saloons were hastily erected along Broadway, the town's main street. Four boasted attached gambling rooms while one brazen saloon owner offered "female boarding" at the corner of Broadway and Cherokee streets.

As many as 150 to 200 prostitutes worked the streets and saloons of Cleveland during this period.[26] Oklahoma was wide-open territory in the years leading up to statehood, and the primary export to Indian Territory remained bootleg whiskey. Tolerance for the lawlessness and bawdy behavior of the unruly territory began to subside with the influx of a more purposeful society of frontiersmen and women.

Those coming from the East did not share the intemperance of the earlier frontiersmen, bootleggers, robbers, and others who made up much of the population early on in the territories. Homes were built, and men and women staked out their futures and that of their children. Town councils were elected or appointed, and schools and churches rose up to overtake the saloons as places to gather and exchange ideas. In short, Oklahoma was on its way to becoming civilized, and that meant "wholesome" business activities. Oklahoma was to become the forty-sixth state, and statehood proponents were not about to have the entire process muddled by a wanton disregard for needed social change.

Even before Oklahoma became a recognized territory, some citizens pressured lawmakers to quell the illegal distribution of liquor into Indian Territory. The first Woman's Christian Temperance Union in Oklahoma was founded in Britton, now part of Oklahoma City, just after the first Land Run of 1889.[27] The temperance movement gained momentum, and by the turn of the century one Oklahoma anti-liquor organization, the Oklahoma Anti-Saloon League, claimed to have more than 15,000 members,[28] all hell-bent to abolish the sale of liquor in the territory. Soon the towns bordering Indian Territory were feeling the wrath of the temperance movement. Towns such as Weatherford, once considered one of the toughest towns of the Old West, were feeling the pinch of anti-liquor forces. In 1898

Weatherford boasted as many as twenty saloons, but by the time the staunch anti-liquor forces marched on the town in 1902, the number of saloons had dropped to seven; three years later that number had dwindled to two.[29]

Even the whiskey towns, with their beginnings deeply rooted in the liquor trade, began to realize that their businesses were doomed, becoming houses of sand. In 1897, opponents of the sandbar saloons built in the Canadian River succeeded in closing them down.[30] A rushing current of righteousness was washing away Sandtown, and in 1898 it was gone.

The temperance movement gained its greatest impetus, however, when the "matriarch" came to the new territory. Carrie Nation set up shop in Oklahoma in 1905, in Guthrie, the first capital of Oklahoma after statehood in 1907. From there Nation published two appropriately titled newspapers, the *Smasher's Mail* and the *Hatchet,* appropriate names indeed, given her chosen methods of dealing with saloons and distilleries. Saloon keepers weren't the only targets of the liquor abolitionists, however.

Carrie visited the Pottawatomie County town of Wanette on February 28, 1905. According the town's newspaper, the *Wanette Winner,* "At once she gave evidence of her personality by slapping a cigarette from the lips of a hotel porter."[31] Two months later, Nation traveled to the mother of Oklahoma Territory whiskey towns, Lexington. There it was reported that she visited two saloons and gave speeches before a standing-room-only crowd at a local meeting hall.

Nation was obviously not a timid woman. Had she been a man trying similar methods to eradicate liquor, she would have been summarily shot and left for coyote food somewhere out on the prairie. Precisely because she was a woman, and because her position was not unreasonable, she garnered the support of politicians and clergy, and was especially influential over other women. Nation feared few reprisals by pro-liquor factions.

Thus her campaign continued. The proverbial handwriting on the wall cast a sober light on the future for towns in and around Oklahoma Territory. A monumentally effective war had been waged on whiskey towns. Bowing to the pressure being persistently applied to local governments to rid themselves of the "new" scourge, a tax was implanted to try to drive the saloons from the territory. Saloons in Ponca City, Stroud, and Prague, to name but a few, were pinched by rising city liquor licensing fees and taxes. In 1900, for example, Ponca City saloons paid as much as $500 a year to maintain their licenses, a tidy sum in early twentieth-century days—nearly $10,000 by today's measure.[32]

In the mid-1890s, towns that hosted anywhere between twenty and sixty saloons almost overnight replaced those establishments with barbershops, schools, general stores, and government buildings. Newspapers soon took up the cause. Before long several publications, once only too happy to run advertisements touting the serving of North Carolina corn whiskey or "the famous white mule whiskey," suddenly refused to accept any saloon advertisements at all.

The anti-liquor movement gained steam as the new century arrived. One O. T. newspaper, the *Prague Patriot,* was running two separate temperance columns written by non-staff in 1904. None of the columns was more enthusiastic in its demand for teetotaling than that of A. J. Snow, editor of the *Appalachia Out-Look.* In one front-page column on the eve of a vote on a liquor issue Snow wrote, "I understand today is the day that the whiskey question is to be settled. That is, whether or not, that Keystone and Appalachia will continue to drench our children with that infernal, destructive, [s]oul-damaging, brain-destroying, God-dishonoring, wife-beatin' [*sic*] stuff."[33] Voters overwhelmingly passed a new proposed state constitution on September 17, 1907. Two months before becoming the forty-sixth state of the Union voters also, although with notably less enthusiasm, voted the Oklahoma and Indian Territories "dry." Every single county in Oklahoma Territory where liquor was permitted that also bordered "dry" Indian lands, voted for prohibition. The new law took effect the day Oklahoma became a state: November 16, 1907.

Prohibition meant the end for many territorial whiskey towns. Corner, Keokuk Falls, and Violet Springs all disappeared entirely. Even Lexington, arguably the birthplace of the infamous Oklahoma Whiskey Towns, saw a decline in population as a result of increasing temperance. And Old Keystone suffered so much in its decline that less than sixty years after prohibition in Oklahoma began in earnest the town had such a small population that it literally sank from all view with barely a whimper with the creation of the new Keystone Reservoir in 1962.

Chapter 5

Billy's Best Friend

With victory against the English in both the Revolutionary War and the later War of 1812, most settlers might have thought that by the late 1870s American territorial conflicts were not very likely. And to a degree they were right. Nevertheless two opposing factions of merchants with cattle interests took exception with each other in an otherwise sleepy little town in New Mexico, and trouble a-plenty was brewing.

What followed was a head-to-head conflict of monumental proportions, remembered in books, in movies, and in many television variations. The Lincoln County War became one of Western lore's most famous, long-lasting, close-in gun battles, on a par with the Earp-Clanton feud of OK Corral fame.

The two factions were made up of cattlemen and business owners whose competitive spirits gave way to base gunplay, ousting of one town sheriff for another, collusion with the governor, and military intervention arguably initiated more because of friendships than by duty under the law. Efforts to get and maintain control of Lincoln, New Mexico's, mercantile trade and cattle operations soon gave way to such business practices as horse thievery, cattle rustling, murderous ambushes, and a gun battle that would last five days, killing at least five men.

One of those who took part in the Lincoln County War bore a name that would be forever emblazoned in the minds of Western enthusiasts. Henry McCarty, by that time known as William H. Bonney and later simply as Billy the Kid, was a key figure during the Lincoln County War. Those who rode with the Kid included three men from Indian Territory, now Oklahoma. One was Big Jim French, the facts of whose life and times prior to and following the Lincoln County War are still much in dispute. The second, Billy's best friend, Frederick T. "Fred" Waite (or Wait), came to be known as Dash Waite probably as a result of his actions at Lincoln during a most heated and deadly exchange. Another of Billy's best friends was John Middleton.

Fred Waite was born in Indian Territory in 1853. He was a

quarter-blood Chickasaw who married an Indian woman and traveled to Lincoln, New Mexico, where he chose to settle. He took a job with John Tunstall, an English rancher. That association would make Waite a significant figure in the Lincoln County War. The war erupted when Tunstall was assassinated by men aligned with a most violent competitor, Lawrence G. Murphy. Murphy was not merely shrewd, but also a cutthroat business adversary who, if he couldn't run a competitor out of town, would hire a sheriff to do his bidding for him.

Waite joined Billy the Kid in making up a group of fighters known as the Regulators. The Regulators were formed to protect the interests of Tunstall and others whose properties were considered fair game by Murphy and his constituents. During their time spent together as members of the Regulators, the Kid and Waite grew to be best friends, according to leading authorities.

The House of Murphy was the business hub of Lincoln around 1877, just prior to and during the Lincoln County War. The "House" consisted of a saloon and general store, neither of which faced any competition in their respective markets. Murphy naturally preferred to keep things that way. Then Tunstall teamed with attorney Alexander McSween, a Scotsman, to open a mercantile store and bank, thus causing a change in the Lincoln County cash flow. Murphy soon recognized the potential effect this competition would have on his empire.

McSween and Murphy held many hard feelings toward each other, but when one needs a lawyer and there is only one at hand, one hires him even if he is planning to throw in with a business rival. That is what Murphy did when he commissioned McSween to collect a $10,000 life insurance policy of a partner, Emil Fritz, who had died in Germany. McSween collected the money without difficulty, but for reasons never explained he refused to turn over the money to Murphy. This infuriated the House of Murphy, and charges of embezzlement were drawn against McSween.[1]

Sheriff William Brady, who was apparently on Murphy's dole, was sent to collect McSween's cattle as a partial payment of the $10,000, but McSween was a step ahead of Murphy and turned over all his cattle to the Englishman, Tunstall. Tunstall's amiable participation in this plot led to his being ambushed by a band of Sheriff Brady's deputies on February 18, 1878. He was killed, and the war was on. Once again McSween was caught in the crosshairs of the House.

This treachery and conniving infuriated Waite and another Indian Territory compadre, Big Jim French, and led to one of the most famous shoot-outs of all time on a main street of Lincoln. The five-day gun battle and subsequent burnout of the McSween house, all of which began on July 15 and ended on July 19, 1878, eclipsed the actions that precipitated that mid-summer nightmare. It began with the assassination of Sheriff Brady in broad daylight several months earlier on April 1, 1878. He was killed by members of the Regulators. As Brady and four deputies strode down Lincoln's main street that morning, Regulators Billy the Kid, Fred Waite, Big Jim French, John Middleton, Henry Brown, and Frank McNab concealed themselves behind an adobe wall outside the McSween store, then ambushed Sheriff Brady and his men.[2]

When the lead stopped flying, Brady lay dead in the middle of the street where the first bullet fired found him. No one to this day can attest to the name of the marksman who felled the sheriff. Two of the concealed Regulators, Waite and Bonney, were injured when they ran to the corpse of Brady. They apparently intended either to retrieve rifles the lawman had confiscated from one of the men earlier, or to collect warrants for McSween that Brady was supposed to be carrying. Also wounded was Regulator Jim French or Fred Waite; history is not clear on which. Deputy Billy Matthews is credited with the shooting, however.

Another deputy, Jack Long, was wounded but survived. A second deputy, George Hindman, was shot in the neck by McNab and fell instantly where he stood. Badly wounded, Hindmann yelled for help, but the only one to answer his cry was Waite, who shot him once more, this time silencing the pleading deputy forever.

As collateral damage from the sudden burst of gunplay, a former justice of the peace named Wilson, harvesting onions across the street, was accidentally shot in the buttocks. The wound from the errant bullet was only slight and the former J. P. survived.

Wounded, French—or Waite—staggered back into the Tunstall store where clerk Sam Corbet hid the fleeing Regulator beneath a trap door that was not discovered by pursuing deputies. Because of that event, Billy secretly rode back into town after dark and successfully rescued the wounded man.

The leader of the Regulators, Dick Brewer, led his group to Blazer's Mill for a meal three days after the Lincoln ambush that killed Sheriff Brady and Deputy Hindmann. But now their number had grown to sixteen. There a classic Old West shoot-out occurred on April 4, 1878. It was one against sixteen, but the one was determined to kill as many as he could for reward money or die trying.

His name was Andrew L. "Buckshot" Roberts, and he had been a member of the Brady posse that gunned down Tunstall in February of 1878. The Regulators, especially Billy, remembered and hated Roberts for that act.

Roberts' checkered path included stints as a soldier, bounty hunter, criminal, and buffalo hunter. He was a native of the South, but no real records exist as to where he was born or even when. Much about Buckshot's life is made up of rumor. For example, there is more than one explanation as to how he earned the nickname, Buckshot. Some versions claim that Roberts received his nickname because: he liked to use a shotgun; his body was riddled with buckshot; or, he beat a hasty retreat from Texas with shotguns blasting after him. Other rumors about Roberts concern his chosen career path, and questions remain to this day.

Was Roberts a desperado and gunman, an army deserter, a convict, a Texas Ranger, or an enemy of the Texas Rangers? What is known for certain about Roberts is that he was a formidable and fearless fighter. Also known is that Roberts' upper body mobility was limited; he had been severely wounded in some unrecorded gun battle. Those wounds prevented him from raising his rifle to shoulder height. Roberts was known for his remarkable accuracy when firing his rifle from the hip. He never backed away from trouble, and in many cases such as seeking out Billy the Kid and the Regulators, he went looking for it. He found it at Blazer's Mill on the morning of April 4, 1878.

Attracted by the $200 reward posted for the murders of Sheriff Brady and his deputy, Roberts set out to collect as much of that money as he could. He knew that the Kid and several of his Regulators were keeping camp at Blazer's Mill, and he headed straight for the place. It did not bother Roberts in the least that those same Regulators were interested in "questioning" him about his involvement in John Tunstall's death.

When Buckshot rode his mule up to the mill that morning, he had but one thing on his mind: kill as many as possible and collect as much of the reward as possible.

So it didn't matter to him that an old friend with the Regulators, Frank Coe, came out to parley with him. A few words were exchanged before some of the other hired guns began to emerge from the mill. At some point in the conversation Dick Brewer, who headed the outfit, made a play for Roberts. The result was one hell of a gunfight.

Roberts managed to wound or kill three of his adversaries before succumbing to a mortal wound. Billy the Kid was not injured in the mêlée and lived to continue to fight in the Lincoln County War.

With Brewer dead, Frank McNab took the reins of leadership of the Regulators.

Fred Waite, one of the men from Indian Territory now with the Regulators, was also in the midst of things when the shooting began at Blazer's Mill. And not unlike everyone else who could do so, Waite scampered for cover while throwing lead in the direction of Roberts.

Waite, it seemed, was better than most at dodging bullets. That ability was again evidenced during the mass escape from the McSween house in Lincoln the night of July 19, 1878, after it was set ablaze by factions loyal to Murphy. Some authorities claimed that is how he came by the nickname Dash.

The other Regulator hailing from Indian Territory was Big Jim French. There is no record that either of the two Oklahomans knew one another prior to joining the Regulators. After all, Oklahoma was still an untamed territory with little law save whatever could be enforced through the United States Federal Courts, and it was not uncommon to have as lawmen former bootleggers and bandits. Waite made his home in the Chickasaw Nation near Pauls Valley. French likely was a drifter with no special place to hang his hat.

Little is known of French's presumably humble beginnings or of what exactly became of him after the Lincoln County War. Some speculate that he rode with Billy the Kid for a short while after the range war ended, stealing horses and other stock. He soon tired of that career, as the story goes, and is said to have simply ridden off into the sunset where his tracks are obscured by the blowing winds of time. Still others say French sailed to South America.

One source whose testimony is difficult to repudiate is Frank Coe, a participant in the Lincoln County War who fought with French and the Regulators. Coe said that French, once leaving Billy's band of stock thieves, returned to Indian Territory, where he continued his wanderings and where he died in either 1905 or 1924, depending on who is telling the story.[3]

During those rough and tumble times, questions of who, what, where, and when seemed not only unnecessary but sometimes downright dangerous. Today, as is often the case with Old West figures, details of French's life and demise were left to his own story, entirely true or not, and rumor.

Although unlikely, it is possible that Big Jim French was half-Cherokee, raised in Fort Gibson, I. T., by his father, Tom, and one source says, graduated *cum laude* from the male seminary in Tahlequah. Despite his lofty academic attainments, French allegedly killed a man in or near Fort Gibson in 1889 or 1891; again the details are obscure.[4]

Was this the Jim French who returned to Indian Territory from New Mexico? Certainly Jim French the Regulator could have been involved in a killing there in 1889 or 1891. The Lincoln County War was well over by then, and several of the Regulators who thought better of joining or remaining with the Kid's stock-theft ring probably did set out to return home. Thus, French the Regulator may have been among those who preferred a familiar home place to a life of raiding and being raided.

French probably would have considered the mystery surrounding his remaining days' whereabouts and activities an advantage in that era. Today it seems a shame to lose the details of a man who figured prominently in the life and times of Billy the Kid and the Lincoln County War.

Another of those riding and fighting with Billy the Kid was Frederick T. Waite. Waite may not share the name recognition the Kid has, but he was as much a part of the killing during the Lincoln County War as one of the Regulators. Waite was about six years older than Billy, and the two men became fast and loyal friends.

Waite was born in 1853 at or very near Fort Arbuckle, Indian Territory, near Pauls Valley; he was a member of the Chickasaw Nation and one-quarter Chickasaw. His parents were Thomas Waite and Catherine McClure Waite.

Fred Waite was sent to Champaign, Illinois, where he attended the Illinois Industrial University. Later he went to Bentonville, Arkansas, for further studies before finishing his education. He graduated from Mound City Commercial College in St. Louis, Missouri, with the equivalent of a modern MBA. After graduation, Waite worked for his father at the family business located on Rush Creek, I. T., near Pauls Valley for about two years before deciding to head west.

He traveled to Colorado before he crossed into New Mexico around 1877, nearly one year before the clash of merchants in Lincoln. He was employed by rancher John Tunstall as a cowhand, but changed job descriptions when his employer was gunned down by Sheriff Brady's posse on February 18, 1878.[5]

Waite was among the group of Regulators—including Billy the Kid—who, on April Fools Day, 1878, hid out in Lincoln inside the Tunstall store, where they lay in ambush for Sheriff Brady and his deputies. Brady, with his deputies Jack Long, George Hindman, George Peppin, and Billy Matthews, all armed to the teeth, took a stroll down the center of town on their way to the courthouse, where they were going to post notice that court was postponed.[6] The five lawmen might not have marched toward the courthouse in such a careless, confident manner had they known what awaited them.

Around 11:00 a.m., as Brady and his men walked past the Tunstall store, Billy the Kid and Regulators Fred Waite, Henry Brown, John Middleton, Frank McNab, and Big Jim French unleashed a firestorm from behind an adjacent adobe wall. Brady was killed instantly, and Hindman died of wounds.

Waite grew tired of living by the gun. As the gang, now led by Billy, began to break apart in 1881, Waite left the group, but not before offering to help establish Billy the Kid as a white member of the Choctaw Nation. Waite would set Billy up with a farm in Indian Territory. Although legend has it he did visit his best friend once while in I. T., only to come away with a stolen horse,

Billy refused Waite's generosity and returned to New Mexico.

Waite finally put his extensive education to use and followed a career path that led to political appointments and elected positions. He remained in his native I. T., where he held positions ranging from saloon owner to attorney general of the Chickasaw tribe. By 1881, Waite was married to Mary E. Thompson, who provided Waite with a daughter, Katie.

In 1888, Waite was appointed by Chickasaw governor William Malcolm Guy as a delegate to the International Convention at Fort Gibson, I. T, and in 1889 he was elected representative of Pickens County. He became speaker of the House, a place of prominence he held for the three sessions that followed. In 1890, Waite attempted to further his political ambitions by announcing his candidacy for the Senate on the Progressive ticket.

On September 24, 1895, at the age of forty-two, Waite succumbed to a bout with rheumatism. Billy's best friend was dead.[7]

Mystery is a constant but elusive companion to several of the former Regulators. Those whose later years are clouded by obscurity include not only Big Jim French but also a one-time Oklahoma man, John Middleton.

In fact, so little is known about Middleton that—with the exception of his activities during the Lincoln County War—even his age remains uncertain. But what has been recorded does provide an interesting glimpse into this man's past, a past made up of murders, war, fraud, and perhaps a stint as a grocery store clerk. Either way, John Middleton did participate in the Lincoln County War, fighting alongside Billy the Kid, Big Jim French, Fred Waite, and others until the group disbanded sometime in 1881.

Middleton may have been the man of the same name who was the cousin of Jim Reed, first husband of the infamous Belle Starr. That John Middleton is thought to have been born in Arkansas about 1855, and Middleton's rap sheet starts at a relatively young age. In 1873 he received his first conviction, although little is known about it except that it occurred in Scott County, Arkansas. He spent one year in the state pen and returned to Scott County where, it is said, he busied himself with the attempted arson of the county courthouse at Waldron.[8]

What is certain is that sometime in the late 1870s a John

Middleton drifted into New Mexico from Kansas, and due to his tough-guy demeanor he caught the eye of John Tunstall, who was in the process of recruiting fearless gunmen for what would later become known as the Lincoln County War. Describing his first impression of Middleton, Tunstall is quoted as having said he was "about the most desperate looking man I ever set eyes on"—which may have been all Tunstall needed to know about him.

Middleton was at Steel, New Mexico, on March 9, 1878, less than one month after the gunning down of Tunstall by Sheriff Brady's men. There he and other Regulators captured Frank Barker and Billy Morton, key figures in that murder. Barker and Morton were killed that same day, after Morton grabbed a gun of one of the Regulators, William McCloskey, and shot him through the head in a failed attempt to escape. And, of course, Middleton was on hand for the ambush of Brady and four of his deputies on April Fools' Day, 1878, also less than one month after Barker and Morton were killed.

Middleton's last hurrah as a Regulator came during the siege of Andrew L. "Buckshot" Roberts at Blazer's Mill. Middleton took a rifle slug to the chest; the bullet tearing through the upper part of his left lung. The leader of the Regulators, Dick Brewer, was also killed. Having shot Roberts early on, the posse is said to have believed that he was near death, and so decided to take Middleton and fellow Regulator George Coe, who was shot in the hand, to nearby Fort Stanton for medical help.[9]

Middleton survived his wounds that day, April 4, 1878, but this is where the rest of his history gets somewhat lost on the plains' dusty trail. Although most historians place John Middleton's death in the year 1885, it is not clear whether the Middleton to whom these historians refer is the same as the "the most desperate looking man [John Tunstall] ever set eyes on" and who fought with the Regulators at Lincoln, New Mexico.

The John Middleton of Regulator fame was said to have left that group as inconspicuously as he joined it, unobtrusively drifting out of New Mexico just as he had drifted into it a few years earlier. It is widely accepted that Middleton shot and killed newly elected Sheriff J. H. Black of Lamar County, Texas, on November 11, 1884, at the request of the deposed sheriff. One year later a John Middleton met and began a trifling dalliance with Belle Starr, whose husband Sam was away from the gang's hideout at Younger's Bend as a prison guest of the federal government.

Then on May 11, 1885, the badly decomposed body of a John Middleton was discovered on the banks of the Poteau River near Keota in the Choctaw Nation of Indian Territory. This John Middleton had been ambushed. His suspected killer? Sam Starr.[10]

However, in yet another account, Middleton separated from the Kid at Tascosa, Texas, sometime in 1878, and proceeded to Kansas where he unsuccessfully tried his hand at being a grocer. Middleton also spent time attempting to wheedle money from John Tunstall Sr., of England, the father of the murdered New Mexico rancher. Ramon F. Adams, in his book *Burs under the Saddle,* makes no mention of Middleton's connection to Belle Starr or I. T.

Yet a third Middleton, known as "Two Gun John," served as a deputy sheriff of Kay County, Oklahoma, and in that capacity was mortally wounded with George "Hookey" Miller, on July 21, 1923, at Three Sand attempting to arrest Jack Burns. The question remains: Were there three gunfighters named John Middleton in the Old West, or were there only two?

Others of more prominence who rode alongside the Kid included Henry Newton Brown, who, after fighting it out in the Lincoln County War, did a bit of wandering, finding employment where it suited him. About 1879, Brown was appointed sheriff of Oldham County, Texas, but lost that job because he was ill-tempered and may have caused as much trouble as he was hired to stamp out. Then in 1881, Brown was hired by Littlefield as sheriff but was once again dismissed for being a hothead. He took a job as cowhand offered by Barney O'Connor, foreman of a ranch in Woods County, Oklahoma Territory. But wanderlust took hold of Brown, and he soon followed the trail to a wild Kansas town just across the border named Caldwell.

Before long, Brown once again pinned a badge to his shirt and took the by-then-familiar oath of office of the peace officer. This time, July of 1882, Brown did rather well at his job, apparently not letting his temper get the better of him. In a few months he was promoted from the position of deputy marshal to that of city marshal, giving him full range of the powers of that job. He hired a man from Texas to be his deputy.

Ben Wheeler (whose real name was Ben Robertson) was known by Brown to be a man who dealt severely with individuals who crossed him. Within a short time the two hard cases managed to rid Caldwell of its rowdiest element.

The townspeople were so taken with Brown's effectiveness as Caldwell's chief law enforcement officer that on New Year's Day 1883, they presented him with a new Winchester rifle. The rifle had a silver plate attached to the stock with an inscription recognizing his "valuable service to the citizens of Caldwell, Kansas." What the smitten citizens of Caldwell, Kansas, didn't know was that Brown and Robertson each worked together on a second job. Such an undertaking would not have necessarily tarnished the folks' collective opinion of the two officers, except that their second job was that of robbing the banks of other towns.[11]

The two men received permission from the town's elders to travel south across the state line on the pretense of capturing a murderer, and while they did in fact dip into Indian Territory, upholding the law was the farthest thing from their minds. Instead they picked up a couple of desperadoes, cowboys by the names of William Smith and John Wesley. The four gunmen then turned their mounts back to the north and into Kansas, where Brown and Robertson would attempt to rob their very last bank.

At the crossroads of present-day U.S. Highways 281 and 160 in south-central Kansas is the small town of Medicine Lodge, approximately seventy miles west by northwest of Caldwell and a little more than thirty-two miles directly north of present-day Alva, Oklahoma, in Woods County. Woods County, incidentally, is where Brown was once employed as a cowhand by Barney O'Connor. And it is entirely possible that that is where Brown recruited his two Oklahoma gunmen. Apparently, it was only coincidence that O'Connor was in Medicine Lodge the day Brown and his accomplices decided to rob the Medicine Valley Bank.

Brown and Robertson rode into Oklahoma Territory on a Sunday in late April 1884, and collected Wesley and Smith. Early the following Wednesday morning, April 30, they staked fresh horses in a canyon near Medicine Lodge and rode into town, leaving Smith to guard the horses. A driving rain kicked up, drenching everything, and showed no signs of letting up.

A little after 9:00 a.m., the three men walked into the Medicine Valley Bank and almost immediately made their wishes known. They confronted bank president E. W. Payne and a cashier named George Geppert. They demanded money, but instead of complying with the bandits' demand, Payne went for a revolver, a mistake on his part. He was gunned down by Brown. Even though Geppert had thrown his hands in the air, Wesley and Robertson pumped lead into him as well. Geppert, mortally wounded, staggered to the vault and managed to throw the lock on the safe, thus thwarting the robbers' intent. Geppert then slid to a sitting position in the vault, where he died.[12]

Brown, Robertson, and Wesley dashed out of the bank empty-handed. Scampering to mount their horses, the trio galloped out of town toward Gypsum Canyon, where Smith and the fresh mounts waited. The citizenry apparently heard the commotion coming from inside the bank and upon discovery of what had taken place became hopping mad. The chase was on.

Led by Brown's former employer, Barney O'Connor, a makeshift and somewhat undisciplined posse took quick shape and galloped after the bandits. The rain continued to drive hard, softening dirt trails and swelling creek beds. Through the pouring rain the robbers made time as quickly as they could. One of the thieves' horses was beginning to fail, however, probably due to slogging through deeply mudded trails at breakneck speeds. Then Brown led his men into a canyon only to discover that he had turned into a small thirty- or forty-foot box canyon. It was the wrong canyon, and a bad move.[13]

He and his men held out for two hours, but it soon became only too obvious that they weren't going to be able to do so much longer. The posse outside the canyon only had to wait: wait for the robbers to use up their ammunition, wait for them to begin to starve, wait for the canyon to fill with flood waters—which it was beginning to do—and drown the bandits.

Brown apparently took note of those same possibilities, and when two hours had passed he threw down his guns and begged for protection against the angry citizens of Medicine Lodge. His comrades followed suit, and with the capture of Smith some time later, all four men were shuffled back to Medicine Lodge, presumably to await trial. However, the irate townspeople had other ideas, and when the foursome was brought in by the posse they were met with threats of lynching and other out-of-court remedies for the evil of their ways. They were tossed into a log building whose former purpose is not known, but whose immediate purpose became that of the town jail.

For a while it seemed that things had smoothed over. The men each ate two meals during their stay and posed for pictures for the local media. They seemed to be considered not much more than an irksome sideshow of some kind. As evening drew its blanket over the town, however, the mood darkened with the setting sun. Around nine o'clock that night three shots were fired; if they struck anything or anyone it was not reported, but the guards were overpowered. The jail was breached, and a seething mob rushed the prisoners.

In the mêlée that followed on that night of April 30, 1884, Brown had anticipated the townspeoples' mood and slipped from his cuffs. He broke for the door, and his getaway would have been clean had it not been for the farmer who unloaded his double-barreled shotgun at him. As if that wasn't enough to kill a man, several rifle bullets thudded into the prone body. Brown was dead. Robertson, who had been wounded during the siege, was taken to a nearby tree and hanged in the company of Wesley and Smith.

In a letter written from the makeshift jail to his wife, whom he had married just one month before the Medicine Lodge incident, Brown offered a rather feeble explanation for his actions: "[I]t was all for you."[14]

Not every one of the former Regulators had such an inglorious demise. Some just wandered out of New Mexico and back to their native lands or simply disappeared from history altogether. Big Jim French may have died in one of a number of unrelated incidents or may have taken passage on a sailing ship to South America. No one can say for sure what happened to him. Likewise, the eternal fate of John Middleton remains a historic question mark. Is he the John Middleton who may have dallied with the infamous Belle Starr while her husband, Sam, stewed in a Kansas state prison and who later was found badly decomposed on an Indian Territory riverbank in 1885? Or did Middleton finish out his days roaming haplessly from Kansas town to Kansas town trying to reinvent himself until his death in 1885? Or was he mortally wounded with Hookey Miller in a 1923 gunfight?

Chapter 6

Oklahoma Bad Girls

Cattle rustling, gun battles with deputy sheriffs, hard-ridden escapes from fleeing posses—these activities were not uncommon for most of the nineteenth- and even part of early twentieth-century Oklahoma. They were not unusual at all, unless this fact is considered: Many of these activities were conducted by women, the so-called weaker sex.

Most True Crime readers and Old West enthusiasts are quite familiar with the names of Belle Starr, Ma Barker, and Bonnie Parker, whose contributions to the flavor, romance, and lore of the era are without precedent. Or are they?

Before statehood, Oklahoma for all intents and purposes had no uniform law enforcement presence. Its earliest settlers were forced to live in the territory as part of a mass removal from eastern lands. Civilization brought with it its constraints of accepted, polite social behavior. Many who sought only solitude and the freedom to live under nature's law—not the nation's law—looked to Indian Territory for refuge and opportunity. Many of these opportunists included a type of woman whose free spirit and determination moved her to throw off the glitter of society for the grit of simplicity.

These were the Oklahoma women who were more at ease with drilling a pursuing posseman than darning a petticoat; women who, like their male counterparts, came to be known by a nickname that shed a little light on their character. Women such as Poker Alice, Cattle Annie, and Little Britches shocked the sophisticated East by emulating the raucous, gun-toting, cigar-smoking, whiskey-guzzling behavior of their outlaw hombres.

These and other women of equally scandalous behavior were active participants in lootings, shoot-outs, and robberies throughout Indian and Oklahoma Territories. These Oklahoma bad girls were just as hotly pursued as their male counterparts and sometimes found themselves doing time in reformatories or prisons. Just like their male counterparts, these women considered none of the perils a deterrent; rather, they found them motivational.

Before this chapter delves into the mythological activities of some of the female criminals of the period, it will take a short ride down history's dusty trail to examine some female killers.

Polly Ann Reynolds

Polly Ann Reynolds was a rather large, unrefined woman. Polly Ann was anything but what her name inspires in thought. She was a woman of generous proportions, weighing in at around 280 pounds. For all her formidable size, she was apparently quick to anger.

Polly Ann's temper got the best of her one New Year's Eve, and she was later hauled into Judge Isaac Parker's court in Fort Smith, Arkansas, charged with murdering a friend. History doesn't say whether the friend was male or female, nor what precipitated the tragic death of Polly Ann's "friend." However, the cause of death is quite clear. "Miss Reynolds . . . was brought to Fort Smith charged with kicking a friend to death at a New Year's celebration," according to historian Fred Harvey Harrington.[1] Judge Parker evidently was not unaccustomed to seeing similar behavior in women brought before him. Apparently Oklahoma and Indian Territories were fertile ground on which female slayers of men were not in short supply. Polly Ann was just one of several femme fatales brought in from the Twin Territories to answer to the courts for their less than prudish behavior.

Alvirado Hudson

For years Mrs. Alvirado Hudson lived a quiet homebody kind of life on the farm with her equally quiet homebody husband, John. Apparently Mrs. Hudson grew weary of a life of splitting wood, scrubbing the washboard, and shucking ears of corn, and so she began shucking her petticoat for a man named Bill Tucker.

Now Bill Tucker was nothing like the farmer to whom Alvirado was married, and with whom she shared a humble existence. In fact, Tucker was already known by Judge Isaac Parker; the "hanging judge" had already sentenced Tucker to the Detroit House of Corrections.[2] When the roving eyes and unfulfilled desires of Mrs.

Hudson eventually fell upon Tucker, she found everything about him to be exciting. The two commenced a most illicit affair, unbeknownst, of course, to farmer John.

And as the temperature heated up during the summer of 1887, Tucker and Mrs. Hudson's affair showed no signs of cooling off. Quite the opposite, Tucker was openly boasting that he planned to kill his paramour's husband. Unaccustomed to such deceit and treachery, John probably wasn't aware that Tucker's blathering was anything more than the ranting of a loud-mouthed braggart.

That June, however, John Hudson was murdered while tending his garden. Mrs. Hudson was then free to marry her "bad boy" lover, which she did.

Even though lawmen, including Judge Parker, were convinced that Bill Tucker and his new bride, the Widow Hudson, were guilty of murdering her husband, evidence against the two was scarce. Bill Tucker, with his track record, seemed the most likely candidate— besides the widow. In January 1888, Tucker was arrested on a charge of train robbery, but even that charge had to be dismissed. Lawmen eventually tagged him with a charge of selling liquor to the Indians; this was one charge that Tucker apparently could not dispute, and so he posted a cash bond to gain release from jail.

Tucker immediately went on the lam, forsaking both bride and bond, and left Fort Smith in a hurry. His freedom was short-lived, and when the deputies caught up to him this time they jailed Tucker on charges of horse theft and robbery. But those charges would have been a walk in the park compared to what the lawmen were really trying to get the court to charge him with: the murder of John Hudson.

Alvirado Tucker, while not completely off the hook for the alleged murder of her former husband, was not as easy to pin charges on. She had no previous criminal record, and even though she was not a particularly well-placed member of the community, she nonetheless was a woman, and harassing her, even in the righteous name of the badge, would have been derided by the townspeople as abusive. For that reason alone, the deputies concentrated their efforts on the previously convicted Bill Tucker.

The new Mrs. Tucker hadn't quite exhausted her conniving ways in the hope of springing her husband from jail. She convinced two small-time hoodlums to help her with a jailbreak. She then turned to a trusty named Charles Wilson, and told him of her plan, which included Wilson's delivering hacksaws to Tucker. Because Wilson maintained trusty status he was allowed to perform small jobs outside the jail as part of his sentence.

Wilson did as Alvirado planned, and on the afternoon prescribed he returned to the jail as he was ordered to do. Alvirado was convinced this was a surefire scheme, so clever in its planning and performance that her man would soon be by her side. She waited.

But the man who came to see Alvirado on that night of anxious anticipation was not Bill Tucker, her husband of ill repute, but a deputy who promptly arrested and charged Alvirado and her accomplices with the attempted jailbreak of Tucker. Trusty Charles Wilson just could not be trusted to stay crooked. Rather than join the ranks of Alvirado's accomplices he instead weaseled his way to the jailer and sang like a canary.

The jailer, a man named Pettigrew, informed Judge Parker of Alvirado's escape plan, and the judge, citing a need for hard evidence against her, told the jailer to allow the plan to go forward. Then, as Trusty Wilson entered the jail, he would be routinely searched, the saws would be discovered, and the plan revealed, naming Alvirado and the two male scoundrels as her accomplices. That plan worked, and soon everybody involved was behind bars. Wilson continued in his status of trusty and, as is the case with most trusties, probably saw to the needs of the new inmates he had just helped place behind bars.

Alvirado was sentenced to one year in the penitentiary for her part in the foiled plan to bust her husband out of jail. Bill Tucker's charge of the murder of John Hudson never did stick, but he was given an eleven-year sentence following convictions in Parker's court on three counts of horse theft and one count of burglary.[3]

Little else is known of Alvirado. She disappeared from history along with her two would-be accomplices.

Fannie Echols

About four years before the shenanigans of the Widow Hudson and the nefarious Bill Tucker, there came before Judge Parker's bench a bright, intelligent, perhaps a little full figured but otherwise attractive girl. This one, Miss Fannie Echols, was charged with murdering a coworker in 1884. This charge stuck, and she became the first female ever to be sentenced to be "hanged by the neck until dead" by Judge Parker.[4]

Echols, it seems, had taken employment out in the Creek Nation with an unmarried coworker by the name of John Williams. Even though the two were not married to each other, they found that living together was, although perhaps somewhat frowned upon, nonetheless a suitably convenient arrangement. Convenient to a point that is, but that point was lost on John Williams, shot as he lay in bed.

It was easy for the townspeople to side with one so bright and lovely, and had it not been for the pesky facts of the crime, Fannie just might have gotten away with murder. But the men of the court saw things in a little different light and presented a straightforward prosecution against her.

Apparently Williams never did develop a jealous streak and threaten to kill Echols as she claimed, although evidence was introduced that he did occasionally whip her "when he happened to be in an ugly mood." But that in and of itself was no cause to kill a man back in those days. After all, it would be about another hundred years before a woman taking matters into her own hands and rendering immediate punishment would be considered a reasonable case of self-defense.

Be that as it may, there was a sore lack of evidence in the illicit couple's bedroom to even suggest that anything more than a verbal row had taken place. According to the officers who looked into her claim, there was no sign of struggle at all. And when sworn to testify, witnesses said the only out-of-the-ordinary sounds they heard was a single pistol shot and Miss Echols shouting exuberantly, "There! I've killed him!"

As if the deck wasn't already stacked against her, when the authorities were summoned to the cabin, they found Williams dead as a doornail, lying in the two lovers' bed "in a sleeping position." Worse yet was that when the scene was inspected more closely, it was discovered that not only had Williams been shot through the torso but that the offending bullet had lodged into the floor directly beneath where he lay. That only meant one thing to Parker and the jury: Echols shot Williams as he lay sleeping like a baby and not, as she suggested, during wild anger brought on by his supposedly jealous nature.

The jury ruled that the homicide was indeed cold-blooded murder. Parker sentenced Miss Fannie Echols to be hanged by the neck until dead. She wasn't alone in her appointment with eternity, however. For on the date ordered, July 11, 1884, Echols would swing with six men: five murderers and one rapist.

Fannie managed to coo her way out of an upcoming necktie fitting by soliciting assistance from a higher power: that of President Chester A. Arthur, who ordered a reprieve. So instead of hanging, she was shipped to the penitentiary at Columbus, Ohio, to serve out her remaining years.

Elsie James

Judge Isaac Parker sentenced to the gallows three other women all of whose sentences were commuted to life in prison. One was described as "a giant of a woman." Elsie James ran her Chickasaw farm with the help of hired men after her husband died. One of the men, William Jones, was rumored to be employed as more than just a field hand.[5]

Then one day in 1887 gigolo Jones came up missing. The veteran deputy United States marshal Henry "Heck" Thomas was put on the case. Thomas learned that in addition to Elsie James being a mountain of a woman she was also a monumental liar.

When asked on three separate occasions what she knew about Jones's disappearance she gave three separate responses, the last of which was that another of her hired hands actually shot and killed Jones and that her only part was to help keep the act quiet. Heck Thomas wasn't buying any of it, and when Jones's body was eventually found and unearthed, the manner of death was quite apparent. There were no bullet holes, but the man's skull had been bashed in by a hefty blow with a blunt instrument. After a few more tries at interrogation Thomas learned that the blunt instrument was what is called a hominy pestle, a wooden device used for crushing wheat grain into a powder for the making of bread. Its shape is similar to that of a rolling pin, and Elsie was notorious for carrying it with her at all times.

Elsie sold the farm so she could hire four of the best lawyers Fort Smith had to offer, but the jury was unaffected by the prominence of the barristers and convicted the widow of murder. Five days before she was to swing from a rope looped over a hefty gallows' beam, President Benjamin Harrison commuted Elsie's sentence to life imprisonment. She was then sent back east to Columbus, Ohio, where Fannie Echols was currently doing time.

Mollie King

Then there is the tale of the frontier hotel chambermaid and the stable boy. Generally this type of pairing has all the makings of a deliciously scandalous affair. But to Mollie King, the chambermaid, and her husband Ed, the stable boy, it became obvious after only a short while that not all about being wedded was bliss. Arguments seemed about the only way the two could communicate with one another, and they soon managed to cool their tempers by agreeing to separate but not divorce.[6]

For Mollie this was a golden opportunity, for it seemed she had a curious streak in her that could only be satisfied in the course of discovering what men other than her husband could do for her in a wildly promiscuous way. Since Mollie worked at a local hotel, the opportunity to satisfy her "curiosity" was no further from her than the next room and the next room and so on.

Eventually Ed the stable boy-husband found out about Mollie's copious couplings in pursuit of customer satisfaction, and this discovery led to more quarrels, which did nothing to resolve the pair's differences. Mollie had a plan that she believed would forever resolve their problem: Kill Ed.

It wasn't very long before Ed found himself recuperating from an ambush his wife had orchestrated, probably with help from one of her admirers. But Ed managed to pull through, surviving that attack and avoiding his charmingly, potentially lethal wife. But one day, Ed having had his usual diet of frontier whiskey—which he consumed mightily—once again fell for a trap set by the seductive Mrs. King.

It was some time later that poor Ed's half-naked corpse was discovered, shot full of holes from behind.

Mollie King was charged with the shooting, along with a man the prosecution said assisted her, one Barry Foreman. The case was tried in 1896, the last year Parker sat on the bench. King and Foreman were found guilty of murder and sentenced to the gallows. But on appeal, the Supreme Court reversed Parker's decision. A new trial was held in 1897, the year after Parker's death, in which Foreman was cleared of any wrongdoing and King received a life sentence.

Poker Alice

"At my age I suppose I should be knitting," quipped Alice Ivers, a habitual gambler. She was born in Sudbury, England, in 1851, the only daughter of a schoolmaster. There she was educated at a female seminary, which, along with her father's strict moral guidelines, imbued her with a strong sense of middle-class values. The Iverses moved to Virginia when Alice was in her late teens, but then moved on to Colorado. It was there, in 1875, that Alice met and married her first husband, Frank Duffield, a mining engineer. Frank liked to spend time at the card tables after work, and Alice was not about to be left home alone darning socks when she could be out with Frank dealing cards. Many evenings the two ventured from their Lake City home to find a card game. It wasn't long before Alice spent as much time during the day playing cards as she did with Frank in the evenings. But that dealing duo came to an abrupt end one day when Frank was killed in a dynamite explosion while at work in the mines.

Unable to find work as a schoolteacher, for which she was most qualified, and needing to fill the loss of her husband's income, Alice turned to the only other thing she knew she was good at: poker. Thus she made her living, and thus she earned the nickname, Poker Alice.

Poker Alice evidently felt the need to take her talent on the trail. She played at games throughout the West to include Oklahoma Territory, where she dealt her hand at tables in Guthrie and other promising towns throughout what would become Oklahoma.[7]

Poker Alice, whose formative refinement kept her from dressing like many other uninhibited women of the Old West, maintained a neat appearance and fashionable attire. But even so, she developed a taste for a good stogie and was seen constantly puffing on a thick, black cigar everywhere she went. To add to that image, Alice was also widely known to carry a .38-caliber pistol mounted on a .45 frame.

In 1880, hearing of a new silver-mining town in Colorado called Creede, Alice left Indian Territory and headed back to the San Juan Mountains where the action was fast, the gambling never ceased, and the silver kept flowing. She took a job managing the card tables at Bob Ford's Creede Exchange, and her reputation as a gambler became all the talk on the card-playing circuit.

The circuit took Alice to Deadwood, South Dakota, where she dealt cards and met her second husband, W. G. Tubbs. Alice and Tubbs became better acquainted one day when, while working neighboring tables, a drunken, disgruntled card player pulled a knife on Tubbs. Alice expertly palmed her .38 and fired off a round, hitting the rowdy miscreant in the arm and thereby settling his complaints.[8]

From that moment on, Alice and W. G. Tubbs folded their professional relationship in favor of a personal one. The two were married in 1907 and left gambling for a homestead just north of Deadwood. The two settled down on their homestead, and for the next three years Alice and Tubbs were out of the gambling game, raising sheep on their land. But in the winter of 1910 Tubbs contracted pneumonia and died in the couple's home during a blizzard despite Alice's best efforts to comfort her man.

Showing her native character and tenacity, Alice loaded the corpse on a horse-drawn sled and drove her dead husband to Sturgis, some forty-eight miles away, to be buried. The price tag of the burial was twenty-five dollars, which she did not have. Rather than have her husband interred in a pauper's grave, Alice pawned her wedding ring to pay for the interment of the second husband she would bury.[9] She later won enough money at her old trade to be able to redeem the ring, which she wore to her death.

Poker Alice kept the homestead she and W. G. had settled while she continued her gambling in Sturgis. The trip, forty-eight miles each way, was too daunting to make daily, so she hired one George Huckert to see to the property and livestock during her absences. Huckert continued to pepper Alice with propositions of marriage, which she repeatedly rebuffed. However, Alice saw an advantage to accepting Huckert's proposition when she calculated back wages of $1,008 which she owed him. "It would be cheaper to marry him than to pay him off," she was quoted as saying, and so she did the former.

Still smoking cigars and still carrying her trusty .38, Poker Alice showed little signs of slowing down. In the 1920s, in her seventies, Alice was operating a roadhouse on the road between Sturgis and Fort Meade. Most of her patrons were soldiers. Alice became particularly annoyed one afternoon with a brawl that seemed to have no end and fired a shot through the closed door of the room where the ruckus was taking place. Unfortunately, in so doing she hit and killed one of the drunken soldiers inside that room. A later inquest cleared her of any wrongdoing, but her roadhouse was closed down by local authorities as a result.

The remainder of her life was spent in relatively quiet fashion, and on February 27, 1930, Poker Alice died. She is buried in the Catholic Cemetery at Sturgis, South Dakota.[10]

Cattle Annie and Little Britches

Two women, girls really, made a rather large nuisance of themselves to early-day Oklahoma peace officers. They were involved in all sorts of crime-related activities including horse thieving and whiskey peddling, but more infuriating to those sworn to uphold the peace was the charge that the two teenage girls were suspected of acting as informants for the infamous Bill Doolin and his gang of desperados. However, today that is a matter of controversy and much doubt among many historians.

Anna "Annie" McDougal and Jennie Stevens would go down forever in history as Cattle Annie and Little Britches. In the name of clarity the authors have relied on the spelling of Anna McDougal, however Cattle Annie's last name also appears as McDoulet or McDouglet.

The tale of Cattle Annie and Little Britches and how they each met, ran off with, rode with, and fell in love with members of Bill Doolin's Oklahombres is fine fodder for any tales of the dames of the Old West. This tantalizing story in all its sordid aspects is, according to one noted historian and author, Nancy Samuelson, one of total fabrication. Nonetheless, it is offered to the reader solely based on its merits of being a good Old West yarn.

Born the same year, 1879, neither girl knew of the other until they were introduced at a barn dance in Oklahoma's Indian Territory in about 1888. As the two grew to become teens, they became close friends, sharing a great deal with each other including a place in history.

Annie McDougal was born to James C. and Rebekah McDougal who hailed from Lawrence County, Kansas. James was a preacher-lawyer in the nearby small community of Fall River.[11] Annie was the third eldest of nine siblings that included an older brother, Calvin, and an older sister, Martha, as well as the younger Claude, Maude, Everett, George, James, and John.[12]

The McDougal patriarch moved his family to Skiatook, Indian Territory, where Annie met members of the Doolin gang. Shortly afterward, she attended a country dance at a small crossroads community south of Pawnee, where she first met one of Doolin's gunmen. Annie was introduced to a bandit by a boyfriend who said that he knew the man was a member of the notorious Doolin gang. Annie fell for the purported gang member instantly.[13] Already in love with the romantic and suspenseful tales of the Doolin gang's escapades, Annie then had her very own bandit on whom she could spend her emotions. Annie was a young teen when she took up with one of Doolin's men, supposedly Red Buck Weightman.[14]

Jennie Stevens (Stephenson) was born in 1879 to Daniel and Lucy Stephenson of Barton County, Missouri. Her only known sibling was her sister, Victoria Estella. In about 1888, when Jennie would have been nine years old, the family moved to the rural town of Sinnett, Oklahoma Territory, in the southeast corner of Pawnee County. Jennie's new home place was not far from a Doolin gang hideout along the Cimarron River.[15]

Since people out on the frontier commonly welcomed strangers who might stop by to water their horses or refresh themselves after a long day's ride, Jennie on several occasions was introduced to members of the Doolin's gang. And it seems that once the gang realized that the Stevens and Jennie could be trusted, they employed the young girl as a seamstress, supposedly sewing up bullet holes in the men's clothing after scrapes with the law.[16]

The Stevens were honest, respectable folks making a living on their modest farm, supplying the surrounding area with produce. They had nothing to do with the outlaw ways of the Doolin gang. Nonetheless they allowed the men to visit, and during these encounters Jennie became completely enthralled with their outlaw persona. As one account put it,

> they would come in from a raid and [she would] hear them related [sic] their experience, every word of which she would drink in as a bootblack does a five-cent detective story.[17]

Her head spinning with the details of the Doolin gang escapades, and her heart filled with the romantic notions of a teenage girl upon hearing such exciting lore, at not quite sixteen Jennie rode out one night with the bandits. But before doing so she tiptoed to the upstairs room of her parents' house where she swiped a pair of men's britches to wear. This made horseback riding less complicated than trying to ride in a skirt. From then on she was called "Little Britches." That maiden voyage into her life of banditry soon ended as a farce. The wide-eyed farm girl managed to lose her horse, and the gang dropped her off at a neighbor's house for safekeeping.

A couple of days later Little Britches returned home, where an incensed and frustrated father waited. He gave Jennie a "sound thrashing" through her "little britches." Her adventure into the realm of the outlawry ended with her being dumped not only by her horse but also by the Doolin gang as well—and all in the same night. And the story is told that she became the butt of much mockery by her friends.

Jennie ran off again. This time, on March 5, 1895, she married a deaf-mute horse dealer, Benjamin F. Midkiff. The two set up housekeeping in a Perry, I. T., hotel. Less than six weeks later matrimonial sanctity was shattered when Midkiff returned home from a horse-buying trip to find that "house" wasn't the only thing Jennie had been keeping at the couple's hotel room. Apparently she had started a practice of "keeping" other men in Midkiff's absence.[18]

Jennie had several such dishonorable episodes, including one in which Midkiff found his young, highly charged wife in Cleveland, I. T., not far from Stillwater, staying in a store with two young men. Midkiff once again gathered up his teenage wife and headed for home, but they "fell out and quit [each other's company] on the road."[19]

During one of her forays up and down the Arkansas River, Little Britches is said to have met and married one Robert Stephens when she was just sixteen years old. That marriage also failed, with Little Britches riding off into the sunset in search of her more romantic notion of life as a female consort to a gunslinger. While her marriages are a matter of record, her criminal record does not portray her as anything more than a whiskey peddler and horse thief. As in the case of Cattle Annie, Jennie's starry-eyed story of her alleged outlaw exploits have been repeated to the point of being accepted in a few circles as factual. Therefore, as with Cattle Annie, Little Britches receives a fair piece of play here.

While in the Osage Nation of Indian Territory north of Tulsa, Little Britches finally made progress in becoming a female outlaw. She conspired with a fellow whose last name was Wilson in a scheme to sell whiskey to Indians. Wilson quickly realized the ease with which Little Britches could conceal her true identity and sex. Her youthful appearance and her preference for men's clothing made it all work.

Wilson put into place a scheme: Little Britches would maintain a day job—as a quiet, unassuming, dress-wearing domestic; at night, however, she would dress in men's clothing and steal away into the Osage and Pawnee Nations and there distribute liquor.[20]

Not only did her disguise keep her safe from her clients, but it also went a long way in keeping her identity safe from the deputies, who sought to stop whiskey peddling to Indians in the territories.

By that time Little Britches and Cattle Annie had forged their mutual friendship and a business partnership through 1895, continuing the illegal sale of whiskey to Indians and horse theft, victimizing unsuspecting farmers throughout the territories. Each girl had her best disguise against the scrutiny of lawmen, posses, and neighbors. With Little Britches it was her child-like appearance and her tomboyish behavior that dissuaded would-be accusers from casting aspersion upon her reputation. With Cattle Annie on the other hand, it was her advanced womanly appearance and adult demeanor that caused none to think of her as a criminal but rather as a pretty, dashing figure of a young woman whom it would be far more delightful to befriend than betray.

Even though the two frontier waifs did not ride with the Doolin gang, they took on the attitude and attire of the gunslingers, cattle thieves, and bootleggers. Both girls' reputations soon were in need of defense. Throughout 1895, both girls remained more than pesky irritations to law enforcement and continuously made newspaper headlines in the Twin Territories from Guthrie to Coffeyville, Kansas. Cattle Annie and Little Britches thrived on the danger and excitement of banditry. The two were living a high life, compared to the farm life each had abandoned.

Cattle Annie and Little Britches enjoyed together their rising star in the eyes of several members of the Doolin gang.[21] Because no one in law enforcement knew exactly who these purveyors of illegal liquor were, due to their disguise as men, Cattle Annie and Little Britches were free to roam about the countryside unquestioned by lawmen.

Soon however, the ruse failed to fool lawmen. Each time one or both of the girls were spotted they were heavily armed with pistols and Winchesters, not a common sight for females at the time. As sheriffs became suspicious they grew less tolerant of the girls' coquettish ways and evasive answers to the simplest questions.

When Jennie's true identity was discovered, quite accidentally, it was revealed that it was she who had been selling whiskey to the Pawnee and Osage Indians, and she was arrested on July 5, 1895.[22] Jennie posted bond and as quickly as she was released rejoined her best friend Cattle Annie in Pawnee territory. The girls wasted no time in going about their business of bootlegging and horse stealing.

Charley Pierce, George "Bitter Creek" Newcomb, and William "Tulsa Jack" Blake, all members of the Doolin gang, were dead following the Dover robbery. Their "sweethearts" in the gang scattered, the girls returned to their old trade of selling whiskey to the Indians and stealing horses, an activity in which they became "very troublesome."[23]

In little more than a month, Little Britches managed to get herself arrested again. On August 18, Sheriff Frank Lake did the honors.

Lake took Little Britches back to the city of Pawnee, where she would be jailed awaiting arraignment. Instead of being fed in the usual manner and place, with bad food in a jail cell, Lake took Jennie to a hotel where she was given a well-prepared meal. Lake may have left Jennie under the guard of a deputy named Canton. Canton was presumably stationed outside the hotel door, and when Little Britches polished off her fine meal she tore her dress from her body, bolted through the back door, jumped on the back of a horse tied there, and galloped off into the night.

As much fun as this passage is, it may have been the product of an eager newspaper industry whose readership was tiring of accounts of the same old crimes committed by the territories' roster of usual suspects. The newspapers pilloried Deputy Canton for his unwitting role in her escape. The papers reported that the horse on whose back Little Britches made her getaway belonged to Deputy Canton. Sadly for him, presumably that is the sole reason his name remains in print today.[24]

Little Britches' newfound freedom didn't last very long. Legend has it that she was being pursued by one of the most expert lawmen of the Old West. Bill Tilghman was one of the famous deputy U.S. marshals known as The Three Guardsmen assigned to Oklahoma and Indian Territories. Tilghman had come up against more formidable foes out on the prairie, and he may not have believed it possible for two young girls to be so full of fight.

Accounts vary of the capture of Cattle Annie and Little Britches. Marshal Bill Tilghman may or may not have bothered himself with the tracking and capture of the two teenage outlaws. Some historians don't mention Tilghman in this last arrest of Cattle Annie and Little Britches. Author Glenn Shirley states that Deputy Marshals Steve Burke, Frank Canton, M. Zuckerman, and Gant Owens actually arrested the girls after several shots were fired.

In keeping with pioneer reminiscences, it is alleged that when Tilghman and another officer, Steve Burke, encountered the duo they found that both girls had had a belly full of judges and jails. This time they were in no mood for coy conversation, choosing instead to spit fire, and it was the mouths of their Winchesters that did the spitting.

The story continues that Burke covered the rear of the Pawnee farmhouse where the teenagers were located while Tilghman, in his usual fashion, barged in through the front door. The girls were sent scattering in all directions before Cattle Annie clambered through a rear window trying to make her getaway. But Burke was waiting for her and pulled her from the window and wrestled her to the ground.

Little Britches had some mighty tough fight left in her, however, and she wasn't about to be taken down easily. When Tilghman went after her as she galloped away on horseback, he wound up dodging lead from Jennie's Winchester.

Reading like an Old West dime novel, based largely on fiction, the story picks up. Little Britches, as one writer stated, repeatedly fired at Tilghman over her shoulder as she raced into the night. But Tilghman, long experienced in such pursuits, pulled his horse to a stop, took good aim with his rifle, and fired. One shot ended Little Britches' run to freedom. Tilghman's well-aimed bullet hit Jennie's horse, sending mount and rider crashing end over end to the ground.

Then, the story goes, when Tilghman caught up to her, she went for her pistol, but he managed to take it from her. Not finished yet, Little Britches took a handful of dirt and threw it in the lawman's face, hoping to blind him long enough to flee, but that trick failed also. When Tilghman grabbed her, Little Britches went for his face and eyes with her fingernails, trying desperately to claw her way to freedom. As enticing as that account is, it is regarded by many historians as pure poppycock. Many agree that the entire event was concocted by newspapermen eager to satisfy the prurient appetites of an East Coast readership hungry for tales from the Old West. With that having been said, the story continues.

None of her wild tactics worked, and just one night after her escape from Pawnee on the back of Deputy Canton's horse, Jennie "Little Britches" Stevens was finally captured on Monday. On August 19, 1895, her career as one of Oklahoma's most active female bandits was over.[25]

The adolescent miscreants stood trial in the Fourth Judicial District Court, at Pawnee, presided over by the Honorable Andrew G. Curtain Bierer. Both were convicted of their various crimes. Cattle Annie was committed to reform school in Framingham, Massachusetts, and Little Britches was handed a two-year term in the Massachusetts Reformatory Prison in Sherborn. By November 12, 1895, Little Britches sat in jail serving her sentence.

However, within a few months, in October of 1896, Jennie

Stevens was released from prison, her family having successfully petitioned for her parole. Little Britches returned to Oklahoma Territory, a changed woman by all accounts. She left behind her old personality and arrived back in the territory dressed in crisp, flowing feminine attire. She married, raised a family, and rejected her former outlaw friends for family and solitude. She is said to have lived out her remaining years in Tulsa.[26]

Anna "Cattle Annie" McDougal didn't fare as well. She too was released on early parole, but feared she couldn't as easily shun the ways of the old days; she refused passage back to Oklahoma Territory and instead chose to remain in the East. She found work in Boston and shortly thereafter in New York. But in two years Cattle Annie would die in Bellevue Hospital of consumption.[27]

Belle Starr

Shed not for her the bitter tear nor give the heart to vain regret;
'Tis but the casket that lies here; The gem that filled it sparkles yet.

That is the inscription carved onto the headstone of one of the Old West's most noted outlaw women, Myra Maybelle Shirley, dubbed "Queen of the Outlaws" and known throughout the land as the infamous Belle Starr. She was born in Medoc, Missouri, along with a twin brother, Edward, on February 3, 1848, to John and Eliza Hatfield Shirley.

The legend of Belle Starr is hardly untold. Because she was such a prominent figure in Old West crime and married the son of the feared Tom Starr of Cherokee Civil War fame (see Chapter 2, "Oklahoma Assassins"), she can hardly go unmentioned here. The circumstances surrounding her death remain a mystery, a riddle that has fascinated historians for years.

Myra Maybelle Shirley was living near McKinney, Texas, in 1865 when old friends, the Solomon Reed family from Missouri, joined them there after Solomon's death. Among the Reed offspring was one James C. "Jim" Reed, who fell in love with and married Myra Maybelle. He was twenty and Myra was sixteen when the two traded vows before the Rev. S. M. Wilkins in Collin County on November 1, 1866.[28]

Another version of this made-in-heaven matrimonial affair has the two eloping with the aid of about twenty former guerilla fighters because Mama and Papa Shirley objected to Myra's having anything to do with Reed. However, Glenn Shirley in his book, *Belle Starr and Her Times,* disputes that there was ever any consternation by Myra's parents about her marrying Reed.[29]

By the end of the following year Belle and Reed, along with the entire household of Reed's mother, Susan Reed, made their way back to their native Missouri. In September 1868, Belle gave birth to a daughter, Rose "Rosie" Lee, on whom she bestowed the sobriquet "Pearl." Rosie, as will be exposed later in this section, didn't exactly live up to her nickname.

Reed tried to keep to the straight and narrow and for a while took a job in sales while in Texas where he sold bridles and saddles for a Dallas manufacturer. But when his mother returned to Missouri with him and Belle in tow, he tried another trade: hog farming.

Legend has it that when her younger brother, Edwin "Ed" Benton Shirley was shot and killed in Texas late in 1866, Belle's dark eyes turned black with revenge. Belle's anger intensified when her husband was shot and killed about seven years later on August 6, 1874. On that black day Deputy Sheriff John T. Morris shot and killed Reed northwest of Paris, Texas.[30]

Apparently Reed became a fugitive from justice after he killed a man who did likewise to Reed's younger brother, Scott, following an argument over a horse race. But Reed's criminal stature grew after he, Belle, Dan Evans, and another person ventured into Indian Territory to the cabin of a government appointee with the purpose of robbing him. Watt Grayson, who lived on the North Canadian River, was a Creek Indian who handled government subsidies for his tribe. This information, once in the hands of Reed and Belle, made Grayson a target. After they tortured the man and his wife, for an unspecified amount of time in various ways, Grayson told them the hiding place of about $30,000.[31]

It was for the torture and robbery of Grayson, as well as a variety of other misconduct that rewards totaling $4,000 were placed on Reed's head. A close acquaintance shot Reed in order to collect those rewards. One account lists the date of Reed's killing as April 7, and not August 6, as other historians claim. There is agreement that Reed met his untimely end near Paris, Texas, and that the year was 1874.

Myra Belle Reed married Sam Starr in 1880, taking her place in history forever as Belle Starr. She already carried the moniker Queen of the Outlaws. Even though she claimed that most of the smears on her reputation were the work of enemies, the name and her vile reputation outlived the notorious female outlaw of the Cherokee Nation.

For a while, Belle lived a secluded life along the North Canadian River in her effort to gain solitude from the gossipers and rumormongers of the day. Belle said she never quite fancied women's societal regulations and thus chose to keep her own company with Pearl, her husband Sam, and her beloved horse. It was from the back of her sorrel horse that Belle Starr was said to have committed many of her probably mythical crimes against unsuspecting citizens of the Twin Territories.

Belle Starr said she was victimized by her female neighbors who persisted in spreading "lies" about her and her home place. Those rumors alleged that Belle entertained quite a few known robbers and highwaymen at her place on the Canadian. Belle authored this missive about her desire to live her years in quiet and peace, intentionally shunning her neighbors for the sake of her privacy and that of her family and chosen friends. It was published sometime later in the *Fort Smith Elevator.*

> On the Canadian River . . . So long had I been estranged from the society of women (whom I thoroughly detest) that I thought I would find it irksome to live in their midst. . . . Surrounded by a lowdown class of shoddy whites who have made the Indian Territory their home to evade paying taxes on their dogs, and who I will not permit to hunt on my premises, I am the constant theme of their slanderous tongues.[32]

Belle apparently had a change of heart one Friday night a week before Christmas Eve, for she and Sam accepted an open invitation from Mrs. Lucy Suratt to attend a dance she was holding on her place near Whitefield on the Canadian. Arriving after dark, Sam had already been drinking and was in a rather foul mood when he saw an old nemesis, a lawman who has been identified in various sources as an Indian policeman, John West.[33]

Sam snarled at West, "You are the son of a bitch who shot me and killed my horse that day in the cornfield." West denied Sam's allegation, but as he did so, Sam pulled his gun and fired one shot at the policeman. West was struck in the neck and fell, but not before he retrieved his revolver from his coat pocket and fired once at Starr. West's shot was a clean one, penetrating Starr's heart. Both men were dead within two minutes of sighting one another at what was supposed to be a neighborly affair.[34]

Belle was widowed for the second time.

Before the new year had concluded, Belle Starr was married again. Her new husband's name was Jim July, but he sometimes rode under the alias of Jim Starr.[35] July was twenty-four years old when he and Belle tied the knot, reportedly well educated and able to speak the languages of all the Indian Territory tribes. He was also under indictment in Judge Parker's court for horse-stealing at the time he moved in with Belle at Younger's Bend. July rode toward Fort Smith on February 2, 1889, to answer the charges made against him. Belle accompanied her latest husband for about fifteen miles of that ride to a community called San Bois and then turned back.

While on her way back to Younger's Bend Belle decided to visit a friend, a woman named Rowe. Also visiting Mrs. Rowe was Belle's tenant, Edgar A. Watson. Watson had only been in the territory about a year. He hailed from Florida and for some time he peppered Belle with requests to lease more of her acreage. Belle showed no interest in Watson's offer, and every time he tossed the question of leasing more land from her she tossed back a firm "No." Watson had a reputation as a somewhat unscrupulous character, and more than that it was rumored that he was wanted back in his home state of Florida for questioning in a murder case.

So on this occasion, when the two coincidentally met at the Rowe place, there was little doubt in Belle's mind that Watson would once again present his offer. This time, however, Watson thought a more indiscreet method might induce the heralded Queen of the Outlaws into compliance. He suggested that he was quite aware that federal agents had been keeping a close eye on her home place and just perhaps he might have something to offer them.

Unshaken and aware of the rumor about Watson and the murder

case, Belle took Watson to task in her usual direct and confrontational manner. "Maybe the officers in Florida would like to know where they could find you," she shot back.[36] Watson left the two women to conduct their visit.

Later that same afternoon two men were at a ferry on the south side of the Canadian when they heard the unmistakable report of gunfire. Within minutes a riderless horse came galloping down the trail past them, jumped into the river, and swam across. It was Belle's saddled white horse, Venus.

Milo Hoyt, one of the men at the ferry when Venus darted past, hurried up the trail in the direction from which the horse had come. Not too far up the trail he made a grisly discovery, Belle Starr lying face down in the mud on a corner of her own property. She had been shot in the face and neck with a shotgun.[37] There was no one around other than the lifeless and now nearly faceless form of the former Queen of the Outlaws. Her body lay sprawled in a muddy roadside ditch.

Pearl was at the Starr place at Younger's Bend when the riderless mare made its abrupt and worrisome appearance. She wasted no time but quickly mounted the animal and made a dash back to where she knew her mother had been. She too soon fell upon the scene of the murder, after which she got word to July, who was in Fort Smith, about what had happened. July bought a jug of whiskey, mounted his horse, and vowed vengeance.

July made the nearly seventy-five-mile trip to Younger's Bend in nine hours. He was aware of the land lease argument, and found tracks which led back to the Watson place from a fence corner near where Belle was blasted out of her saddle.

Armed with that information and a Winchester rifle, July headed straight for Watson's home. Someone, presumably not July, had ·inspected Watson's shotgun and found that both barrels had been "freshly discharged."[38] That information, along with the now widely accepted rumor of the land lease argument and the tracks from the murder scene to Watson's home, provided more than enough evidence in July's mind to convict Watson on the spot. And when he reached the home of Watson, and Watson stepped out to meet him, July did just that. July shouldered his Winchester and accused

Watson of killing his wife. "If you kill me, you will be killing an innocent man," Watson said.

In a rather uncommon display of coolheadedness, July didn't shoot the man through the heart as he probably had planned, but instead he told Watson that he was arresting him, a "citizen's arrest." The formality of a warrant being overlooked, Watson nonetheless agreed to accompany July to the court at Fort Smith. Once there, July did swear out a complaint against Watson.

United States Commissioner James Brizzolara heard the testimony against Watson, all of which was from the mouth of July and all of which the commissioner deemed purely circumstantial if not purely conjectural. The neighbors not only refused to say anything against Watson, but also told the court that he was a quiet, decent, hardworking farmer. The paucity of evidence persuaded Brizzolara to dismiss all charges.

July wasn't so lucky. His charge of horse theft was still pending in Parker's court, so rather than face the tenacious old judge, July decided to jump bail and hightail it out of there. But that may not have been the only reason Jim July was in such a hurry to put measurable distance between him and Parker's court and his battery of marshals.

It is said that after Watson's release he became pretty loose-tongued with a deputy named J. R. Hutchins. Watson told Hutchins that on the day of Belle's murder, around three o'clock, July came to him and asked to borrow his shotgun. Watson told the deputy that July claimed he wanted the shotgun to kill a wolf that had been eating his chickens. Watson said he loaned the gun to July and that when July returned the weapon about one hour later, both barrels had been fired.

It wasn't long after that, Watson told the deputy, that he learned that Belle Starr had been shot. Watson presented Hutchins with two spent shotgun shells. It was evidence that could easily have been fabricated, but Hutchins took what he had learned to Judge Parker who said he saw no reason for the farmer, Watson, to lie. Parker ordered Hutchins to go to Younger's Bend to investigate further.

Hutchins questioned the man who first came upon the murder scene, Milo Hoyt. Hoyt told Hutchins another story concerning July which might have made a conviction a little closer to a reality. Hoyt said that not long before the shooting, July approached him and offered him two hundred dollars to kill Belle Starr. Hoyt said he refused, and July spurred his horse angrily and rode off saying, "Hell, I'll kill the old hag myself and spend the money for whiskey."[39]

When Hutchins questioned Hoyt as to why July would want to kill his own wife, Hoyt said Belle had found out about a certain young Indian girl July was fooling around with; as punishment she refused to accompany him to Fort Smith to help in his defense against charges pending there. Upon hearing all this, Judge Parker issued a warrant for the arrest of July and sent Hutchins and another deputy marshal, Bud Trainor, to bring him in once they concluded other official business in the Chickasaw Nation.

July was aware that the two men would soon be searching for him so he left Younger's Bend, which had become a preferred lair among the bandit friends of Belle Starr, given its place of relative seclusion on the Canadian River and not too far from the town of Briartown. He headed deeper into Indian Territory to the town of Ardmore. The deputy marshals soon picked up July's trail, however, and caught up with him. July was ordered to surrender, but his answer was short, spurring his horse and reaching for his guns. But it was Hutchins who fired the first shot, and July fell from his horse, seriously wounded. He died a few days later in Fort Smith.

Watson eventually left the territory and went back to Florida, where he was mysteriously gunned down inside his own home nestled deep in the Everglades. His murder has never been solved.[40] The infamous Belle Starr was laid to rest in a very irreligious unceremonious fashion. Her daughter Pearl planted the Queen of the Outlaws in the back yard at Younger's Bend behind one of the cabins.

Flora Quick Mundis: A Girl Named Tom

Flora Quick was born into a wealthy family in Holden, Missouri. Her father, Daniel Quick, was a wealthy stockman. When he died, Flora inherited his fortune and a husband, a ne'er-do-well by the name of Ora Mundis.

In late November 1892, together the two blissful newlyweds ventured to Guthrie, in Oklahoma Territory, where they lived pretty high on the hog until the money ran out. At which point, so did Ora. Strapped for cash, Flora became a madame and began running a "boarding house" at the intersection of Fourth and Grant Streets for women only. However, some unknown dispute with a customer caused Flora to abandon the enterprise. Flora wandered around the territories for a while, supporting herself by stealing horses from ranchers in Logan, Canadian, and Oklahoma Counties and reselling them to a not very savvy clientele.

Flora gave herself the alias Tom King, hoping to confuse the law by dressing in men's attire and impersonating a male bandit. Once the gold-digging first husband ran off, Flora met and kept close company with Earnest "Killer" Lewis. Together the duo rode the countryside robbing trains, stealing horses, and indulging in all sorts of undignified behavior. But the two bandits were anything but efficient in their chosen career paths.

Lewis and Flora apparently decided to rob the No. 408, a passenger train regularly making a run between Red Rock and Wharton (now Perry). Trouble was, they recruited a moron to hide on and stop the train, and the event was anything but successful. Apparently the inside man, named Manvel, tripped over his dangling Knights of Pythias sword as he started toward the conductor. He was quickly tackled and shackled by some of the passengers until U.S. Deputy Marshal Heck Thomas arrived to relieve them of their quarry.[41]

Manvel's hat was said to have been so threadbare that his hair was protruding from most of it. And his footwear were a pair of old worn-out plow shoes. Manvel was summarily committed to an asylum in Illinois.[42]

The law eventually caught up with Lewis in Bartlesville, I. T., where he had been running a saloon in addition to his mouth. By the time two deputy marshals came upon Lewis, it was November 16, 1907, the day of statehood for Oklahoma. Lewis, if he were so inclined to do so, didn't get much time to celebrate the momentous occasion as he was shot and killed by deputies Fred Keeler and George Williams after an altercation.

Just as Killer Lewis found little time to celebrate the Twin Territories' union and inclusion as part of the great United States of America, neither did Flora waste any time mourning the death of her lover. Under her alias of Tom King, Flora kept on stealing the occasional horse, but she had no trouble switching identities while supplementing her income by prostituting herself now and then. She even managed a couple of jailbreaks.[43] Because Flora was uniquely aware of her "carnal agility," there is room for serious doubt whether those were jailbreaks at all, but rather Flora's use of her feminine attributes to induce the jailers into releasing their charges, claiming they had "escaped."

Two noted U.S. deputy marshals, Heck Thomas and Chris Madsen, were carting Flora/Tom to jail in a wagon. "What's the name of the jailer where you're taking me?" inquired the rambunctious prey. When Madsen asked why she wanted to know, Flora coolly replied, "Because every jailer in Oklahoma has his price. If I know which one this is, I'll know his."[44]

But all this Tom King foolery eventually caught up with Flo, and after one arrest in 1894, she became pregnant. Due either to the embarrassment of her claims that it was a jailer at the prison who impregnated her or simply the expense and trouble of having a prisoner deliver in jail, the expectant, cross-dressing, horse-stealing, train-robbing, whoring Flora Quick Mundis was released.

There remains today speculation that Flora may have been the "sixth man" of the Dalton gang. She was an attractive, small-framed woman "who could be a real charmer," furthering the rumor that she may have also been Bob Dalton's sweetheart. Another rumor surrounding Flora Quick Mundis is that her real name may have been Eugenia Moore. And to further complicate matters, another persistent rumor is that she wasn't any of those people but actually Emmett Dalton's future wife, Julia Johnson.[45]

As was not unusual in those times for those people who chose to live in relative obscurity, Flora's disappearance from this earth is just as puzzling as her true identity may continue to be. Glenn Shirley, in *Heck Thomas*, writes that after Flora became pregnant, she moved to Tombstone, Arizona, where she was killed while committing a holdup dressed as a man and calling herself Tom King.[46]

Another source has Flo quitting the bandit business altogether and settling down to a nice quiet life as a housewife. Yet another version has Flo getting killed in Wichita, Kansas, in 1893,[47] during a holdup there. Or she might have fallen victim not to a bullet, but to cancer, dying at Silver City, New Mexico in 1892.

How she finished her wild life is unclear, but Flora Quick Mundis—alias Tom King, et al.—left a tangle of fact and fable regarding her world which continues to stir up dust devils in the minds of some historians even today. The prevailing view is that she was shot and killed by William Garland, a boyfriend and fellow dope addict. As one writer put it, "Flo—or Tom King—was quite a character, and the West was a little less wild when she finished her earthly race."

Blanche Caldwell

Another Oklahoma woman who stood by her "bad" man was Garvin County native Blanche Caldwell. Born on January 1, 1911, she was twenty years old when she married Clyde Barrow's brother, Marvin Ivan "Buck" Barrow in 1931 at the small community of America, Oklahoma. She hailed from near Pauls Valley. In the spring of 1933, Blanche finally met her celebrity outlaw brother-in-law, Clyde Barrow, and his partner in crime and love interest, Bonnie Parker.

While in Oklahoma, the foursome decided to vacation in Joplin, Missouri, and took an apartment. Blanche got her first taste of gang violence in Joplin, when local authorities, who may have been tipped off that the rented living quarters housed the gang, kept a vigil on the place at 3347 1/2 34th Street.[48] And on April 13, 1933, all hell broke loose. After the sudden outburst of gunfire, two lawmen lay dead while Blanche, Buck, Bonnie, and Clyde managed a clean getaway.

The gang busied themselves with robberies and other crimes throughout the Midwest. On June 24 and 26 the four bandits committed robberies at Enid, Oklahoma, and at Oklahoma City.[49] Blanche claimed that in that same month the four traveled to Sallisaw, Oklahoma, in a vain attempt to team up with Charles Arthur "Pretty Boy" Floyd.

For years Blanche was estranged from her mother, probably due to the company she kept, and even when Blanche lay terminally ill, she refused to allow her ninety-three-year-old mother to visit her. Her mother, as in most cases, got in the last word when she visited Blanche for the last time by attending her funeral on December 24, 1988.[50]

Zerelda James

A woman who never participated directly in the crimes of her two sons nevertheless deserves at least a mention here. Zerelda Cole James is worth mentioning strictly because of her two notorious sons, Frank and Jesse.[51]

Zerelda's death came in February 1911 while she was on a train traveling through Oklahoma after visiting her one-time bandit son, Frank. Frank had elected to settle in Fletcher, Oklahoma, where he chose to make a living busting sod as opposed to busting banks. The train was headed back to the James family farm near Kearny, Missouri , from Fletcher when Zerelda dropped dead in a Pullman car. Now as part of the criteria for gaining a place in this book, one must have lived, ridden, or robbed in Oklahoma or the early Twin Territories. As Zerelda died while in transit from Oklahoma to Missouri, she qualifies as a kind of itinerant corpse.

She was buried alongside her other son, Jesse, who was killed by Bob Ford in St. Joseph, Missouri, in 1882. Medical witnesses said Zerelda James Samuel died of an apparent heart attack. She was eighty-six.[52]

Pearl Starr

Remember Rosie "Pearl" Starr, daughter of the hard-riding, straight-shooting, Queen of the Outlaws, Belle Starr? Belle insisted on calling Rosie "Pearl" because of an intense adoration she had for her girl child. But after Belle's unsolved murder and Sam Starr's death, Pearl became a flighty and seemingly eager, soiled dove.

Pearl and her brother, Eddie, left the home place along the Canadian River. Because it was the headright (property and minerals rights recognized by the U.S. government) of Belle's deceased Cherokee husband, Sam Starr, the land automatically went back to the Cherokee Tribal Council. As a result, neither of the young Starrs had a place to call home. Eddie eventually found home in the Ohio State Penitentiary for bootlegging whiskey to the Indians, leaving poor, pitiful Pearl nearly an orphan. But Pearl was not without resources, and it wasn't long before she embarked on her life-sustaining trade as a prostitute.

Taking the moniker Rosa Reed—her father Jim Reed was Belle's first husband—she moved to Van Buren, Arkansas, where she inaugurated a career in prostitution. She did quite well, becoming one of the most attractive and sought-after "boarders" in the house of Madame Van.[53]

Pearl was just twenty-three years old when she came out from under the protective veil of anonymity, and moved to the larger, more affluent town of Fort Smith. She boldly advertised herself as the daughter of the infamous Belle Starr and set up shop in the "Row," an area of Fort Smith where bordellos were located. Rosa's Place, as Pearl dubbed her newly opened house of whores, was located at 25 Water Street, only three blocks from the courthouse and the man who presided there, Judge Isaac C. Parker. Once having earned a goodly sum of money, Pearl, being a loyal sibling, hired a team of lawyers who won her brother's freedom in 1892 from the Ohio State Penitentiary. One year later in 1893, Eddie received a pardon from President Benjamin Harrison.[54]

Full of pride and gratitude, Eddie Reed rushed to be with his sister in Fort Smith, full of heartfelt thanks. When he saw how she "earned" the money that paid for the lawyer who argued for his release, however, he just as quickly rejected his sister and her generosity.

The experience must have been so traumatic as to cause Eddie to be scared straight. For a while he completely reinvented himself, even taking a job as one of Judge Parker's deputy marshals. In October 1896, he killed two former Judge Parker marshals, brothers Zeke and Dick Crittenden. The Crittenden brothers were creating quite a drunken row in the town of Wagoner, I. T., Eddie's new home. The Crittendens were blowing off steam when one of them wounded a resident by the name of Burns with an errant shot. Starr wanted it stopped. The Crittendens didn't. Reed shot and killed them.[55]

Word quickly spread as to who the man really was, the son of the "famous" Belle Starr. Eddie found that he couldn't intimidate everybody, and when he tried to shut down a saloon in Claremore a bad thing happened. One story has it that Ed Reed was only doing his job. He was attempting to arrest two store owners, Joe Gibbs and J. N. Clark, for selling whiskey, but the two men let a shotgun voice their objections, cutting Reed nearly in half. Another version says that Reed was seeking revenge for the death of his father-in-law, who was dying of bad whiskey supplied by Gibbs and Clark and that he was cut down when he entered the store to arrest the two men. Ed Reed is buried in his wife Jennie Cochran's family cemetery located south of Claremore in Tiawah.[56]

As for Rosie, the "Pearl" of Belle Starr's eye, it is said she was eventually run out of town on a legal rail that she tired of battling. She abandoned Rosa's Place and sought a secluded life in the small town of Douglas, Arizona. There she died on July 6, 1925.[57]

Chapter 7

Bonnie and Clyde and Them

Perhaps the first boy-girl robbery team in America was Flora Quick Mundis and Earnest "Killer" Lewis, who committed their various vagaries by horseback in early Oklahoma; but scarcely forty years later another more celebrated duo would capture the interest of lawmen and romanticists nationwide.

Bonnie Parker and Clyde Barrow held a nation's heart and ire, depending on one's socioeconomic bent at the time, as they spent significant quality time in Oklahoma, using Highway 69 as their personal road to fame and fortune. Originally dubbed "The Texas Road," Highway 69 is the long stretch of blacktop that still cuts through eastern Oklahoma from stem to stern. This was the road often used by Bonnie and Clyde as they commuted from jobs in Missouri and elsewhere to their families living at the opposite end of the highway in Texas.

Oklahomans had long accepted that theirs was "a land conceived in violence" and that it too was "the last frontier of the outlaw. . . . These seemed to thrive there in great numbers."[1] Bonnie and Clyde were among the worst of this bad lot.

Barrow was born on March 24, 1909, in Teleco, Texas, the third youngest of eight children whose father, Henry, was a sharecropper. His full name was Clyde Chestnut Barrow, but he preferred to be called Clyde "Champion" Barrow. By the time Clyde reached twelve years of age, his father gave up on farming and moved the family to a spot in West Dallas where Barrow the elder opened a service station. Barrow's mother's name was Cummie.[2]

With a checkered academic past, Barrow found himself spending more time in downtown Dallas police headquarters than the Cedar Valley School. Just beyond the fifth grade Barrow dropped out of school altogether, and with his older brother, Marvin Ivan Barrow, also known as Buck or Ivy, was arrested for dealing in stolen turkeys. From there the two Barrow boys, the seedlings of the Bloody Barrow gang, advanced their careers and reputations by turning to auto theft and even safecracking. Buck and Clyde were arrested eight times in the course of their misspent youth but were allowed to go free each time.[3]

Bonnie Parker was also a native Texan, born at Rowena on October 1, 1910, to J. T. and Emma Parker. Her father was a bricklayer. Bonnie was the second of three children in the Parker clan. In 1914, when Bonnie was about four years old, her father died, and the family moved to Cement, a community near Dallas, where they lived with Emma's parents. Bonnie was enrolled in school in Cement and by all accounts was a pretty good student. Bonnie's downfall wasn't a penchant toward an easy buck or crime. Instead, the young girl kept her head in the clouds with images provided by romance and true confession magazines. In 1925, Bonnie was barely fifteen when she met Roy Thornton. The two were married a scant one year later, but the honeymoon was short-lived. Thornton soon found himself in the hoosegow, serving a ninety-nine-year sentence at Huntsville on a charge of being a habitual criminal.[4] There was no divorce, but sometime in 1930 Bonnie met Clyde, and outlaw history was about to get a new chapter.

After a spate of incidents in Texas that landed Barrow in a number of jail sentences and nearly an equal number of jailbreaks, things turned deadly in one of those "incidents." Barrow had teamed with a young Oklahoman named Raymond Hamilton. Together, the two small-time criminals catapulted their status to the big leagues when during one of their holdups one John Bucher was murdered. The date was April 1932, and this was reportedly the Barrow gang's first killing.[5]

Four months later the gang's reputation and their bounty as wanted criminals would rise sharply, after what took place at a country dance in the otherwise quiet hamlet of Stringtown, Oklahoma. It was August 5, 1932, the first time the Barrow gang conducted any criminal activity in Oklahoma. Situated above the Texas-Oklahoma border along Barrow's favorite roadway, Highway 69, Stringtown was just another grocery store, filling station, and post office along the main route used by motorists traveling either into or out of Texas and Missouri. For some reason Barrow, Hamilton, and a third man some believe was Ross Dyer, stopped at Stringtown the night of a country dance. Nobody knows why Barrow or Hamilton attended the dance at all that evening. What is known is that while they were in a stolen car, the man believed to have been Dyer left his two compatriots in the car drinking whiskey while he went inside.

Sheriff C. G. Maxwell and a deputy, Eugene Moore, evidently took notice of the two men and approached to question them. Barrow and Hamilton opened up on the two lawmen, killing Moore instantly, and seriously wounding Maxwell.[6]

Despite wrecking one hijacked car and losing a wheel from a second, the two gunmen were able to successfully flee to Dallas where they scooped up Bonnie and continued their killing spree. Before 1932 came to a close, the Barrow gang was charged with killing three more Texas men.

Hamilton soon left the Barrow gang and set out on a solo career but was captured in Michigan not long after he turned in his resume. Meanwhile, Clyde's older brother, Marvin, set his sights on marrying Blanche Caldwell, a rural Oklahoma girl with no criminal past. The two were sentenced to a lifetime of wedded bliss on July 3, 1930, at a place near her home in America, Oklahoma, a Garvin County town. Blanche was the daughter of Matthew and Lillian Fountain, and she had no idea that when she married Marvin "Buck" Barrow he was already an escaped convict.

But as a testament to his devotion to his new wife, when Blanche pleaded with Buck to turn himself in to the authorities, he did just that. He was once again incarcerated at Huntsville, admitted on December 27, 1931. On March 22, 1933, Buck was pardoned. Much to her dismay however, Blanche found herself in the company of Bonnie and Clyde once again. This time she was in deeper than just being a hapless sister-in-law because after April 13, 1933, the law considered her a willing member of the Bloody Barrow gang.

That day in Joplin, Blanche received her baptism of blood into the gang, a shoot-out with lawmen at a rented residence that ended the life of two officers.[7]

The forays continued. The gang was cited for bank robberies in Indiana, Minnesota, and Arkansas, and murdered Alma, Arkansas, town marshal, Henry Humphrey near Fayetteville.

Those the Bloody Barrow gang intimidated, threatened, or killed were not the only victims of the bandits' ill-mannered behavior. In June of 1933, Bonnie was badly burned on one of her legs in a car wreck near the small Texas town of Wellington. By that time the group had added a fifth member: a sixteen-year-old car thief named William Daniel Jones who often went by the sobriquet, W. D. or "Deacon" Jones.

At the scene of the car wreck in which Bonnie was burned, farmers rushed to provide any assistance they could. Their kindness was repaid by Barrow or Jones shooting at one of the good Samaritans, a woman who lost her hand.[8]

Soon afterward, Jones and Barrow managed to kidnap two lawmen, stealing their car in the process. With their new hostages, Sheriff George Corry and Marshal Paul Hardy, the gangsters fled to a spot near Erick, Oklahoma. There they met up with Buck and Blanche. The two lawmen were tied to a tree with barbed wire.

The Barrow gang slipped quietly into Enid, Oklahoma, where they are credited with robbing a National Guard armory of a large cache of weapons and ammunition. While in Enid, the gang also relieved a Dr. Julian Field of his car and medical supplies. Listed as stolen by the Department of Defense, in the armory raid of July 7, 1933, were several Browning Automatic Rifles (BARs), forty-six Colt .45 automatic pistols, and several thousand rounds of ammo. At least that's what the authorities reported. Buck Barrow, even on his deathbed in Perry, Iowa, insisted that he bought the weaponry from a soldier at Fort Sill, in Lawton, Oklahoma, for $150.[9]

The Barrow gang soon made their way to Platte City, Missouri, where they rented a hotel room for a little diversion from the drudgery of life on the lam. Not long before holing up in Platte City the gang had to first replenish their coffers, which they accomplished by withdrawing brazenly from the tills of three Fort Dodge, Iowa, filling stations.

The authorities caught up with the gang of five at the Platte City Motel, surrounded the place, probably announced their presence and their intent, and within seconds a gun battle was on. The gang somehow managed to survive this shoot-out as they had done in the Joplin episode, and when the smoke cleared the police officers were left empty-handed.

But Buck was seriously wounded. The gang escaped to Dexter, Iowa. There on July 24, 1933, just five days after the Platte City raid, they again encountered a determined police posse who this time surrounded the bandits' wooded hideout. Clyde, Bonnie, and Deacon Jones made good their getaway, but Buck and Blanche were nabbed by the invading officers. Buck died five days later in Perry, Iowa, of the wounds he received in Platte City. Blanche, the girl from Garvin County, Oklahoma, who had only known trouble to be too little rain for the sorghum crop until marrying into the Bloody Barrows, was sentenced to serve a prison term in Missouri. Blanche was paroled in 1939.[10]

With Buck dead, Blanche in jail, and Jones having split from the gang, all that remained of the Bloody Barrows was Bonnie and Clyde. Evidently, the two desperadoes got that sentimental feeling and were desperate to visit dear old Mom. So, just after robbing an Overton Township refinery on November 15, the pair arranged a secluded visit with their mothers in Wise County, north of Fort Worth. The homecoming was cut short by gunfire when Dallas County authorities ambushed Bonnie and Clyde while en route.

Deacon Jones was apprehended in Houston and received a fifteen-year sentence for his part in the murder of a deputy in West Dallas. Then he received a two-year federal term on a conviction of harboring Bonnie and Clyde. Jones had claimed that while he joined up with Bonnie and Clyde at age sixteen, he repeatedly tried to abandon the group but was held under the threat of death. It didn't work.[11]

Bonnie and Clyde vanished from the scene for a while. The two may have spent time recuperating in the Cookson Hills in Eastern Oklahoma with "Pretty Boy Floyd's people," according to Bonnie's sister, Billy Parker.[12] The gang was on the mend once again, however, even with the death of Buck and the early retirement of Deacon Jones. Unscathed by the loss of membership, on January 16, 1934, Barrow, Bonnie, and a James Mullen broke former gang member Raymond Hamilton out of the Eastham, Texas, prison farm where he was serving 263 years for murder and robbery.

Finding pistols planted at strategic spots around the prison farm, presumably by Bonnie, Hamilton and an accomplice, Joe Palmer, dashed toward the sound of a honking horn after killing one prison guard and wounding another. With officers in hot pursuit of the fleeing men, Barrow and Hamilton covered their break by spraying BAR fire toward their pursuers. Three other convicts found early parole thanks to the Barrow gang's prison break. Two were soon recaptured;[13] a third, Henry Methvin, joined the gang.

The gang stayed pretty busy in Texas, robbing an armory on July 20, and then a bank in Lancaster, Texas on the twenty-seventh of the same month. A violent dispute over how the spoils of the Lancaster robbery should be divided arose between Barrow and Hamilton. The result of that toe-to-toe was that Hamilton left the gang for good as did Joe Palmer. Methvin stayed.

The Bloody Barrows gave credence to their morbid moniker, and before the month of April expired killed three more lawmen. On April Fools' Day 1934, the trio gunned down two Texas Highway Patrol troopers. Six days later in Commerce, Oklahoma, they shot Constable Cal Campbell. Campbell along with Police Chief Percy Boyd, responded to a nervous motorist's tale of a stack of guns inside a stranded vehicle. Campbell was killed. Boyd too was hit by flying lead, but since he was not seriously wounded, the gang took him hostage.[14]

Boyd was later released in Fort Scott, Kansas, without further injury. He was, however, given instructions to settle a running dispute Bonnie had with the press. Bonnie hated a nickname reporters had given her after a picture was circulated showing her toting a BAR while pressing a cigar between her lips. The nickname given was "cigar-smoking-gun moll Bonnie Parker." Seizing the opportunity to refute the charge of cigar smoking (she evidently wasn't too concerned with being labeled a murderer), Parker told Boyd to set the record straight. "Tell the public I don't smoke cigars," she said. "It's the bunk."

Five days after killing Campbell on April 1, 1934, and after releasing Boyd, Barrow, or someone using his name, sent Henry Ford a soaring endorsement of the Ford V-8. The letter, the authenticity of which is in some doubt, was mailed from a post office in Tulsa.[15]

But, on May 23, 1934, Bonnie and Clyde were killed. The Texas prison break—which included murdering one of the guards—was a fatal mistake for the couple.

Lee Simmons, the head of the Texas Prison System at the time, was so incensed at the murder of one of his guards that he convinced former Texas Ranger Frank Hamer to come out of retirement to track down the killers. Hamer must have gotten to Methvin, the gang member who along with Bonnie and Clyde was tagged for the murder of two Texas Highway Patrol troopers and the Commerce constable. Actual accounts of the circumstances are sketchy but, according to one scenario, Methvin and his parents ratted on Bonnie and Clyde in a successful bid to keep Methvin from being convicted of the murders. That scheme worked, and Methvin received immunity once the information he provided proved reliable and lawmen successfully ambushed Bonnie and Clyde.

It did not help Methvin in Oklahoma where he was tried for the murder of Constable Campbell and received the death penalty. Methvin appealed, and his sentence was reduced to life imprisonment. He left the Oklahoma Department of Corrections prison system a free man after ten years.[16]

Tips received as a result of FBI Special Agent L. A. Kindale's negotiations with informants led Hamer and his posse of five lawmen to an ambush site where the story of Bonnie and Clyde would end. With Hamer were: Manny Gault, a Texas Prison System employee; Bienville Parish, Louisiana, sheriff Henderson Jordan and a deputy, Prentiss Oakley; and Dallas County sheriff deputies, Bob Alcorn and Ted Hinton.

Bonnie and Clyde barreled down the road between Gibsland and Sailes, Louisiana, apparently headed to the Methvin place. Lawmen opened up on them with a hail of gunfire. For the first time and the last time in their careers Bonnie and Clyde were the victims of their own tactics. The pair never got off a single shot amidst the several hundred fired at them. The car alone received 167 bullet holes. Predictably, the car absorbing all that lead was a 1934 Ford Desert Sand V-8,[17] one of Clyde's favorites.

Pretty Boy

And then there was Charles Arthur Floyd, sometimes called "Pretty Boy." Early in 1911 Walter and Mamie Floyd decided they had had enough of the post-Civil War South. The couple sold their Georgia farm and livestock and followed other family members to Oklahoma. Walter's sister and parents, Charles and Mary Floyd had made the move years earlier as had Mamie's parents, Elmer and Emma Echols.

The Floyds had six children in tow when they arrived in Hanson, Oklahoma, a small railroad town near the Arkansas River. One particularly wide-eyed, rambunctious, beefy child, a seven-year-old named Charley, was especially enthusiastic about the new adventure.

Charley wasted no time in setting out to discover as much of the surrounding area as he and his brothers could possibly cover on foot. Charley, Bradley, and the youngest boy, E. W., raced off in all directions on these boyish explorations. They came back home having seen or heard of other communities of Sequoyah County with unforgettable names like Akins and Lone Oak, Paw Paw and Blackjack, Sallisaw and Seven Oaks. The Cookson Hills, north of Hanson, would one day figure prominently in the life of young Charley.

Not long after their arrival, Walter borrowed a horse and rode out to scout the new countryside, a promising vista of growing fields and healthy cattle. He then leased acreage and bent his back as a tenant farmer. Walter quickly made a success of the place, acquiring livestock and poultry, raising grain and cotton and hay. Mamie, in addition to raising her brood of six—three boys and three girls—was quite happy canning fruits and vegetables and becoming a respected member of the Hanson Baptist Church.[18]

The children participated in the Floyd family way of life, with the boys helping Walter in the fields and the girls doing their assigned duties helping Mamie to maintain a tidy household. On June 25, 1912, a seventh sibling was added to the ranks of the brood: a girl named Mary Delta. Even with the addition of another to their ranks there were always plenty of chores for all.

Up the road from the Hanson place was the town of Sallisaw, Oklahoma, and a grocery store there owned and operated by J. H. Harkrider, who had come to Indian Territory in 1899 from Arkansas. In his earlier years, while running a shoe and harness shop, Harkrider had repaired a saddle brought to him by one of the territory's most wanted outlaws of the time; Henry Starr. It was from this venerable, capable storekeeper that Charley Floyd cut his teeth—his sweet tooth actually—on the beginnings of a life of crime. It seems Charley had a penchant for the iced cookies Harkrider kept on his shelves and lifted a few boxes without payment. Charley was not quite ten years old at the time.[19]

Charley's father Walter "came to Jesus," as the saying goes, one summer day just after the arrival of daughter Mary Delta in 1912. Walter allowed a preacher to dunk him in the muddy waters of the Big Skin Bayou Creek. Except for a rare outing with his sons at fishing and hunting and a little pull from the white lightning jug every now and then, Walter was mostly all work. No matter how dirty, gritty, or muscle-pulling the task was, farm kids in those days knew there would be no recreational swimming in the creek, no sitting under a shade tree with a cool watermelon, and above all no going into town, until all the chores were done. And always, it seemed, the boys needed more chores.

"That single maxim was ingrained in them as much as all four Gospels and the Ten Commandments combined."[20]

But Oklahoma rural life then also tolerated "social banditry." Since Civil War Reconstruction days, an occasional bank or railroad raid was considered an acceptable practice by many in Arkansas, Missouri, and Oklahoma. By 1912, just one year after the Floyds moved into the new state, Oklahoma held the record as having the highest number of bank robberies in the country.[21]

To what degree this fact and the legendary tales of Jesse James, the Doolin, Dalton, and James-Younger gangs made an impression on eleven-year-old Charles Arthur Floyd cannot be calculated. But even in the years preceding the Great Depression, the sharecroppers and tenant farmers had a growing dislike for such moneyed establishments as banks. Those institutions were seen as soulless bullies who would indiscriminately cheat them at every opportunity. Banks were looked upon as being no better than the big railroads that fenced off the grazing lands of the hardscrabble farmers. Robbing a bank then in Oklahoma was considered by many to be "the ultimate expression of protest." Social bandits were generally considered by certain elements to be among the "good guys" in rural Oklahoma. The Floyds were apparently among those who saw nothing wrong with a man who had the guts to rob a bank in order to better his own plight.[22]

The lure of the bandits' lifestyle was pulling hard at young Charley during this impressionable, early stage of life. At first the attraction played itself out in boyhood pranks and pilfering. Later, around the time he turned twenty, Charley's appetite for fast times—infused by a desire for fast women and fast cash—would only be satisfied by armed robbery.

Figures such as Robin Hood and Jesse James—Floyd's favorite—became heroes to young Charley and for much of the surrounding countryside as well. In later years during the Great Depression, men such as Ford Bradshaw, a Cookson Hills native and gang leader, often put on huge community meals lasting several days after some of their "withdrawals" from area banks.[23]

No wonder then that some neighbors of Bradshaw, Floyd, and other bandits not only turned a blind eye to their misdeeds but almost endorsed them. When the bottom fell out of the stock market in 1929, many of the farmers who had been eking out a living and who had placed their meager savings in banks were suddenly destitute. When those banks went belly up, many farmers lost everything. Worse yet, cotton prices fell to an all-time low, decimating that market.

With some desperate farmers having encumbered their family farms with one, two, or sometimes three mortgages, on a crop that they couldn't sell, it was only a matter of time before foreclosures started. Rural folks began a powerful dislike for banks. So when Cookson Hills bandits robbed a bank, some area residents thought it was a righteous payback. After all, it was just "rich outsiders" and large corporate banks that were being victimized. Many people of the Cooksons weren't about to turn down a few dollars in help from some local boys who demonstrated a healthy dose of courage and humanity.[24]

During this period, for example, Ford Bradshaw was once arrested for robbing a bank in Henryetta. The case went before a jury in Okmulgee, where after just twenty minutes of deliberation the jury intoned: "Not guilty." This, even after two clerks who witnessed the robbery positively identified one of the hold-up men as Ford Bradshaw.[25] In an area whose unemployment reached 40 percent, the strong sentiment regarding banks as more an enemy than the hold-up men becomes a little clearer to the outside observer.

Bradshaw came by his talent for robbing banks and peddling whiskey naturally. His father, Jim, a blacksmith by trade, also dabbled in bank robbing. He served eighteen months of a five-year term for robbing the bank at Vian, the family's hometown, in 1920.[26]

One member of the Cookson Hills gang, headed by Bradshaw, was a rodeo performer named Charley "Cotton" Cotner.[27] Born in 1900, he was a boyhood friend of Charley Floyd. Years later Cotner would join Bradshaw, "Pretty Boy," and Clyde Barrow on J. Edgar Hoover's list of the American West's "Most Wanted."

Cotner was arrested with seven others in a raid on a farmhouse in Mannford, Oklahoma. Led by Sapulpa police chief Floyd Sellers, twenty-eight federal, Kansas, and Oklahoma lawmen conducted the predawn raid on March 15, 1934. Cotner was sentenced to serve twenty to a hundred years in the Kansas State Prison. He died there in 1954.[28]

Floyd, Barrow, and Bradshaw would all die in 1934. For Bradshaw the end came the morning of March 3, 1934, at a roadhouse near the small town of Arkoma, just inside the Oklahoma border with Arkansas. Lawmen got word of a man going crazy in the place and sent a detail of men to investigate. The joint's manager, Bob Harper, met the officers outside. Bob's brother, Bill, owned the club and was also an auxiliary Le Flore County deputy sheriff.[29]

Inside, the officers saw a man attempting to teach an errant slot machine a thing or two with a baseball bat. He was quickly subdued, cuffed, and relieved of a bulletproof vest he was wearing. It was at about this time, as things returned to near normal, that the club's owner, Bill, showed up. As the other officers were leading Bradshaw outside, he struck Bill Harper in the face and made a dash for the back door. Harper leveled his .45 at the fleeing, cuffed man and shot him three times in the back. Bradshaw fell to the ground and rolled over on his back. Harper stood over him and took dead aim. Realizing what Harper was about to do, Bradshaw pleaded, "Don't do that." Harper fired two more shots into the man.[30] None of the officers knew that the man who was pleading for his life was the notorious Cookson Hills bad boy, Ford Bradshaw.

When Bradshaw's identity was eventually learned, lawmen across the country hailed the event as a good thing for law enforcement and the nation. Upon hearing of Bradshaw's death, a spokesman for the Department of Justice said that he welcomed the outlaw's demise. Likewise the Muskogee County sheriff, V. S. Cannon, said, "I'm glad they got him. He was a bad apple."[31]

Regardless of what the law thought of Bradshaw, he was apparently a popular young outlaw. More than 1,200 viewed the body at the Vian funeral home while 1,500 more made their way through the home of the Bradshaw family where the casket sat in a breezeway.[32]

Even though the law was all but giddy at Bradshaw's death, some were not particularly happy with the way in which he was cruelly exterminated. On the Tuesday following Bradshaw's funeral, Bill Harper was given a hearing at Poteau on a charge of murder. In the end, the judge merely revoked Harper's liquor license.[33]

Similarly, Pretty Boy Floyd was gunned down by lawmen as he attempted to flee, dashing through a cornfield outside Clarkson, Ohio.[34] An estimated 20,000 to 40,000 mourners attended the graveside services for Pretty Boy held on October 28, 1934, in Akins, Oklahoma, a small community near Sallisaw. Although it was a Sunday, and hot, they came by the thousands. It was the largest funeral in Oklahoma history.[35]

Newspapers across the country compared Floyd to Jesse James, his idol. Before his death Floyd once wrote a thank-you note to one Ohio newspaper making the mythical connection. That was written in September 1934. The following month Floyd was killed by law enforcement officials led by famed FBI man Melvin Purvis during the Ohio roust.[36]

Floyd had been on the lam in the farm country near the towns of Calcutta and Clarkson, living off the land, staying low. He came upon the farm of Mrs. Ellen Conkle and asked for food, which she provided as was the custom.[37]

Floyd dined on Mrs. Conkle's back porch sitting in a rocker reading the *East Liverpool Review.* After finishing spareribs, potatoes, and rice pudding, Floyd asked Mrs. Conkle if perhaps she couldn't help him get to Youngstown. She said she couldn't but said her brother, Stewart Dyke and his wife, Florence, might be able to help once they finished their farm chores. Dyke however said that was too far to go as late in the evening as it was.

He did offer to take Floyd (whose identity was kept from all present) as far as Clarkson where he and Florence lived. Floyd accepted and loaded his stocky frame into the backseat of the man's Model A Ford. The car had barely moved when two Chevrolets appeared in the distance. Melvin Purvis and his men had arrived. The federal agents and policemen who made up the posse boiled out of their cars, and Purvis twice commanded the hard-running Floyd to "Halt!" Purvis's next command would be to his ready and aiming officers: "Fire!"[38]

From Horseback to Cadillac

"In Oklahoma you could do anything you was big enough to do," claimed Joe Newton.[39] And one of the era's most successful Oklahoma gangs, in terms of spoils gotten while shunning violence to get it, was the Newton Boys. Up from Texas, these four brothers could arguably be called the most safety-conscious train and bank robbers of the times. While it is true that Jess, Joe, Willis, and Wylie (called Doc) carried weapons, only the pistols were deadly, the shotguns were loaded with non-lethal birdshot. "We wasn't like Bonnie and Clyde," Willis Newton said. "We never wanted to kill anybody."[40]

And perhaps just as interesting, Joe and Willis spent the most time ever behind bars at McAlester for an Oklahoma bank robbery they didn't commit. The one bank robbery Joe was in on in Oklahoma occurred long before the Newton Boys became a gang. But by then their reputations had preceded them, and when one old Oklahoma sheriff needed a little political capital, he allegedly recruited witnesses to testify against the two brothers. They did, and Willis and later Joe, upon his return to Tulsa from Mexico, were convicted. The effort did little for the incumbent sheriff, and he was replaced by his political opponent who later helped to arrange for the brothers to be paroled.

Willis was born near Dallas in the small town of Cottonwood on January 19, 1889. He was one of eleven children born to Jim and Janetta Pecos Anderson Newton. Jim Newton fancied himself a horse trader but never made good at it and instead roamed with his large brood from one leased place to another, mostly raising cotton. Janetta was an avid reader. Her favorite genre was crime novels and newspaper stories of Old West bandits, the likes of Jesse James and the Daltons. It was his mother's interest in the Old West outlaw figures that captured the rapt attention of Willis at an impressionable age. "She read every outlaw story that came along. Read nothing but outlaw stories. . . . Then at night when we went to bed she'd tell us the story, and she could tell it word for word."[41]

The boys worked alongside their father in the cotton fields following the plow. Occasionally they got work as ranch hands and bronc busters. But some of the growing boys knew the life of a Texas itinerant farmer was less than what they hoped for. Willis knew it best of all. "I wanted something . . . and I knew I would never get it following a mule's ass and dragging cotton sacks down them middles."[42]

In and out of Texas prisons for one crime or another, Doc, Jess, Willis, and Joe eventually make Tulsa, Oklahoma, their new home. By October 1920, Doc, Willis, and a fellow named Brent Glasscock were acting as a team, already successfully pulling off bank robberies in Illinois and Detroit. When Jess joined the group the following spring, Willis felt the band was complete. "I had my bunch then," Willis said.[43]

Within four years of the gang's arrival in Tulsa, the gang would commit America's greatest train robbery ever. Despite Joe's reservations, the gang saw the heist of the Chicago, Milwaukee & St. Paul mail train as the one job that would get the Newton boys out from behind the mule forever.

The event netted the group as much as $3 million, but the "sweet taste of success" was to be short-lived. As Willis put it, "Maybe we shouldn't have tried one like that, but I'd always wanted to do a million dollar robbery."[44]

During that June 24, 1924, mail train robbery at Rondout about twenty-five miles northwest of Chicago, Doc was shot by the one gang member who was not kin, Glasscock. Glasscock was supposed to have stayed with Joe Newton during the holdup. Inexplicably, Glasscock instead ran toward the front of the train where Doc had positioned himself. Glasscock found himself on the side of the train opposite to where Doc was. "And he had to go up there and crawl under the train to get to where Doc was," Joe recounts in *The Newton Boys.*

"Maybe in the dark he didn't recognize Doc. He must have knowed that for one of us to get shot was the best way in the world for him and all the rest of us to get caught," Joe said. But what really had the rest of the Newtons scratching their heads was that Brent Glasscock not only shot Doc about five times, he just left him lying there.

"Then what's harder to understand is he seems to have left Doc there. Maybe . . . he thought that we'd have to take him to a hospital . . . so he decided he'd just keep shooting and sure enough kill him and figure we'd bury him somewhere and nobody'd ever know."[45]

The gang finished the robbery and after instructing the clerks to help load the sixty-one sacks of registered mail into two waiting Cadillacs, loaded the injured Doc into one of the Caddys and sped off into the night. The Newtons had upgraded their style of transportation from their early horseback days as minor criminals, to major players driving Cadillacs.

Even though they used Cadillacs for the greatest train robbery of all time, the gang usually preferred the Studebaker automobile with the Big Six or Special Six engine, they claimed.[46] Due to the seriousness of Doc's injuries, which required medical attention, the gang was eventually nabbed and charged in the $3 million caper. Glasscock not only shot Doc but he spilled the beans to a postal inspector as to the whereabouts of the loot, to get a lighter sentence.

The two surviving Newtons, Joe and Willis, spent much of their remaining years back in their home country of Uvalde, Texas, where they kept watch over their bee hives. Willis Newton died on August 22, 1979. He was ninety. Joe, the last of the gang, died on February 3, 1989. He had just celebrated his eighty-eighth birthday.[47]

Previously unpublished portrait of Harry Aurandt (Ron Trekell Collection)

Tulsa, 1889 (Ron Trekell Collection)

Rare photograph of Christ Madsen, Deputy U.S. Marshal (Courtesy of Armand DeGregorias)

William Tilghman (Courtesy of Armand DeGregorias)

James Franklin "Bud" Ledbetter (Ron Trekell Collection)

Henry "Heck" Thomas (Courtesy of Armand DeGregorias)

Pauls Valley native Fred Waite with a companion presumed to be fellow Lincoln County Regulator Henry Brown (Courtesy of Haley Memorial Library)

Crawford Goldsby "Cherokee Bill" (Ron Trekell Collection)

Jesse James (Ron Trekell Collection)

Henry Starr (Oklahoma Historical Society)

Arizona "Ma" Barker (Ron Trekell Collection)

Herman Barker (Ron Trekell Collection)

Previously unpublished portrait of Fred Barker (Ron Trekell Collection)

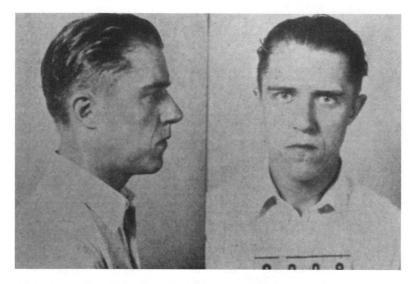

Alvin Karpis (Ron Trekell Collection)

Matt Kimes in handcuffs, 1927, with Okmulgee County Sheriff John Russell on the right (Courtesy of Michael Koch from *The Kimes Gang*)

Al Spencer, left, with Joe Clark, 1908 (Courtesy of Lenapah Historical Society)

Headquarters of the Barker gang, 401 North Cincinnati, Tulsa
(Ron Trekell Collection)

Bonnie Parker and Clyde Barrow
(Dallas Public Library)

George Barnes "Machine Gun Kelly"
(Ron Trekell Collection)

THE BUCK GANG.

Maomi July.   Sam Sampson.   Rufus Buck.   Luckey Davis.   Lewis Davis.

Rufus Buck gang (Oklahoma Historical Society)

Frank James (Western History Collections, University of Oklahoma Library)

Cole Younger (Western History Collections, University of Oklahoma Library)

Quintet hanged on September 23, 1875, in Fort Smith, Arkansas (Fort Smith Historic Site)

Chapter 8

Woulda, Coulda, Shoulda

Prior to statehood the criminal element of the Twin Territories swelled. Indian and Oklahoma Territories were burgeoning with outlaws of various experiences, expertise, and talents. Some of the crimes attempted during the run up to statehood were so poorly planned as to be almost comical. These were the work of the Woulda, Coulda, Shoulda outlaws.

Alphonso "Al" Jennings was born in 1861. A Virginia native, he was educated at West Virginia State University where he attained his law degree. He moved to Oklahoma Territory and took the job of county prosecutor of Canadian County in 1892. By 1895 Jennings had joined his brothers, Ed and John, in their private practice in Woodward.[1]

That same year John and Ed and another prominent attorney, Temple Houston, son of famed Texas statesman, Sam Houston, were in a local saloon following a particularly contentious courtroom hearing. Likely fueled by liquor as much as ego, the three attorneys became embroiled in a heated disagreement spurred by the earlier courtroom drama. The intensity of the argument inside the saloon escalated into a three-way gunfight. Ed was killed, and John was wounded. Houston holstered his firearm and walked away from the fracas completely unscathed.

The incident must have motivated Al Jennings deeply for in the following year, 1896, he was found working at almost the opposite end of the state at the Spike S Ranch, about six miles south of Bixby. He was joined there later by another brother, Frank, who had been working as a deputy clerk in the district court of Denver, Colorado.[2]

While working as cowboys on the Spike S, the Jennings brothers met a new hire, Richard "Little Dick" West. Before hiring on with the Spike S, West had been a member of the infamous Doolin Gang from 1893 until 1895. West participated in the renowned Ingalls, O. T. (Oklahoma Territory), shoot-out in which three lawmen were killed.[3]

West was one of only two members of the Jennings gang with any experience in banditry. The other outlaw of equal talent was Dan

"Dynamite Dick" Clifton. Two other men, brothers and both former lawmen, joined the gang but only after their law enforcement careers ended with charges of embezzlement. Patrick and Morris O'Malley had both worked for Marshal E. D. Nix. Morris had served as Nix's deputy while Patrick was a posseman.

Both men were unceremoniously relieved of their respective positions, having been charged with padding the tab. It seems they were rather creative when it came to adding up the mileage and witness fees actually incurred while on the hunt for bad guys. The O'Malley brothers exaggerated the statistics, were found out, and were fired.[4]

Al Jennings bridled this ragtag bunch of *coulda*s into what one source describes as a Three Stooges style of bandit gang. So profoundly inept was this Oklahoma gang that one of the group's experienced outlaw members, Little Dick West, stomped off after a miserably failed train robbery attempt. Dynamite Dick Clifton had walked off several days earlier. However both bandits veterans agreed to reunite at the Spike S at a later date.[5]

The outlaws kept to wooded terrain, rocky creek bottoms, and sympathetic friends, all the while fearing imminent capture. Al Jennings and Dynamite Dick were being pursued for the robbery of a post office in Foyil, Cherokee Nation, that they had committed in the summer of 1897. That robbery followed the plunder of two general stores and the holdup of the Corner Saloon in which they not only took from the till, but also relieved a sizeable crowd of patrons of their money. The thieves also absconded with "a quantity of whiskey."[6]

Jennings later claimed the Foyil robbery was just an experiment. One member of the gang brought into camp a "set-screw" used for removing the lock from a safe. Al simply wanted to see how the device worked and so employed the tool during the Foyil post office heist. Jennings made off with $700 from "the experiment"; enough, he said, "just to pay expenses."[7]

By mid-July, veteran U.S. deputy marshals James F. "Bud" Ledbetter and Paden Tolbert of Muskogee were trailing Jennings and his accomplices.

The two deputies dogged the bandit gang for months throughout the Northern District of Indian Territory but with little effect.

Jennings and his bunch remained an elusive prey, partly because they traveled under assumed names and partly because they never stayed in any one place for more than a few days.

Ledbetter testified at a later trial to his hampered efforts in apprehending the gang. "We made numerous inquiries, but never did get information of their staying at one place over three or four days at a time, and that was at the mouth of Little Spavinaw."[8]

The Jennings gang stayed ahead of pursuing lawmen for months, robbing, or attempting to rob, one country store or buggy driver after another. Their successes were so few that it is in the gang's failures that the story really lies.

What appeared to have been a well-laid-out train robbery at Edmond was anything but. On August 16, 1897, conductor Frank Beers and engineer John Rains stopped the southbound Santa Fe passenger train at Edmond. After the train's water supply was replenished, the locomotive chugged on toward Oklahoma City, about fourteen miles to the south.

Three masked, armed men climbed over the tender and made their way to the cab. There they drew down on Rains who was alone. At a point three miles south of Edmond the bandits ordered the train stopped. As the train came to a halt, four men sprang from the tall grass at the side of the tracks and made a beeline for the express car: So far, so good for the bandits. Beers had been traveling in one of the train's cars, and when the locomotive made its unscheduled stop, he climbed down and began to go forward to ask Rains why the train had stopped. Beers got his answer when one of the bandits fired a couple of rounds in his direction. He was told in terms very sincere to get back on the train.[9] Still at this point the holdup had all the signs of a professional heist.

Other gang members kept curious passengers and would-be heroes inside the passenger cars by repeatedly firing Winchesters and yelling strongly worded advice against coming outside. The outlaws then started pumping lead right through the express car as a means of convincing the guards inside to open up. With rounds from their Winchesters whirring past the two men inside, Messenger W. H. May and Route Agent Lytle, rapidly complied and opened the door behind which sat a Wells-Fargo safe.[10]

Things were going rather well for the Jennings gang at this point. Three of the bandits entered the express car and told May and Lytle to get out. Work began on opening the safe. The three men were later described to marshals in precise detail, down to the number of days of growth of their beards. Because of that accurate description it was determined that the robbers included none other than Frank Jennings, Dynamite Dick Clifton, and Little Dick West. The other three who had commandeered the locomotive were later identified as Al Jennings and the O'Malley brothers.[11]

Dynamite Dick assessed the safe and affixed two dynamite sticks to its door. The result of the explosion? Absolutely nothing. The safe remained completely intact, and after several more attempts to loose the door from its hinges the safe proved to be much too formidable. Disgusted, the robbers left the train and bid the crew a good night before disappearing into the dark. The luckless crew then lit out for the Baker place.

Sam Baker was a reputed gunfighter who came to Oklahoma Territory from his place of origin, Cooke County, Texas. Baker moved to Bond Switch, now Onapa, where he owned a farm. His brother-in-law, Willis Brooks, also rumored to be a Texas gunfighter, lived just west of Eufaula. The Brooks brothers had long ago befriended a young Little Dick West when West was sweeping out saloon floors in Decatur.[12]

Both West and Dynamite Dick were able to secure many a free meal from Brooks and Baker. West kept in touch with both men during the years he rode with Bill Doolin. Following the humiliation of the Edmond debacle, the gang laid low, camping near Baker's farm. Within two weeks of miserably failing to rob the Santa Fe passenger train, the gang made plans to rob a train on the Missouri, Kansas & Texas Railroad line.

A site was selected not far from Bond Switch (Onapa), about twenty-seven miles southwest of Muskogee. This time there would be no foul-up. A pile of railroad ties was stacked on the tracks. When the outlaws heard the train coming, they set fire to what they believed was an effective barricade. The engineer was no stranger to holdups and barricaded railroads. When he saw the tell-tale orange glow up ahead he knew what he was in for. Rather than fret he shoved the throttle to full ahead. The powerful locomotive exploded through the barricade "scattering railroad ties like matchsticks."[13]

The bewildered outlaws headed for parts to the southwest, traveling through the Seminole and Pottawatomie Indian lands on their way to the Chickasaw Nation. They chose an easier, stationary target to rob, the train station at Purcell. But rather than making a haul here, they were forced to decamp when they were spotted by a night watchman who notified the local sheriff. He gathered an armed posse, and a brief chase ensued.[14]

The badmen escaped without incident, but by that time the gang was desperate. They had little money left among themselves, their clothes had been unwashed and unmended for weeks, and their only meals had been foraged from farmhouses.

By then the gang was hungry for a good meal and any success. But it would not come. The relentless Al Jennings planned still another train robbery, despite the gang's penchant for failure. This one, he assured his beleaguered band, would yield a $90,000 payload. Jennings had received word that a consignment of coins totaling that astronomical sum would be on board a Rock Island passenger train on the morning of October 1, 1897.

At a place eight miles south of Minco (now Pocassett) Jennings and the gang persuaded a few section workers to flag the train to a stop. Jennings thought to provide a disguise for himself, as by that time he was well known among train conductors. He fashioned a "mask" from a bearskin saddle pocket (bag) by cutting two eyeholes in it and pulling the thing over his head. But at one point during the robbery the cleverly devised contraption fell off his head and revealed his true identity to the conductor, a man by the name of Dacy.[15]

Passengers on the Rock Island sat in fear after hearing the first dynamite blast. But that was only a warm-up compared to the next explosion, which shook the entire train and blew the car containing the safe to pieces. But the safe, as in the MK&T robbery attempt, withstood the explosions. With the putrid taste of humility and abject failure fresh in the outlaws' mouths, they chose to pilfer the express car. After not finding anything of value there except a passel of registered mail, they turned to robbing the passengers. The heavily armed bandits ordered everybody off the train and then proceeded to line them up against a barbed wire fence. There were about 115 persons on board that train, about 20 of them women.[16]

While several of the bandits covered the passengers with their weapons, one of the outlaws took a feed bag around to each of the passengers and ordered them to dump any valuables they might have into it. The take amounted to about $400 and some jewelry. It seems the $90,000 bonanza had eluded them.

The Rock Island Railroad put up a $500 bounty for each of the desperadoes, while the American Express Company offered $300 a head. If all were captured and convicted then the amount of money to be awarded would have been a substantial $4,800.

Motivated to capture these boys was none other than noted deputy U.S. marshals Henry "Heck" Thomas and William Matthew "Bill" Tilghman. Both famed lawmen were on a special train that departed Guthrie, accompanied by a dozen armed men and their horses. At Oklahoma City, Tilghman transferred to the Choctaw line, by which he was to head to Pottawatomie Indian country in the event the gang chose to flee in that direction.

They didn't go the direction the posses were hoping they would. Instead Jennings and his ragtag band of brigands made their way to Cushing. Lee Nutter was co-owner of Cozier & Nutter, a small mercantile operation in Cushing. Nutter occupied quarters at the rear of the establishment. Shortly after midnight on October 29, Nutter was awakened by someone tapping lightly on his bedroom window and calling him by name. Convincing the proprietor that they were in urgent need of funeral clothes for a recently deceased person, the four men persuaded Nutter to open the shop to them. Later he would realize that the four were Dynamite Dick Clifton, Al and Frank Jennings, and Little Dick West.[17]

Nutter had deposited the day's earnings in the bank earlier that day. Otherwise the thieves would have made off with about $350 from the store's till. Instead they were forced to go away with some coats, hats, and gloves, fifteen dollars they picked from Nutter's pockets, a jug of whiskey, and, as a bonus, some bananas.

Dynamite Dick and Little Dick West then parted ways with the Jennings and O'Malley brothers near Tulsa, presumably carrying part of the foraged fruit. Dynamite Dick Clifton was shot to death soon after he left the gang for semiretirement, holing up with a woman friend and her young son in a remote cabin several miles west of Checotah.

Deputy marshals George Lawson and Hess Bussy trailed Clifton to the cabin after an earlier shootout that left Clifton's arm broken from a gunshot. The deputy marshals called to the cabin for Clifton to surrender. Their demands were met with silence from within the lair. Bussy and Lawson made repeated threats of setting the cabin ablaze if they were not obeyed. Finally the woman and the boy appeared at an open doorway. The officers threw down on them with their guns and instructed them to set fire to the cabin themselves. The frightened boy and his mother refused. The marshals then threatened to kill them if they did not comply. But again the pair refused.

When the officers repeated their command one last time along with the promise to kill the boy and his mother if they refused, the door burst open and Dynamite Dick charged the two officers with his gun blazing. Since Dick had the use of just one hand due to his earlier scrape with these two officers, he was not much of a match for the two lawmen who quickly shot him to death. Dynamite Dick Clifton was dead just seconds after he charged outside his hideout.[18]

Ledbetter received word that the gang had stopped at a blacksmith shop in Red Fork, near Tulsa, on November 28. Posing as cowboys, the riders had sought to have one of the horse's shoes repaired. They claimed to be hired hands on their way to the ranch of Red Hereford. For whatever reason, the suspicious smithy didn't buy the boys' false claim.

Once the riders left Red Fork, the blacksmith notified Tulsa District deputy marshals Lon Lewis and Joe Thompson. Just before sunset the marshals headed south out of Tulsa. They were accompanied by Gus Thompson, Joe Thompson's sixteen-year-old son, John Mclanahan, and Jake Elliot. On the road at about midnight the posse was joined by Ledbetter and Tolbert up from Muskogee.[19]

The posse lay in wait above the Hereford ranch until daylight. They sent Joe's son to the main house on the pretense of needing to borrow a wood maul and an iron wedge. When he returned to the lawmen he informed them that the gang had left the Hereford place after staying just long enough to eat dinner the previous night.

By the time the posse picked up their trail again, it led straight to the Spike S Ranch of John Harless, the gang's old haunt. In *More Burs under the Saddle,* author Ramon Adams doubts that a gun battle ever took place. Adams contends that on the day the posse confronted the men, Jennings and his gang gave up without a fight.

In *West of Hell's Fringe,* from which most of this material was taken, Glenn Shirley sets the scene of a cold November night when things really heated up. According to Shirley, the posse closed in on the Spike S under cover of darkness. It was November 29, 1897. Shirley writes that Ledbetter had earlier recruited a neighboring farmer by the name of Kelly to approach the house and pretend that he had got lost in a sandstorm and needed help in finding his way. Once inside, Kelly was to take note of what or whom he saw there. Kelly did as he was instructed.

The outlaws had just finished supper when Kelly knocked on the door and was admitted. But Mrs. Harless commented after his departure that it seemed almost unnatural for Kelly to be lost, saying, "As if he didn't know this country as well as I know my kitchen." The gang's suspicion rising, Morris O'Malley was then posted in a wagon as a sentry.[20]

O'Malley was taken by surprise as Ledbetter managed to sneak up on him and stick his Winchester against him with orders to climb out of the wagon and keep quiet. He was bound and gagged and placed in the Harless barn for safekeeping. Ledbetter then posted the possemen at all corners surrounding the house and waited for morning.

Mrs. Harless's brother, Clarence Enscoe, exited the house to fetch a pail of water and realized that O'Malley was not in the wagon. Enscoe walked into the barn and into a trap. He too was bound and gagged by lawmen and was laid out in a stall along with Morris O'Malley.

Mrs. Harless sent a hired girl, Ida Hurst, to summon Enscoe and O'Malley for breakfast. She returned to say she received no response to her beckoning. Mrs. Harless threw on a shawl and strode to the barn in search of the two men. Once she was inside, Ledbetter stepped up behind her and introduced himself. He told the woman to go back inside the house and inform the remaining gang members to surrender. Ledbetter instructed Mrs. Harless that in the event the others refused to surrender, she and Ida should leave the house and take cover behind the stone walls of the family cemetery.

That's what happened, and Al and Frank Jennings and Pat O'Malley responded to Ledbetter's call for surrender with a hail of gunfire. "From sixty to one hundred shots flew in both directions, thick and fast," Al Jennings is quoted as saying.[21] All three men managed to escape by making a mad dash from the rear of the house to an orchard. Two possemen, Lewis and Elliot, fired on and wounded each of the refugees even as they dove for cover in a bank of trees.[22]

The trio commandeered a wagon driven by two Euchee Indian boys and eventually made their way to the home of Willis Brooks, the long-time friend of Dynamite Dick Clifton and Little Dick West. But because Dynamite Dick was dead and Little Dick was no longer part of the Jennings gang, Brooks had little interest in helping the outlaws. He sent them to Sam Baker. Baker went into Checotah to fetch a doctor for the wounded outlaws but then began to assess the penalty for harboring federal fugitives. He then contacted Marshal Ledbetter and made arrangements to deliver the fugitives to him.

On the morning of December 6, 1897, with a wish of "good luck," Baker waved at the departing crooks with instructions on which trail to take to pull off a clean getaway. Unbeknownst to Jennings, Baker had already told Ledbetter that he would be sending the gang down that same trail. This, according to *West of Hell's Fringe,* is where the posse threw down on the outlaws. Seeing they were caught red-handed, the gang gave up without a shot.[23]

Al Jennings was sentenced to life imprisonment on February 17, 1899, but with the help of friends he was able to persuade President William McKinley to commute that sentence to five years. Jennings was released from prison on November 13, 1902. Frank received a five-year sentence.[24]

Al Jennings went on to run for Oklahoma County attorney in 1910 and for governor in 1914. He was defeated in both attempts.[25] He later traveled to Hollywood, where he played a major role in the movie *Beating Back,* in which he portrayed himself.

Al Spencer

Another enterprising Al was Al Spencer, whose first criminal high jinks—which resulted in his arrest—was rustling cattle in Nowata County, Oklahoma, in 1916. Spencer was sent to the

Oklahoma State Penitentiary on March 3, 1920, where he was to serve three concurrent ten-year sentences and one five-year sentence for larceny of domestic animals and grand larceny.[26]

While in prison Spencer met Frank Nash, known as "Jelly" Nash, who was serving time for robbing a bank in the small town of Corn, Oklahoma. While on a leave of absence granted by the warden in December of 1922, a privilege not uncommon for the era, Nash joined the Spencer gang. Spencer had already escaped prison on January 17, 1922, after having received at least two leaves of absences from Warden William S. Key.[27]

The following year, the Al Spencer gang ran rampant, robbing banks in as many as three states from January to June. Spencer was variously labeled with such sobriquets as "King of the Osage," "Phantom Terror," and "Wild Rider of Oklahoma."[28]

On January 15, 1923, the gang held up the State Bank of Cambridge in Kansas. Then they withdrew money from a bank in Gentry, Arkansas, on the first of March. They hid out near Row, Oklahoma and wound up shooting it out with Delaware County Sheriff Maples and two deputies.[29] The gang managed to escape, and was suspected of robbing banks in Nelagoney, Pawhuska, Talala, Lenapah, and Broken Bow, all small Oklahoma towns. Later, they were reported to have robbed the banks in Elgin and Towanda, Kansas.[30]

But, like his predecessors, Spencer's ego lured him to make a spectacular name for himself. He decided that rather than robbing two banks in the same town on the same day as the Dalton gang had attempted, unsuccessfully and fatally, in Coffeyville, Kansas, Spencer would rob a train. The site of the robbery would be somewhere around Bartlesville, Oklahoma.[31]

Moved by ego rather than logic, Spencer concocted a scheme of fantastic proportions. So overblown was his desire to be recognized as a thief of tremendous courage and daring that he boldly invited many of his cronies to watch this next job. Spencer told his friends where and when this caper would occur in such detail that no one could possibly miss the time or location. Unfortunately for Spencer his invitation at the last minute reached the attention of area law enforcement officers who were only too eager to attend without the formality of an invitation or an RSVP. Unfortunately they arrived too late.[32]

Shortly after midnight, August 21, 1923, Al Spencer and his gang struck. A Katy (Missouri, Kansas, Texas) train was robbed. This was the last train robbery in Oklahoma, and an estimated $20,000 in Liberty bonds was "liberated" during the heist.[33]

Almost immediately a posse gathered in Bartlesville, hopped aboard a special locomotive coach, and descended upon the scene of the robbery at the small town of Okesa. The law enforcement community acted swiftly, and before September came to a close a grand sweep collected nearly all of the Al Spencer gang. All, that is, except for Spencer.

His ability to elude pursuers and a vow never to be taken alive were both taken very seriously by the men charged with bringing him in. Deputy U.S. Marshal Luther Bishop, acting under the direction of U.S. Marshal Alva McDonald, devised a plan to ambush Spencer and kill him if necessary. The problem was that no one knew where Spencer was hiding. Bishop enlisted the aid of Stanley Snyder, an underworld figure familiar with Spencer and associates. First however, Bishop had to secure Snyder's release from the Pawhuska jail. He was being housed there in connection with the Katy railroad robbery at Okesa as a member of Spencer's gang.[34]

Six heavily armed men accompanied Marshals McDonald and Bishop to a spot on a trail about three miles south of the Kansas border near the Osage-Washington County line in Oklahoma, about ten miles from Bartlesville. The posse included Bartlesville police chief L. U. Gaston, Pawhuska policeman Billy Crowe, railroad detective Joe Palmer, Burns Agency detective C. F. Raub, postal inspector D. W. Adamson, and Ed Robertson.[35]

In his first book, *Alive If Possible, Dead If Necessary,* Dee Cordry describes what happened next:

> They concealed themselves behind damp bushes and waited as a light rain fell. At dusk, Al Spencer was spotted walking along the trail. He had a rifle cradled in his arms, ready for instant use.[36]

The similarities of this ambush to that of the one that brought down Bill Doolin were not merely coincidental. Bishop was keenly aware of the tactics of the Doolin ambush and deliberately employed them here. Suddenly finding himself confronted with the posse, Spencer raised his rifle and got off a single shot, ignoring an order to halt. He was cut down in a fiery barrage within seconds. On Spencer was found ten $1,000 Liberty bonds, or half the take of the Katy robbery, and a .38 revolver.[37]

Al Spencer went down in history as the man who pulled off the last train robbery in Oklahoma only to be stopped in his tracks with the help of a snitch and relentless lawmen. After all his disreputable service to law enforcement, Stanley Snyder was later shot in the back on May 9, 1924, by his wife, Aileen, whom he was in the act of thrashing in the couple's Bartlesville home.[38]

The Narrow Gauge Kid

There is a name out of the Old West that *shoulda* conjured up all sorts of romantic ideas of a fast-shooting, hard-riding, quick-fisted man in black. But the nickname Narrow Gauge Kid bestowed upon William "Bill" McElhanie would be the only really memorable contribution to his notoriety.

Even though he was said to have ridden with the Dalton gang, his accomplishments as a bandit proved far less than what one might expect from a member of that notorious bunch. Unclear is whether or not McElhanie participated in the robbery of a Southern Pacific train in Alila, California. In fact there is some doubt as to whether it should be attributed to the Dalton gang at all.[39] Had McElhanie participated in the robbery of train No. 17 on February 6, 1891, his status among outlaws *woulda* been duly recognized.

Because history doesn't align itself with speculation, McElhanie's biggest known "accomplishment" in banditry was that of stealing clothes in August of 1893 and stealing some hogs in Pawnee County in December of 1896—hardly the things legends are made of.[40]

McElhanie's demise was as unheralded as his career as a criminal. His lifeless form was discovered near Red Fork, now a part of Tulsa, in March of 1897. A single gunshot to the back of his head had done him in.

Elmer McCurdy
A Short Life: A Longer Career

Those who don't believe in a life after death have obviously never heard the story of outlaw Elmer McCurdy.

He was born in Maine sometime around 1880 to Sadie McCurdy; the name of his father is unknown. In 1903, he left Maine after learning the plumbing trade and moved west, taking jobs as itinerant plumber in both Cherryvale, Kansas, and Webb City, Missouri.[41]

McCurdy joined the army in 1907, and on November 7, 1910, was discharged from the Quartermaster Corps. That was probably the last legal means of making a living McCurdy ever practiced. Just three days after his discharge, McCurdy and another man were arrested and convicted on a charge of possessing burglars' tools. From there McCurdy's career path spiraled pathetically, almost comically, downward until even after his death he was held out to ridicule and scoff, as we will see.

During his lifetime, McCurdy bungled one attempt after another at becoming a formidable foe to the rich and powerful whose trains always ran on time but whose schedules McCurdy couldn't keep straight. McCurdy's mixture of enthusiasm and daftness even led him to rob the wrong train. On October 4, 1911, the MK&T train traveling through Okesa, Oklahoma, was boarded by McCurdy. He was looking for a big payoff. The train, he believed, was carrying a cargo said to be in the thousands. But McCurdy commandeered the wrong train and came away with just forty-six dollars and two bottles of whiskey.[42]

Just a few minutes after McCurdy let that train chug on down the line, the express train he thought he had stopped went rumbling by at a high rate of speed with the much-sought-after payload safe and sound. In McCurdy's world missed opportunities were beginning to add up faster than the booty he hoped to get from those opportunities.

In an earlier train robbery, McCurdy stopped a locomotive near Lenapah, Oklahoma, his new base of operation. McCurdy got wind of a safe containing more than $4,000. He and three other men brought the Iron Mountain Railroad train to a stop. Upon locating the safe, McCurdy put nitroglycerine to its door. But once again McCurdy let enthusiasm overtake common sense. He overestimated the amount of explosives needed, and as a result the safe disintegrated and the money inside was blown far and wide. The express car it was in was blown to smithereens. The outlaws came away with roughly $450 for their efforts.[43]

McCurdy's skills did not improve with time or experience, from which he learned very little. He was killed on October 7, 1911, just three days after the ill-timed robbery of the wrong MK&T train near Okesa on October 4. Death is generally a hindrance to fortune hunting, but for this uncelebrated member of the *Woulda, Coulda, Shoulda* gang, it was in death that his greatest adventures lay ahead.

McCurdy was killed after three possemen found him near Pawhuska at the Charley Revard ranch in the early morning hours of October 7. The ensuing gun battle left only the luckless McCurdy dead. His corpse was taken back to Pawhuska where it was dumped at the Johnson Funeral Home. Possibly fearing that no relatives would come by soon to claim the body, the undertaker embalmed it with arsenic; it was a practice then used if a body needed to be preserved for long periods of time pending next of kin identification.[44]

In the next five years the body became known as "The Embalmed Bandit" and stood in a corner of Johnson's mortuary where locals often entered to view the stiff. Then on October 5, 1916, Johnson received a phone call from two men, Charles and James Patterson, who pretended to be Elmer's brothers. They convinced the Osage County attorney to allow them to take the body home to a worried and sick mother. On October 7, 1916, Elmer was on his way to Arkansas City, Kansas.[45]

Elmer wasn't headed home to a worried and sick mother with two bighearted brothers at the dead man's side. However, he was in fact going on the road and into show business.

James Patterson it seems was the owner of a traveling carnival show. Charles was a salesman for Lesh Oil Company, living in Arkansas City, when James brought his show to town. Charles told James of the mummified bandit down in Oklahoma, and together the brothers concocted the sibling scheme, which would make the corpse a headliner for the show.

McCurdy did his standup routine at Woodward, Oklahoma, for a week before he and the rest of the troupe headed south to Texas. Elmer was a hit. He stayed with the show for six years until the owners sold the operation in 1922. Elmer again attained top billing, starring alongside wax replicas of such prominent men as Jesse James,

Bill Doolin, and the Daltons, all mere replicas of themselves.

McCurdy's theatrical career was experiencing a long, successful run. He was later with Louis Sonney's "Museum of Crime," the outfit that bought the Patterson Carnival Show. In 1971 the Museum of Crime was sold to Ed Liersch.[46]

McCurdy, or more aptly the mummified corpse of McCurdy, had been in show business for nearly fifty-five years—longer than his criminal career and even longer than his life span of thirty-one years. Elmer wasn't through yet. Though his looks were deteriorating somewhat with age and decomposition, McCurdy was to have one more "starring" role. This time he would be on network television.

Elmer's shriveling corpse had been reduced to the role of just another frightful prop. The remains were hanging around, by the neck, in a fun house called "The Laff in the Dark," a wax figure exhibition that was the brainchild of Ed Liersch and his partner, D. R. Crydale, who had opened the shop along the Long Beach Pike in California.[47]

The fun house closed after approximately five years and was subsequently leased to Universal Television Studios, who chose it as a site for filming an episode of the *Six Million Dollar Man.* Elmer's standup routine was once again resurrected and, as the story has it, he was being lowered from the spot where he swung when an arm fell off, revealing that this was no ordinary wax prop. The startling reality came when the man attempting to lower Elmer from the makeshift gallows observed what looked like human bone and muscle tissue inside the dismembered arm.

After a coroner's investigation, it was determined that no bizarre criminal act had been uncovered, and the body of Elmer McCurdy was returned to Oklahoma where he received a fine funeral in Guthrie, complete with a black horse-drawn hearse and a fine white pine casket provided by the Gill-Lessert Funeral Home of Ponca City. The date was April 22, 1977.[48]

McCurdy's final resting place is at Guthrie's Summit View Cemetery, Boot Hill section. And even though McCurdy never achieved the status he was hoping for during his lifetime as a bandit, he was buried alongside one whom he likely saw as a standard-bearer of the trade. The inept Elmer McCurdy now lies beside none other than the infamous Bill Doolin.

J. Earle Smith
Final Payment to an Aspiring Mob Lawyer

J. Earl Smith of Tulsa died on August 18, 1933. The cause of death was anything but natural. Smith had long-standing ties to one of the nation's first super-gangs of the 1930s: the Ma Barker gang.

Smith was retained to represent one of the notorious gang members, Harvey Bailey, at a Tulsa court hearing, but Smith forgot to show. Dissatisfied with the docketing practices of their attorney, two members of the gang resolved the matter without the legal remedy of a court sanction or bar complaint. On August 18, 1933, lawyer Smith's body was found shot to death in Catoosa.[49] The crime was never officially solved.

The two Barker gang members authorities wanted for questioning about Smith's murder were Harry Campbell and Glenn Roy Wright. They were also wanted for questioning in the murder of a Miami, Oklahoma, man, William Witten, who police believed was killed during a robbery in nearby Picher four months earlier in May.[50]

Chapter 9

The Adaptable Henry Starr

Technological advances came slowly to Oklahoma in the early and mid-twentieth century. While the automobile was widely used back East and on the opposite shoreline, in California, many Oklahomans were satisfied with the time-tested method of getting around: the horse. Another great discovery, electricity, didn't reach much of rural Oklahoma until Congress passed the Rural Electricity Act of 1936. And even then kerosene and oil lanterns continued to supply many farm homes with the necessary amount of illumination.

Horses were still widely used into the twenties as the preferred power for pulling a plow or a wagon loaded with grain or cut wood, since most farmers deemed the animal trustworthy. Except for the occasional thrown shoe, the horse, unlike its modern-day counterpart, the tractor, was virtually maintenance-free. Commercially, horses had achieved celebrity status with use by the Wells Fargo stagecoach line with its many noted teams of blues (grays), buckskins, and blacks. And of course all across Oklahoma horses were known to pull an occasional "surrey with the fringe on top."

Horses remained the favorite transportation of the mounted bandit too, through the early part of the century. Even though Henry Ford's Model T gained immense popularity nationwide after the car became available to the masses in 1908, the horse was everything the Oklahoma bandit needed.

But in 1916 all that would change, and a national trend would begin to emerge in the way criminals would flee the scene of the crime. On October 18, in a small Kansas town, an event would forever change not just the efficiency of the bandits, but the face of a nation. America was entering a new era, one of electricity, telephones, and automobiles. Bandits began to realize the advantages of changing from horseback to horsepower.

Law enforcement, especially in rural Oklahoma, hadn't quite caught up to the automotive age. Even in a time when a telegraph or telephone call would sound the alarm that a bank or train station or hardware store had been held up, the lawman receiving such messages could do little more than mount his trusty steed and gallop after the automobile carrying the criminals.

Although the introduction of automobile-assisted robbery is often attributed to Henry Starr in Oklahoma, the change from horseback to horsepower was first tested at Coffeyville, Kansas. Thieves targeted the Isham Hardware Store, the very store where citizens helped themselves to guns in defense against the Dalton gang's raid on Coffeyville a scant twenty-four years earlier in 1892. The culprits this time were members of the Poe-Hart gang.[1]

Adolphus Lane Poe was born in Travis County, Texas, in 1876. He purportedly rode with an uncle in the Oklahoma Land Run of 1889, which opened the unclaimed Twin Territories to settlement. Perhaps finding farming too painstaking a living, Adolphus—called "Pony"—and his brother Bill were charged with stealing a herd of horses in less than five years after entering Indian Territory. They were caught, tried, and sentenced by none other than the "hanging judge," Isaac C. Parker. In about three years both men were paroled.

The Hart brothers, William and Harry, were twins. They were the products of an English immigrant, George W. Hart, who arrived in 1894. The family settled on Labette County, Kansas, as a residence before ending up in Centralia, a tiny farming community and whiskey outlet located midway between Nowata and Vinita in what was then Indian Territory.

George died young of a heart attack. The old adage that a boy suffers from the lack of a father figure was never more evident than with the Hart twins. Just after their papa's death, William and Harry set about burglarizing local merchants and were responsible for, or suspected of, several other forms of mischief. In one act of mindlessness, William "Will" Hart shot a Big Creek schoolteacher who had the audacity to discipline the boys' sister.[2]

By 1915, the Harts had met Poe. It was a time when the army conducted an expedition against Mexican revolutionary Pancho Villa after he raided Texas, stealing horses with which to supply his army during Mexico's Civil War. U.S. Army general John J. "Black Jack" Pershing set up horse-buying stations at Fort Reno, Oklahoma, Fort Scott, Kansas, and Fort Sumner, New Mexico. Pony Poe patriotically responded to Pershing's call for horses by setting up a large-scale horse rustling operation. He planned to sell the stolen animals to Pershing for use by the U.S. military.[3]

In addition to the Hart brothers, Pony Poe enlisted two of his nephews: Oscar Poe, who was abandoned at Pony's doorstep by a widowed sister-in-law when he was only thirteen years old, and Johnny Ferrell.

Everything was in place to put the gang on a moneymaking track stealing and selling horses when, in mid-December 1915, their plans abruptly changed. Oscar and William, whom Pony had dispatched on a "procurement" trip, were promptly captured and tossed into a Nowata, Oklahoma, jail on charges of horse theft.

After that incident, the gang turned its attention predominantly toward robbing businesses and banks. The very first known bank robbery wherein the automobile and not horses was used in the getaway occurred in Centralia, Oklahoma on November 18, 1916. The Poe-Hart gang was accused of that feat. Counting on a swift getaway, thanks to the Ford touring car, the gang conducted a number of successful robberies throughout Oklahoma. They started with the bank at Alluwe, a small town about eleven miles southwest of Nowata, where Oscar Poe, Will Hart, and a recent addition to the gang, Jess Littrell, made off with an estimated $2,500.[4]

In spite of several run-ins with lawmen in which various gang members were captured or killed, the gang was successful in robbing five banks in the few short months between November 1916 and January 21, 1917. January saw the end of the Poe-Hart gang when Oscar Poe and William and Harry Hart were killed in an ambush.[5]

The gang enjoyed short-term success primarily because the car in which the bandits rode was faster than the lawmen's horses. By then the automobile was on the fast track to once and for all replacing the horse as the favored means of outlaw escape.

Enter long-time bandit Henry Starr, with criminal antecedents dating back to just after the Trail of Tears. They began with Tom Starr, Henry's grandfather, the much feared assassin of more than thirty Cherokee people Tom believed responsible for the deaths of his father and brother during the Cherokee Civil War of the 1840s. Tom Starr himself was Cherokee and had vehemently opposed other

Cherokees of the John Ross faction, during the early struggle for political dominance in Indian Territory. In 1880, Tom's son Sam Starr married Myra Belle Shirley, later and better known as Belle Starr, Queen of the Outlaws.[6]

Although Henry was no stranger to fear and intimidation thanks to a long line of family role models, he had the intelligence to take notice of improvements to his chosen profession. The successes of the Poe-Hart gang were apparently not lost on Starr.

But Starr was not without an impressive dossier of his own. He was born in 1873, and beginning in about 1890, compiled a list of bank robberies perhaps unmatched by anyone since. He himself, near death, proclaimed his accomplishments by boasting, "I've probably robbed more banks than any man in America."[7] He was probably right.

Henry Starr and his gang were suspected in the robberies of nine banks in Oklahoma in 1914, from September to December. They robbed their tenth bank in Owasso, a town located about twenty-five miles north of Tulsa, on January 5, 1915.

Robert Lee Williams became the third governor of Oklahoma on January 11, 1915. The next day, Henry Starr celebrated the event by robbing the bank in Vera. A $1,000 reward was promptly issued for the capture of Henry Starr; dead or alive.[8] Starr continued his exploits with aplomb until he, like the Dalton boys, decided to rob two banks at the same time in the same town. The town whose banks Starr chose to hold up was Stroud, Oklahoma.

On March 27, 1915, Starr led a gang of six horsemen into the town, situated halfway between Tulsa and Oklahoma City. The double holdup initially appeared to be a success. The two teams of robbers had taken human shields, disarmed one shotgun-wielding citizen, and were making their way to their horses with hostages and loot when seventeen-year-old Paul Curry appeared with a rifle.[9] Curry sniped at the bandits, hitting gang member Louis Estes in the neck and sending a round through Starr's left leg, shattering it. Both bandits lay immobile in the street and were subsequently arrested. The others managed to escape.[10]

Six years passed before Starr and his cronies made the great transition from men of horseback to men of horsepower. Five years previously the Poe-Hart gang was the first to use automobiles in robbery.

Although he was not the first, Starr, nicknamed "The Bearcat," is certainly one of the most celebrated bandits who transitioned from "Old West" outlaw to "motorized bandit."[11] On February 18, 1921, he once again set out to commit a bank robbery with three associates. For their first motorized bank robbery, the Henry Starr gang chose People's National Bank, located in Harrison, Arkansas.[12]

Starr's first motorized holdup would be his last. Forward-thinking W. J. Myers, the former bank president, foreseeing such a possibility as an armed robbery, had a door installed in the back of the bank's vault. Inside the door he kept a loaded shotgun. During the robbery, as Starr and his three associates were busy gathering up the spoils and keeping employees under the gun, Myers was able to make his way to the door inside the vault. He opened the door, got his shotgun, and opened fire. Only Henry Starr was hit.

Starr's wounds would prove fatal, and he died four days later, refusing to identify his accomplices even though they were only too eager to leave him lying sprawled across the bank's floor. Henry Starr, the nephew of the Queen of the Outlaws, was interred at a cemetery in Dewey, Oklahoma, just up the trail from Bartlesville, forever putting an end to the legendary family's lives of crime.[13]

Arkansas Tom

Arkansas Tom was another transitional bandit who robbed his way across two centuries. His real name was Roy Daugherty.[14] He was present at the bloodbath at Ingalls, Oklahoma Territory, in 1893, as a member of the Doolin gang.[15] It was his sniping from an upstairs hotel room that killed three lawmen. Daugherty was captured, convicted of manslaughter, and handed a fifty-year prison sentence. Paroled in 1910, he set up shop as a restaurateur in Drumright, Oklahoma, before going to Hollywood where he acted in Westerns.[16]

For a while it seemed that Roy had survived his criminal past. Then the call of Missouri and home lured Daugherty back to his old ways. In December 1916 he was implicated in a Neosho bank burglary and arrested. Daugherty was found guilty in February 1917 by the Newton County Circuit Court and sentenced to eight years in the state penitentiary at Jefferson City.[17]

Paroled in 1921, Daugherty appears to have gone straight for a time. He held various jobs in Kansas, Oklahoma, and Missouri and was living a clean, uncomplicated life with a cousin at Galena, Kansas, until the afternoon of November 26, 1923. That afternoon, around two-thirty, four men barged into a bank at Asbury and robbed it. Two of the four men were apprehended and began serving fifty-year prison sentences by the summer of 1924.[18] Police wasted no time in apprehending a third gang member. Soon a canary began to sing, and Arkansas Tom would once again be implicated in a robbery.

Police found Tom taking refuge at a friend's residence. He fired on the approaching officers but was shot and killed while babysitting on August 16, 1924. Arkansas Tom had managed to survive a lifetime as a highwayman, train robber, and bank robber in the days of the Old West, but he simply couldn't survive the Roaring Twenties.

As Glenn Shirley poignantly writes in his fascinating book, *West of Hell's Fringe:* "The death of Arkansas Tom Daugherty brought to an end the story of the great horseback gangs west of Hell's Fringe."[19]

Chapter 10

Celebrity Outlaws

The period between the 1850s and the 1870s proved to be a rather fertile time for birthing bandits whose later careers and violent exploits have been criticized, romanticized, or moralized in all manners of media beginning with the Dime Novels to the more recent efforts of the Big Screen and TV. Names such as James and Younger permeated print and film media for decades. Depending on which side of the law one stood, the men and their gangs were celebrated either as criminals or as celebrities, or a dubious combination of both.

The reputation of the gangs became the standard which all others employed in the same trade strove to achieve. Romanticized as Robin Hoods of their time in present-day Oklahoma, the Doolins and Daltons enjoyed a relatively free run of the Twin Territories in the late 1890s. The outlaws were sheltered and shielded by locals, some family and some friends, who perceived the gangs' actions as their own vicarious blow against big banks, real estate speculators, and railroad companies.

Bill Doolin rode with the Dalton gang until its leader, Bob Dalton, drew up plans to rob two banks simultaneously at Coffeyville, Kansas, in 1892, according to Leon Metz. Metz writes that two of the men, believing such an attempt was nothing short of suicide, Doolin and Bob Dalton's brother, Bill, refused to go along with the scheme. That decision saved the two men's lives since the only Dalton gang member at Coffeyville to survive the attack was the youngest of the pack, Emmett Dalton.

Doolin went on to become a preeminent gang leader of the 1890s. His gang included desperadoes as callous as the countryside had ever seen in other gangs. Most were Dalton gang members. Bill Dalton joined Doolin after the Coffeyville fiasco. Other hard cases making up the group included Little Bill Raidler and George "Red Buck" Weightman (sometimes spelled Waightman). Added to the list were Dan "Dynamite Dick" Clifton and Richard "Little Dick" West, both of whom later joined the untrained and ill-fated Al Jennings gang.

153

Charlie Pierce, George "Bitter Creek" Newcomb, and William "Tulsa Jack" Blake—actually a Kansas native—made up some of the group. Another member of the gang known for his accuracy with a rifle, Roy Daugherty, also known as Arkansas Tom, who was born in Missouri in 1870, rounded out the infamous Doolin gang.

Those who settled the Twin Territories, which later united and became Oklahoma, often saw big business as a meddlesome outsider who looked only to take advantage of the dirt-poor farmers. Even early day federal law enforcement had its detractors since it originated from outside the territories at a place called "Hell on the Border," Fort Smith, Arkansas.

Whether lore, legend, or lies, the gangs enjoyed a celebrity status unparalleled by most others despite the best efforts of later crews to emulate the earlier "Celebrity Outlaws." Mounting resentment from banks and railroad companies toward the Dalton gang and the Doolin gang brought announcements of reward money being offered for the heads of the gangs, dead or alive. The tactic worked as a great motivator, and lawmen had little trouble adding recruits to posses.

Bill Doolin was gunned down outside Lawton, O. T. Most agree the date was August of 1896, forever putting an end to his gang's organized activities.[1] Bill Dalton was killed two years earlier, in June of 1894, twenty-five miles from Ardmore, O. T., at the farm of Houston Wallace. Members of a new gang Dalton had organized a month before his death eventually dispersed. One of the members, Jim Night, was apparently shot by a Tulsa, Oklahoma, drugstore owner when Night attempted a robbery there in 1929.[2]

Oklahoma and Indian Territories in the 1890s were not without their share of "offspring," gangs or individuals whose acts of violence or downright depravity would earn for them their own distinguished places in the annals of crime. Most lacked the support of an empathetic community their crime-bent forebears had previously enjoyed. That lack of sentimentality for these latter-day bandits may have had its roots in the manner by which some of the gangs or individuals committed their crimes.

Brothers Victor and Jim Casey each made claim to land opened up to white settlement during the Oklahoma Land Run of 1899. Their respective parcels were established on Mustang Creek in Canadian

County near the town of El Reno. El Reno still exists today and is located along Interstate 40, about twenty-five miles west of Oklahoma City.

Not satisfied with their own sections of land, the brothers were later charged with murdering two of their neighbors in an attempt to acquire their claims.[3] Jim Casey was captured and sent to cool his heels in the jail at Guthrie, the provisional capital of Oklahoma Territory.[4]

In addition to the murders of their farmer neighbors, the men were being held for shooting a deputy named Ferris, once they had sneaked back to El Reno from their hiding place somewhere around Arapaho. It seems the men had a grudge against Deputy U.S. Marshal Christian "Chris" Madsen and were on a mission to kill him.[5] It is unclear why they settled on shooting Ferris, who survived the attack.

Jim Casey escaped jail but was recaptured and sent to the more secure facility in Oklahoma City. He spent time there with two other crime brothers: Will (sometimes referred to as Bill) and Bob Christian. Will Christian, also known as Black Jack and 202 (because of his weight), was charged with shooting to death deputy sheriff Will Turner on April 27, 1895, in Oklahoma Territory.[6] The three men made a daring jailbreak, which cost the lives of Oklahoma City police chief Milt Jones and escapee Jim Casey.

One innocent citizen was shot, by deputies' fire not by bandits', and one of the Christian brothers was wounded. Although badly bleeding, Bob managed a harrowing escape after highjacking a blacksmith's wagon.[7] His brother Bill climbed onto Chief Jones's horse and galloped out of town as fast as his stolen mount would run, but Jim Casey lay dead with bullet wounds to the head just above the ear and through the neck. He died almost instantly.

Another inmate sharing space in the Oklahoma County jail with the Christians and Casey was Obe Cox who was awaiting trial for horse theft. Cox had initially agreed to go along with the three men in their escape attempt but chickened out at the last minute.[8] The innocent who was wounded as a result of the fire from one of Chief Jones's deputies was Gus White, a carpenter. With White was Ella Hurt. The two were minding their own business, taking a pleasure ride in White's buggy on Grand Avenue at around 6:30 p.m., Sunday, June 30.[9]

The pair encountered Bob Christian and Jim Casey, who commandeered the buggy. Stunned, White and Hurt sat there while Christian took control of the reins and struck the horse. The horse was a young two-year-old and evidently unaccustomed to all the excitement. Rather than bolting, which is what the two escapees apparently thought he'd do, he simply froze to the ground he was standing on and didn't move a muscle.

While the stalled horse facilitated the death of Casey and the wounding of Christian by a deputy's bullet, the steed's stand also caused White to be hit. White suffered one leg and one abdomen wound, neither of which proved very serious, and several more holes were created in the clothes he was wearing by the wild shots of the deputies. Ironically, Ella Hurt was not hurt in the exchange.[10]

Later implicated in aiding in the escape were four known supporters of the Christians who, one local newspaper said, were "among the worst of the Indian Territory desperadoes." These four included John Fessenden, John Reeves, Doc Williams, and Ben Brown.[11]

Most surprising, however, was later testimony concerning the involvement of Deputy W. H. Carr, to whom Bob and Bill Christian surrendered after allegedly killing Sheriff Will Turner near Violet Springs in April. And it was in Carr's custody that Bob placed his revered white-handled Colt .45 revolver, decorated with an eagle's head, upon his surrender. It was the same revolver later used in the Christians' and Casey's great escape on an otherwise quiet June afternoon in Oklahoma City.[12]

Suspicions grew and questions were raised as to what plausible circumstances could have put that weapon once again in the hands of badman Bob Christian. What was clear was that whatever those circumstances may have been, they resulted in the murder of the city's beloved police chief. It was only at the arrest of one Jessie Findlay (sometimes spelled Finlay and Finley), that the truth came to light.

Findlay was an innocent-looking young woman who was Bob Christian's sweetheart. She took advantage of her blameless outward appearance during Bob's and Bill's incarceration, presenting herself not as Bob's gal but rather as sister to the two brothers. Findlay,

Fessenden, and Reeves, Bill Christian Sr., the brothers' father, and a couple of additional sympathizers, Tullis Welch and local tough guy Louie Miller, all had easy access to the prisoners while they were under the guardianship of deputy marshal Carr and jailer J. H. Garver, Findlay would later testify. It was during several such periods of access that individually or in groups this sextet would deliver a variety of items such as tobacco, clean linens, and three loaded revolvers, including Bob's own white-handled .45.[13]

At just about six-thirty on Sunday afternoon of June 30, 1895, Jailer Garver, as was his custom, had previously turned the prisoners out of their individual cells and into a common hallway between the cells so that the men could stretch their legs, swap tobacco products, or conduct any number of social activities. Garver was going into the common area where he would herd the bandits back into their cells when Garver's wife came calling. She was just inside the jail's office when Garver entered the corridor where the prisoners were milling about and called after her to close the corridor door behind him. Why Garver didn't do that himself is a matter for suspicious minds to ponder.

At that point the Christians and Casey jumped him, and while he was occupied with the Christian brothers, Casey ran out of the cell area, dashing by the shocked Mrs. Garver who, it was later admitted, forgot to fasten the door after her husband entered the hallway that held the captives.

To her credit however, after Casey sprang free and out of the jailhouse, Mrs. Garver recovered from the initial fright and threw the bolt on the door, thus preventing the Christians from joining their comrade.

Just at the very moment she got the door secured, back came Casey who "placed his revolver against her head and ordered the jail door opened at once. She complied and the Christians, who had succeeded in overpowering the jailer [*sic*] ran out."[14]

Bob and Bill Christian survived the frantic jailbreak, and despite being severely pummeled by the pair, Garver survived. The two met up again at a dugout twelve miles east of Pauls Valley. From there they and their assemblage of sympathizers-turned-gang-members headed west, stopping in Arizona.[15]

While working as a bronco buster on the Mud Springs ranch at

Sulphur Springs, Arizona, Bill recruited three other cowboy fugitives into his new gang that along with brother Bob made up the "High Fives," named for a popular card game of the time.[16]

Their collective successes were few, and peril and death comprised the gang's list of achievements. The gang staged a series of robberies throughout Arizona that included banks, trains, and stores as its victims. But hardly one year after forming the High Fives, Bill Christian was chased down and killed by Deputy U.S. Marshal Fred Higgins,[17] near Clifton, Arizona, in April 1897.[18]

Other members met similar ends. Code Young was shot and killed while involved in a train robbery the gang was conducting. A like end came to George Parker, who was silenced forever by fellow gang member, George Musgrave, who believed Parker had ratted on the gang. Parker was a former Texas Ranger who made a career switch.[19]

Bob held the gang together for a while after the death of his brother, but his enthusiasm in being the leader of the High Fives eroded completely with his arrest in Fronteras, Mexico, on November 25, 1897. Bob apparently got himself involved with some kind of fracas on Thanksgiving Day while in Mexico and was subsequently jailed.

Before U.S. authorities could complete the extradition process, Bob escaped jail and hightailed it to parts unknown in "deepest obscurity." That was the last time Bob Christian was seen or heard from. With his disappearance the High Fives gang disbanded, and Oklahoma's hunt for the bold, bad Christians was over.[20]

Bob Rogers may have been born in 1873 and would die a young man of only twenty-two years, but the time in between was full of acts of despicable proportions that would make him one of the most contemptible and feared desperadoes of the territory.

Having been born in Northwest Arkansas and raised around Washington and Benton Counties, Bob and his two younger brothers, Sam and Jim, moved into the Cherokee Nation with their father, Frank. At some point, Bob began working as a cowhand on ranches around Nowata, a small community south of Coffeyville, Kansas. His earliest recorded offense came on November 10, 1891, when he was arrested by Deputy U.S. Marshal Bynum Colbert for assault with intent to kill.[21]

Young Bob was taken to face the charges at Fort Smith. He was freed on bond within a few days of the arrest. After his release Bob took the trail home to the Cherokee Nation, where he put together a band of brigands in the fashion of the Daltons. His troupe held a cast of characters that were as eager to scrape off the cow manure from their boots and wipe the sweat of a hard day's work from their brow as he was. Bob Rogers had his gang.

They included Bob Stiteler, Willis Brown from the Chelsea area, "Dynamite Jack" Turner who hailed from the Eureka, Kansas, area, and his brother Kiowa Turner.[22] Soon the gang felt the long arm of Deputy U.S. Marshal Henry "Heck" Thomas, and the whole bunch was arrested and taken before "the hanging judge" at Fort Smith. Judge Parker took pity on nineteen-year-old Rogers and his crew. After sentencing the sorry lot to a term in the federal reformatory, he released the teenage gang on probation. Parker admonished Rogers, "This is your first offense. . . . If you continue in this path of life, death may be the penalty."[23]

Forty-year-old Deputy Constable Jess W. Elliott of the Cherokee Indian Police out of Vinita, was on orders to serve legal papers at the small wild town of Catoosa, where he arrived on Tuesday morning, November 3, 1892. Today the Rogers County city is known for its major inland port on the banks of the Verdigris River.

In addition to being a sworn peace officer, Elliott was a seasoned ten-year attorney, practicing law in both the Cherokee and U.S. courts. The long ride south from Vinita to Catoosa must have been particularly parching as one of the first stops Elliott made was to a local watering hole where he promptly got drunk. Unfortunately for Elliott he was in with some bad company at the saloon because also on hand and every bit as drunk as the lawman was ill-tempered, quick-fisted, and mentally demented Bob Rogers.[24]

Equally liquored up, the two men became entangled in a dispute of now long-forgotten origin. At one point Rogers determined that enough talk had passed and proceeded to knock the stuffing out of the lawman. Some of the saloon's patrons had enough of their wits about them to be able to see that Elliott had long since stopped being able to defend himself against Rogers. They managed to pull Rogers off Elliott and hustled the young cowhand outside to his horse. They kept Elliott in their collective "protective custody" until he was able to stagger to his horse and trot down the road and out of town. Rogers wasn't the type to forgive and forget, and what he did next crossed the line between a romanticized robber and the pure, unadulterated meanness of a maniac.

Rogers fell monumentally short of reaching similar fame as the Dalton gang following one particular display of rage. Rogers may have known that when Doolin gang member George "Red Buck" Weightman gunned down an elderly preacher who protested Weightman's stealing of his horse, Bill Doolin and his second in command, Bob Dalton, became angry. The shooting of the preacher followed an 1895, Dover, Oklahoma, train robbery. According to Art Burton, in his book, *Black, Red, and Deadly,* Doolin tossed Weightman his share of the spoils and sent him on down the trail alone.[25] Evidently Rogers skipped that chapter in the highwaymen's manual.

Not satisfied with the severe pummeling he had given Elliott in the saloon, Rogers hid along the trail leading back to Vinita that he knew Elliott would have to take. As Elliott neared the spot where Rogers had secreted himself, the madman dashed from behind a lair of bushes, grabbed Elliott's horse's reins with one hand and pulled the startled constable from the saddle with the other. Once Elliott was on the ground, Rogers pulled a knife and slashed the lawman's throat in three places.[26]

The brutal homicide of Constable Elliott was not without witnesses. A traveler saw Rogers ride off, leaving his victim against a post spewing blood from his gashed throat, "as if he were vomiting blood."[27] Elliott was dead within minutes of the attack. As monstrous an event as that was, it wasn't the worst part of it.

Shortly after the attack, a few neighbors gathered and with a local doctor, whose last name was Warren, decided they would stay with the body until Deputy U.S. Marshal John Taylor arrived. He had been called for by some of those gathered. The group of men with the good doctor milled about the area and as dark began to fall, they built a fire. Until Taylor arrived, there wasn't much they could do except try to protect the corpse from would-be corpse robbers, coyotes, or other vermin, so they waited.

Just after nightfall the sound of thundering horse hooves lifted the gaze of the clustered men to a sight that shook them all. Bob Rogers burst into the open on the back of his galloping horse, jumped the fire, and scattered the citizen sentinels in all directions.[28] Peering from behind whatever cover they could hastily find in the dark, a few remaining witnesses were horrified by what they saw next. Rogers jumped from his horse and began kicking the dead body repeatedly in the head. Not finding relief there, Rogers then stomped the dead man's chest and ribs, smashing and disfiguring the corpse. At one point Rogers hunched beside the corpse, took Elliott's hat and placed it on his own head as he rifled the body's clothing, examining papers he found in pockets. Rogers then climbed on his horse and rode off, just moments before Deputy Taylor arrived.[29]

After a series of depot and train robberies, one of which ended with the bandits literally holding the bag—an empty bag—a spate of successful holdups emboldened Rogers to lead his gang in the high art of bank robbery.

Following the robberies of the depots at Chelsea and Blue Jacket, on July 13, 1893, the gang entered the Mound Valley Bank at Labette, Kansas, and robbed it of a few hundred dollars. U.S. Deputy Marshall Heck Bruner and his brother Wood Bruner and "Dink" Douthitt set up surveillance on a farm owned by George Harlan, a few miles west of Vinita, a place where they believed the Rogers' gang was apt to rendezvous. Their patience paid off when toward evening two of the gang's confederates unsuspectingly rode to the farmhouse. As the pair of brigands approached, the officers stepped from their cover, identified themselves, and ordered the men to surrender. The two young criminals responded in the usual manner by taking up their rifles against the lawmen, an act that resulted in the quick death of outlaw Ralph Halleck and the serious but nonfatal wounding of Bob Rogers' younger brother Sam.[30]

Rogers and the gang had learned a thing or two about what makes a good train robbery, such as don't let the train blast past the holdup site as did the MK&T at Kelso, five miles north of Vinita, the previous year. As a result they managed a more successful train robbery on Christmas Eve, 1893.

The Arkansas Valley passenger train was held up at Seminole Switch by Rogers and his band of marauders just as darkness set in on the eve of peace and goodwill toward all. Everything of any value was handed over to the bandits. The Rogers gang got away with money and mail from the express car and took jewelry, watches, and overcoats and even garnered a few pocketknives from the passengers. Of course they also made off with any money the holiday travelers may have had on them. They finally released the train after about an hour and a half and allowed it to be on its merry Christmas way to its destination of Fort Smith.[31]

Gang leader Bob Rogers was captured twice by lawmen. The first incident occurred when he and a man named Bob Stiteler were surprised at the home of Rogers' brother-in-law, Henry Daniels, but Rogers struck one of the lawmen and managed to escape. Stiteler, who fled with Rogers, was recaptured that same night and was transported to jail at Fort Smith.

But on the night of March 14, 1895, Bob Rogers' luck appeared to have run out. He was asleep in an upstairs room of his father's house at Horseshoe Mound, about twenty miles south of Coffeyville and just inside Indian Territory. Deputy Marshal Jim Mayes got wind of the bandit's whereabouts and set out with a posse to apprehend the young scoundrel at Frank Rogers' home. They arrived in the wee hours of March 15, 1895. Once there, Mayes deployed his men so that the house was completely surrounded, and with eight members of the posse, Mayes walked to the front door and knocked.[32]

Eventually Mayes was let inside the house, where he called up to the upstairs bedroom for Bob to surrender. Instead, Rogers invited the deputy to come up and get him. Apparently three brave but perhaps not very effective strategists, deputies W. C. McDaniel, C. E. Smith, and Phil Williams, volunteered to do just that. Frank Rogers, the outlaw's father, took the lead, holding a lit lantern.

When they reached the top of the stairs and peered into the room, their trusty lantern providing illumination paled next to the bright muzzle flash of Rogers' two revolvers. The first bullet hit Deputy McDaniel square in the heart, putting an end to his career in law enforcement; the second bullet tore through Smith's right arm from the wrist to the elbow. McDaniel fell into Smith, who was the caboose of this train wreck, and the two men tumbled back down the stairs. Frank Rogers was also retreating as fast as he could.

Bob Rogers grabbed the dead lawman's ammunition belt and Winchester and began pouring hot lead through the floorboards, causing everyone to retreat to the outdoors.[33]

Then the fight was on. Having learned of McDaniel's assassination, the posse outside fired incessantly, putting several hundred rounds into the room. Mayes ordered his men to cease firing, and when quiet was restored he yelled at the defiant Rogers to surrender. Rogers hollered back that he would come out if he were allowed to bring his rifle; amazingly, Mayes said if Rogers kept the muzzle trained on the ground, he could bring it out with him.[34]

Rogers had already proved that he was a thief without honor. His latest release from the jail at Fort Smith was due in part to the $8,000 bail put up by his uncle, Robert W. Rogers, of Arkansas. However, it was widely believed that Bob Rogers also may have turned on his own gang members in return for an early release. In addition to his early release, Rogers was given part of the reward money offered for the gang's capture and received immunity on all charges up to that point.[35]

Ken Butler writes in "The Devious Outlaw Career of Bob Rogers," "The label of traitor became firmly affixed to the name of Bob Rogers. Having never been popular in the Cherokee Nation, he was now considered to be the absolute scum of the earth." That Friday morning of March 15, 1895, every distrusting posseman was looking through the sight of the rifle he trained squarely on Rogers.

Mayes approached the front porch where Rogers stood, still obediently pointing the rifle he carried at the ground. Just a few words were exchanged between the two men when Rogers inexplicably and suddenly jerked the weapon upward. Before he could utter another word or squeeze off a single round, a hailstorm of bullets pierced the thug, forever ending Bob Rogers' menacing ways.

Despite all the accusations that so freely flowed at Bob Rogers, the posse that killed him had no warrants for his arrest.[36]

Bill Cook was another colorful character whose gang's exploits never garnered much notoriety, perhaps because most of the offenses were alleged rather than proved.

Born on December 19, 1873, along the banks of the Grand River about four miles north of Fort Gibson, Cook's criminal career lasted just six months before his capture, trial, and conviction in 1895. He died one month after his twenty-seventh birthday while serving a forty-five-year term in federal prison at Albany, New York.[37]

In June of 1894, Bill, his brother Jim—four years Bill's junior—and a third young tough named Crawford Goldsby, nicknamed Cherokee Bill, were riding along a trail about fifteen miles north of Tahlequah, Indian Territory. There they met several riders of the Cherokee Light Horse, Indian police.

The officers recognized Jim Cook, seventeen at the time, and said they had a warrant to arrest him for horse larceny. As so often happened with so many others faced with a similar predicament, rather than simply complying, all three went for their guns instead. Cherokee Bill, it was later learned, fired the shot that killed lawman Sequoyah Houston.[38]

The three shooters fled and escaped into a thicket that even to this day is a blinding curtain of foliage. That foray upon the good men of the Cherokee Light Horse forever insured that the three relatively unknown hoodlums would rise to the top as the law's "most wanted." One explanation for the quick-draw response was that Bill was worried the posse knew of his troubles earlier that year.

Cherokee Bill was part Cherokee, part white, part black, and part Mexican, and all temper. His parents separated when he was a teen, and he found trouble to be a constant companion. When he was just eighteen, Bill found trouble beyond his imaginings when at a dance at Fort Gibson a black man named Jake Lewis apparently took issue with Bill. A fistfight ensued, and the stronger Lewis was pummeling the daylights out of Cherokee Bill. The next morning, Cherokee Bill encountered Lewis again. This time Bill pulled his pistol and shot Lewis one time in the stomach. Leaving the wounded man for dead, Cherokee Bill fled. Lewis eventually recovered from the wound.[39]

Now on the trail facing the Indian police, Bill Cook and his companions made a momentous decision. They fired on the Indian police, killing Officer Houston; their die was then cast, and the three rode together until captured or killed.

Others either known or suspected as having ridden with the Cook brothers at one time or another included the likes of: Sam McWilliams, known as The Verdigris Kid; Lon Gordon; Thurman

"Skeeter" Baldwin; Elmer "Chicken" Lucas; and one George Sanders. The roster of Cook confederates also included such stalwart characters as Jim French and perhaps the indefatigable, adaptable Henry Starr. One source states that Starr rode with the group prior to 1894 before he had assembled his own crew.[40] A few others came and went, but these were the most steadfast loyalists of the group.

In the short six months Cook and company operated, no fewer than eighteen run-ins with the law were, at least, attributed to them. Seven of those eighteen were said to have been committed by "persons unknown," although the blame was not so uncertain, and the Cooks received it. The outlaws as a gang, or as individuals belonging to the Cook gang, were identified as participants in robberies at Wetumka, Nowata, and Okmulgee. In several more incidents involving the robbery of persons and/or places, the gang was alleged to be involved, but no positive identification was ever made.

Some of those holdups in which the Cooks were suspects but never identified were by far the most successful. For instance, the July 9, 1894, robbery of an unnamed Muldrow man that netted the thieves a reported $1,000 was thought to be committed at the hands of the Cook gang. So too was the Fort Gibson, Arkansas Valley, depot robbery that occurred on the night of October 4, 1894, about ten o'clock. In that robbery the thieves made off with about $300. And then there was the robbery of the J. A. Parkinson store in Okmulgee during a town baseball game in which $600 was reported missing. In that theft the names of Cook, Goldsby, Baldwin, and one Snyder were tossed around as being likely suspects; but again their involvement was not proven.[41]

The robberies in which the band or certain members of the group are identified show an embarrassing lack of craftsmanship. By way of example, Cook and three others are identified as would-be holdup men of the Arkansas Flyer railroad train, as it went south past Nowata on the evening of October 22, 1894. The men attempted to throw a switch that would divert the locomotive onto a siding, forcing the conductor to throw on the brakes. At least that's what the thieves thought they were doing. Instead, the switch thrown directed the train onto the main line, so that all the bandits could do was watch as the speeding locomotive streaked on down the line.

The following month, Bill Cook and three *compadres*—Baldwin, Snyder, and a fellow named Farris—were positively identified in the holdup of the McDermott Trading Post, a modest establishment south of Okmulgee. In that episode the bandits galloped away with a whopping $27.55 and some unspecified store merchandise.[42] In the months that followed, the hapless Cook gang began to unravel. As a gang they weren't very successful but splintered into factions or acted as individuals. Independently, they fared even worse.

The summer of 1894 proved a bad one for the Cook gang. In July, Elmer "Chicken" Lucas was captured at Chandler, as another member, Curtis Dayson, got nabbed at Sapulpa. Lon Gordon was killed west of there, and death overtook another sometime member whose given name was Munson. Snyder and Farris were apprehended at Wichita Falls, Texas, while Baldwin was captured in Clay County, Texas.[43]

Jim French was killed at Catoosa while attempting the robbery of Patton and Company General Store. His demise came on February 7, 1895, almost one month after Bill Cook's capture and incarceration. The Verdigris Kid and Sanders were both killed while attempting a bank holdup at Braggs on March 28, 1895.[44]

Baldwin's prison term was commuted by President Theodore Roosevelt in 1903. Fellow gang members Lucas, Dayson, Snyder, and Farris served their full terms. When they were released from prison, they left the Twin Territories for good. Bill Cook died of what was then known as the "prisoners' ailment"—consumption—on February 7, 1900, thus ending his short life on the outlaw trail.[45]

From the start, Oklahoma and Indian Territories were teeming with bandits. Several outlaw sibling gangs emerged as the Twin Territories' most dangerous groups. It is true, however, that there were loners out on the plains and in the craggy river bottoms and rocky hillsides who stirred up equal amounts of trouble for citizens and business entrepreneurs and the ever-diligent posses. Those lone wolves will be dealt with in the next chapter.

Before statehood was recognized on November 16, 1907, Oklahoma was divided into the two territories. Named for a Kansas jurist, John Guthrie of Topeka, the town of Guthrie in central Logan County was capital of Oklahoma Territory from 1899 until statehood, giving up that prestigious title in 1910 to Oklahoma City.

Guthrie had not lost its entire political prowess as it was named county seat of Logan County, a distinction it maintains today.[46]

A short distance up the trail from 1899 Guthrie, a somewhat older settlement was put on the map with the establishment of the Mulhall post office on June 6, 1890. This farming community settlement took its name from successful rancher and showman, Col. Zack Mulhall.[47] It was near here at another small spot in the road, Rose Hill, where Luther Martin came to live with his two sons in about 1899.[48]

William, called "Will," was the older of the Martin boys, born in 1871. He was followed by Samuel, called "Sam," in 1875. When the Martins arrived in Rose Hill, the brothers were in their mid- to late twenties, respectively. They apparently saw what a lot of the more well-intentioned settlers saw in the territories: opportunity. Will and Sam Martin saw their chance not in the fertile lands and plentiful waters suitable for grazing and farming, but rather in the back roads adjoining remote farm lands. This place was teeming with opportunity, the opportunity to steal.

Will and Sam pulled their first recorded heist the same year they arrived in Oklahoma Territory: 1899. They decided that one of those nearly isolated dusty trails would be as good a spot as any for hijacking.

Charles and Dora Hull and the couple's young daughter were riding along in their buggy on Monday, May 22, 1899, when Charles suddenly noticed an armed man standing in the road. The man's unexpected appearance, coupled with his armament, alarmed Hull, and he proceeded to whip his horse straight past the stranger. A shot rang out from the thick brush along the roadside, which sent a bullet zipping past Hull's head and into the clay banks on the opposite side of the road.[49]

Hull immediately pulled his buggy to a stop as the shooter emerged from hiding on horseback. The family had little of value on their person at the time of the heist, so in order not to have the day a complete loss, Sam and Will attempted to extract money from the Hulls at a future date through extortion. The Martin brothers came up with the idea of telling Charles Hull that if the stated amount of money was not delivered to them, "We'll blow your family to hell."[50] The amount the extortionists demanded was $150.

Two days later at the farm of Clarence Simmons, about nine miles west of Mulhall, authorities located the Martin brothers and attempted to serve them with an arrest warrant. Serving the warrant were Logan County sheriff Frank Rinehart and deputies Charles E. Carpenter and Joe Reynolds. Rather than give up to the lawmen, both Martins made a dash for a rear door of the farmhouse in an attempt to escape; and both were shot.[51]

Despite his injuries, Sam managed to make good his escape. Brother Will was shot up too badly to continue his run for freedom and was summarily arrested and taken back to Guthrie after being treated for his wounds by a Dr. McPeak near Mulhall.

Then on June 23, 1899, Will waived preliminary hearing and was released from custody with no further action in the extortion case being sought. Likewise, Sam was never charged with any involvement in the same incident. As mysterious or suspicious as that failure to prosecute might seem, one attempt to explain the court's lack of action appeared in the Mulhall *Enterprise* newspaper. It stated that the Martins were first-time offenders and, as if that was the deal breaker, "were misrepresented" legally,[52] an apparent tongue-in-cheek reference to the paper's endorsement of the alleged shoddy counsel the Martin brothers received.

Nearly three years would pass before Will and Sam Martin began stirring up trouble again. This time, in the fall of 1902, they robbed a Colorado bank with companions "Indian Bill" Smith and a vagabond female known only as "Gypsy," who would later claim to have married Sam.

Carlton, Colorado, was the site of the Martins' latest offense. Indian Bill and Gypsy were caught, questioned, and readily gave up the Martin boys as the masterminds of the deed.[53] The Martins were back on the scout once again, and it didn't take them long to return to their old haunts in Oklahoma.

Having left their most recent members stewing in a Colorado jail, the outlaw brothers soon recruited an old acquaintance who was thought to have harbored the boys in their early days at his farm near Mulhall. Clarence Simmons abandoned his farm, wife, and children, and rode off with the Martin brothers.

On Monday evening, March 2, 1903, the three desperadoes

struck. In far northeastern Kingfisher County, just a few miles south of present-day Enid, there nestled peacefully the small railroad town of Hennessey. The town got its name from Pat Hennessey, a freighter who was killed in an Indian massacre on July 4, 1874.[54] That peace was shattered on a March night in 1903. It would mark the Martins' inaugural step into the realm of holdup men.

The Rock Island Railroad depot at Hennessey was a two-story affair complete with living quarters upstairs for the station agent. It was this station the Martins, accompanied by Simmons, chose to rob. Attempts to open the safe were futile. The disgruntled bandits found only $8.35 for all their trouble. A young African-American boy named Gus Cravatt chose that most inopportune moment to return a lantern that he had borrowed from the station agent. Cravatt apparently surprised the trio and was instantly gunned down. He died from his wounds.[55]

The three outlaws raced off to the Osage country, where they found refuge so dense that even at close range, if silence were maintained, a person could not be found.

Glenn Shirley's, *They Outrobbed Them All: The Rise and Fall of the Vicious Martins*, used as the primary reference in this chapter, presents yet another example of their audacity. They did indeed "outrob them all," and they did it in one day, June 14, 1903. The Martins set up a kind of toll booth on the road that ran between Pawhuska and Bartlesville. With them was Clarence Simmons, and the three men merely put the touch on passersby as they came down the road. One of the Martin brothers would stop the unsuspecting travelers, and then another brother would lead them off into the thicket where Simmons was waiting. There the voyagers would be relieved of anything of value until in one single day the men had robbed some one hundred victims, including a former deputy U.S. marshal and eight men and women traveling from Ohio.

Almost two months later while on the scout the trio stopped at a farm about two miles southwest of Pawhuska on August 2, 1903. There the men demanded to be fed. The desperadoes were tracked by U.S. Deputy Marshal Wiley G. Haines, Chief of Indian Police Warren Bennett, and Constable Henry Majors.

The lawmen received word (there are varied accounts of how they were alerted, but no two agree) that the men were camped at a place called Wooster's Mound, southeast of Pawhuska.[56]

The gun battle that followed took less than a minute and resulted in the immediate death of Will Martin, brought down while trying to reach his horse. Sam was hit in the right shoulder and in his left wrist, which shattered from the impact. Sam hit the ground and, as Marshal Haines approached, he rolled over and squeezed off one more round. This one, exploding through the marshal's right shoulder knocked him to the ground. As Sam took aim to finish off Haines, Bennett charged the prone bad man, kicked the rifle from his hand, and took aim with his own weapon. With Bennett's gun pointing neatly between the eyes of the wounded outlaw, Bennett dared Sam to make another move.[57]

Twenty-seven shots were fired during the barrage; only six of them being fired by the outlaws. Clarence Simmons made good his escape. Haines was in serious peril from the bullet that tore through his shoulder and on toward his spine. The bullet was a copper-jacketed variety which, after ripping Haines's shoulder, passed around the lower part of his neck before fragmenting into several pieces, rupturing blood vessels in his lung.[58]

Bennett cut as much of the lead out of his wounded companion's back as he could, using a pocketknife. Incredibly, Haines quickly recovered from his wounds and was soon hot on the trail of another Oklahoma Territory bad man, Walter McClain, who had escaped from the Guthrie jail with Bill Doolin. Sam Martin died of his wounds on the Sunday after the Wooster's Mound fight, on August 9, 1903. His last words were, "Guess I've been on the wrong trail." He and his brother Will are buried in Potters Field at Summit View Cemetery in Guthrie.

Clarence Simmons disappeared for nearly sixteen years until he resurfaced in Boonville, Missouri, pawning himself off as one Jackson J. Smith. Many of the locals of Boonville were not fooled by this masquerade, recognizing the old outlaw from previous times. Simmons had been living in Jacksonville, Florida, where he was married.[59] Simmons was acquitted of the Cravatt murder in Hennessey and also of the charges associated with assaulting a federal peace officer at Wooster's Mound. He wasted little time in returning to Florida.

Chapter 11

Lone Wolves

Wolf: any of several large predatory canids (genus *Canis*) that live
and hunt in packs. . . . 2: a fierce, rapacious, or destructive person.
Lone wolf: a person who prefers to work, act, or live alone.
—*Merriam-Webster Online Dictionary*

Beattie, Kansas, is a small agricultural town, situated near the
crossroads of State Highways 99 and 36 in the far northern reaches of
the state. It is about twenty-five miles south of the Nebraska line and
just a few miles east of Big Blue River and the town of Marysville.

Sometime in the year 1875, a Beattie merchant and his young son
left Beattie, where the elder man had a clothing store, bound for Texas.
The fifty-six-year-old merchant, James Harris, and his twelve-year-old
son likely saw the journey to Texas from Beattie as one that presented
equal parts hardship and happiness. Only when the wayfarers reached
Indian Territory, however, did the true meaning of hardship reveal
itself in a most ugly and inhuman form. Its name was Aaron Wilson.[1]

Not much is known about why Harris decided to leave Beattie,
packing everything—lock, stock, and barrel—into a wagon accompanied by his son and three horses to travel the remarkable distance
of some 470-plus miles to Texas. Harris's projected path appears to
have been designed to take him and his son along a route providing
as much safety as was available, stopping at or near towns or military
posts along the way.

There is no mention of the difficulties the Harris party endured at
the outset of their trip. Bad weather, broken wagon wheels, and
gimpy horses were as much a part of long-distance travel during that
era as sunrise and nightfall.

Even so, the shopkeeper and his young son made it all the way
beyond the future site of Oklahoma City, O. T., and on the night of
October 12, 1875, camped just twelve miles from Fort Sill near present-day Lawton.[2] The spot where Harris and the boy slept was just
about thirty-five miles north of the Red River and Texas.

Aaron Wilson was a young black man, living among the Penateka Comanche on the Anadarko Agency in September 1875. He had been a soldier who was discharged (circumstances not known), and as the Harris party moseyed by, Wilson took notice. One hour after the merchant with his worldly belongings and his only son passed, Wilson, in the true fashion of a lone wolf, without saying a word to anybody in the camp, mounted an old gray horse and clomped off in the direction Harris had taken.

He followed the wagon for two days before finally making the decision to stop in and introduce himself. The Harrises' hospitality would prove to be a most unfortunate gesture: It brought terror and death to the two unsuspecting Kansans. Harris and his son had made it as far as the region known as Hell's Fringe. More precisely, they were just west of it when they unknowingly welcomed wickedness into their camp.

Wilson readily and gladly partook of the filling meal Harris and his son offered him. He then snuggled cozily by the warm fire, in blankets provided by Harris, for what should have been a long night's sleep. At around midnight, the long night's sleep would be forever for the two hospitable travelers.

One reason James Harris may have been so accommodating was that Wilson was still wearing his old army uniform, and Harris probably felt fortunate to have made his acquaintance. That feeling of complacency would be a death knell. With everyone settled in to catch some shut-eye, Wilson feigned slumber while keeping one eye on the snoozing patriarch and his offspring. Around midnight Wilson slithered from beneath the borrowed blankets, and in the dancing shadows cast by a waning campfire made his way ever so quietly to the travelers' wagon.

Careful not to wake the Harrises, Wilson reached into the wagon and withdrew an ax. Just about midnight Wilson hacked James Harris to death with his own ax.

The elder Harris's death throes scared the young Harris boy to an upright position. By then Wilson had probably turned toward the youngster, still holding his father's ax in his bloody hands. The twelve-year-old pleaded for mercy. A moment passed with the boy and the murderer looking at one another, and it may have appeared to young Harris that his impassioned plea for his life had registered.

The boy ran into the cover of darkness and the surrounding woods. Wilson merely walked back to the wagon very calmly and very deliberately, reached in, and pulled from it James Harris's shot-gun.[3] Wilson then entered the woods in pursuit of the fleeing young-ster. When he found the boy, he leveled his father's shotgun at him and fired. The boy fell dead about 175 yards from what had been a slumbering, safe camp with his father and the soldier.

Wilson wasn't through yet. The chronology of the next set of events is not entirely certain, but it is without question that some-time after his treacherous murder of his hosts, he took clothing from the wagon and changed from his old uniform. Later that night Wilson, while wearing clothes he had stolen from the wagon, scalped the two corpses.[4]

The killer then rode back to the Comanche camp where he brazenly displayed his trophies and boasted of the killing of two white men, leaving out the heinous details of the crimes. Wilson apparently thought this act would be seen as a blow against the infil-tration of the whites and thus would ingratiate him into the hearts of the Comanches. The chief of the Penateka band was anything but pleased, however. He recognized the horses that Wilson brought back to the Indian camp as those belonging to the two travelers who had passed by without trouble just three days earlier.

The chief didn't much like the idea that such an extreme breach of hospitality had been committed against the two white visitors and that Wilson would somehow assume that these actions were pleasing to the Comanches. Rather than reward Wilson for his deeds, the Comanche chief reported the incident to the authorities. When Wilson learned of the chief's actions he fled in the hope of avoiding justice, but was apprehended within two days by soldiers sent from Fort Sill to investigate the matter.

Wilson was tried at Fort Smith by none other than the "hanging judge" himself. If there was ever any doubt in Wilson's mind as to how closely Judge Isaac C. Parker's ominous nickname described the judge's sentencing practices, he found out on April 21, 1876, when the trap door of the gallows gave way beneath his feet.[5]

A Boy Named Blue

Today, one can travel east from Claremore, Oklahoma, about sixteen miles and run into State Highway 69 at Pryor, located on what was once known as "The Texas Road." A similar distance northwest of Claremore, on State Highway 169, is Oologah, where one will find the home—or almost home—of two famous Oklahomans. Oologah is Cherokee for "Dark Cloud," and was named for a Cherokee chief.[6]

While Claremore is honored as the home of Oklahoma's Favorite Son, Will Rogers, in truth Oologah is the closest town of any size to the famed humorist's birthplace. Claremore and Oologah are both in Rogers County, but Claremore holds the distinction of being the county seat.

One other now-famous Oklahoman with origins near Oologah is Bluford Duck, better known as Blue Duck. Long before Oologah was an established community with a post office in 1891, Blue Duck was born.[7]

The Blue Duck many modern readers first met was a fierce, stalking, ruthless killer in Larry McMurtry's popular novel, *Lonesome Dove.* In reality, there are very few similarities between that character and the one who actually existed. Unless, that is, one considers the fierce, ruthless, and unprovoked murder of a teenager and the attempted assassination of the boy's hired hand and another man who just happened to be working in his own field.

That is just what the record shows for Blue Duck in the summer of 1884 while he and a companion were riding through the Flint District in the Cherokee Nation.

Blue Duck was born to Dick Duck, on June 17, 1859. Nothing is known of Bluford until he committed cold-blooded murder in the Cherokee Nation on June 23, 1884. He had just celebrated his twenty-fifth birthday. Blue Duck and a friend, William Christie, not believed to be a close relative of the famous Ned Christie, were riding together after a night of celebrating Blue Duck's birthday. They were quite given up to spirits, the distilled variety. Having fortified themselves copiously, the two came upon their first victim, a young farmer whose name was Samuel Wyrick.

Wyrick had done nothing to provoke Blue Duck or Christie, and in fact he probably didn't even take notice of the two mounted and inebriated Indians until the shots rang out. For no apparent reason, Blue Duck emptied his pistol in the direction of Wyrick, killing him on the spot.[8]

Blue Duck's appetite for blood was not satisfied with the "harvesting" of the young farmer from his field. Blue Duck reloaded his weapon and commenced firing on Wyrick's hired hand. The birthday celebration, if that's what it was, wasn't over yet. The two outlaws continued to ride over hill and dale and eventually came upon another unsuspecting farmer. It was a neighbor of Blue Duck's, but that apparently made no difference, for he fired several rounds at the man but missed.[9]

Both revelers were apprehended and tried in Judge Parker's court during January 1886, but only Blue Duck was convicted of murdering young Samuel Wyrick. He was sentenced to hang on July 23, 1886.

Blue Duck probably would have hanged as sentenced, but for a shrewd maneuver on the part of his lawyer, Thomas Marcum. Marcum somehow arranged for the widely known, so-called Queen of the Outlaws, Belle Starr, to pose for a photograph with Blue Duck. The ploy was to demonstrate what Marcum lamented as "the plight of the young man."[10]

Evidently the photograph worked, and Blue Duck's death sentence was commuted to life imprisonment at Menard Penitentiary in Chester, Illinois, where he was received in 1886. Bluford "Blue" Duck died of the common "prisoners' disease," consumption, in 1895 shortly after being paroled.[11]

George "Red Buck" Weightman

In the fall of 1890 it was the misfortune of George Weightman (Waightman) to make the acquaintance of an impressive deputy U.S. marshal by the name of Heck Thomas.[12] Thomas was working the Cherokee Nation in Indian Territory that fall when he encountered Weightman and a passel of mules he was stringing along behind him. The encounter was to Weightman's misfortune because the mules in his possession had got there only by way of a recent theft he had committed. Thomas arrested him on the spot, and Weightman was tried and convicted at Muskogee, where he received a nine-year sentence to federal prison to be served in Detroit.[13]

Weightman was an interesting character. Born somewhere in Texas, he later drifted into Oklahoma where his reputation as a wanton killer and horse thief preceded him. He was a short, stocky, muscular fellow who was not only profoundly disagreeable, but who also had only an iota of social skills, and he wanted to keep it that way. His upper lip was festooned with dark red whiskers, and his ample head hair was equally tinted, hence the nickname, Red Buck.[14]

Red Buck, being the disagreeable sort that he was, decided that prison life would be just too . . . disagreeable. So, while en route to Detroit via a special railroad prison car leaving Lebanon, Missouri, Buck escaped the moving train by hurling himself through a window, or so the story goes. The commotion leading up to his dive to freedom left two other prisoners dead as bullets went whizzing through the car. The diversion the two dead prisoners involuntarily provided is likely what gave Red Buck the distraction and time needed to plunge to safety.

From that day in 1890 until 1893 when Red Buck joined up with the Bill Doolin gang, little is known of his criminal activities. For about two years, Red Buck ran with the Doolin outfit, though he was neither liked nor trusted completely. Red Buck's instincts told him to act alone, and he often tried to commit crimes the Doolin gang wanted no part of. He was, at heart, a loner. It was at Ingalls, in Oklahoma Territory, that he would prove to be a Lone Wolf more than at any other time he was with Doolin and his Wild Bunch.

Red Buck's name probably wouldn't be remembered much beyond the red brick grave marker scratched with his moniker if it hadn't been for his participation at Ingalls. And it was there that he showed he had little sentimentality for anyone but Red Buck.

When the Ingalls fight was over, three brave deputies were dead, as was a citizen named Walker. Flying lead had also claimed a horse that was hitched in front of the Ransom and Murray Saloon. For all the collateral damage, only one bandit, Roy "Arkansas Tom" Daugherty was captured.[15]

At the outset of the fighting, gang member George "Bitter Creek"

Newcomb took the first bullet from the approaching lawmen. Bitter Creek was leading his horse when he and Deputy Dick Speed spied each other, at once taking aim and both firing a round. Newcomb's rifle caught the slug, which shattered its magazine and sent a piece of metal into Newcomb's leg. He then turned his mount and galloped for the safety of some nearby timber.[16]

Bitter Creek didn't make it to the woods, thanks in part to a second wound courtesy of a Winchester fired by posseman Tom Houston. Newcomb fell from his thundering horse short of his mark. When the rest of the gang, sans Arkansas Tom, eventually reached a point of seclusion, gang leader Bill Doolin asked where Bitter Creek was; everyone was aware that Arkansas Tom was occupied and could not rejoin the gang presently. Red Buck showed his true colors when he gruffly responded, "Hell. We ain't got time to fool with him."

Doolin, who had previously formed an ill opinion of Red Buck, made his opinion clear as Red Buck started to ride off, leaving Ingalls and the absent comrade.

Doolin drew his revolver, one fable relates, and with a quick retort sent Red Buck's hat sailing. "Come back here you yellow dog! We're not leaving Bitter Creek and that girl behind."[17]

"That girl" was one Rose—or Rosa—Dunn, often described as the Rose of the Cimarron, who was a "tenant" of Mary Pierce's O.K. Hotel. She was said to have been in love with Bitter Creek, after possibly having been the mistress of Bill Dollin, or so legend purports. She later married a fellow named Noble, moved out of Oklahoma, and lived an exemplary and "noble" life.[18]

Incidentally, it was in the O.K. Hotel where Arkansas Tom lodged himself, successfully sniping from his perch in the gable ends and attic at the lawmen below.

Even though Doolin had a strong dislike for Red Buck, the surly, ill-tempered shootist remained with the Wild Bunch for nearly two more years; then came the last straw. It happened just after the gang had robbed a Rock Island train of several thousand dollars on April 3, 1895. Three territorial towns lay along one straight road, heading north. The towns are still in existence today. On what is now State Highway 81—a nearly perfectly straight vein coursing through the western half of Oklahoma—lie Dover, Kingfisher, and El Reno.

Doolin and his gang, which to his dislike still included Red Buck, chose a place near Dover to stop and rob the train. Dover was a few miles from the Rock Island station and about thirty-five miles north of El Reno, leading Doolin to believe that he had chosen a pretty good spot for the heist.

In El Reno a bucketful of trouble lay in waiting for the Wild Bunch in the form of a seasoned lawman, U.S. Deputy Marshal Chris Madsen, one of the famed Three Guardsmen. Because of the newfangled invention, the telephone, the Wild Bunch had barely ridden off with their plunder when Madsen received word of the robbery. He immediately took charge of a locomotive, commandeered a boxcar, and cleared the tracks north via telegraph, giving his engine a full-steam-ahead shot at Dover. With seven other men, their horses, and a strong armament, he headed north.[19]

Red Buck never expected anyone to be close on their trail so quickly, but Madsen and his posse were at the crime scene within a few short hours of the act. Doolin and company were camped nearby, evidently not expecting such an efficient response from law enforcement. Once arriving on the scene, Madsen split his group into two sections.

The posse swooped down upon the bandit camp and opened fire. Instantly, Tulsa Jack Blake's and Red Buck's horses were felled by rifle fire, and Tulsa Jack was permanently retired with the help of a lawman's bullet.[20] The hyena of the group, Red Buck, was on foot as the battle raged, and he soon felt the loneliness of being an unpopular guy even within his own ranks.

The gun battle lasted nearly an hour, with an estimated two hundred rounds fired during the fight. One gang member lay dead, and two others were wounded; the rest ran. They were short of horses, and Red Buck stood flat-footed, watching in despair while his buddies galloped to freedom. Then, as if he either didn't know or simply didn't care, the man Red Buck would have abandoned at Ingalls came racing back at full clip. Bitter Creek swooped Red Buck up behind him, and the two raced off safely.[21]

Red Buck soon showed why he was too low for even a gang of thieves. The Wild Bunch, four men atop three horses, was making a slow journey of it when they happened upon a cabin in the woods belonging to an itinerant preacher. His name, unfortunately, has long been forgotten, though the incident surrounding him hasn't. As the gang passed the old-timer's cabin, Red Buck eyed a lone horse belonging to the old man. A horse would ease the embarrassment and discomfort of sharing a mount with Bitter Creek, so Red Buck proceeded to make the horse his. The commotion of roping the animal and attempting to saddle it brought the older man outside to investigate. When he realized he was rapidly losing his only horse, he at once complained.

Red Buck turned to the old minister and without a word drew his six-shooter and shot the unarmed preacher to death. Then with as little concern as he showed when he killed the defenseless old man, Red Buck threw on the saddle of his newly acquired horse, bridled him, mounted him, and commenced to ride.[22] He did so as if he'd done nothing more than win an arm-wrestling match.

The callousness of that act shocked even the other cold-blooded outlaws. The gang rode only a little ways before Doolin turned his horse into the direction of the others and ordered all to dismount. When they did, Doolin divided the loot from the Dover robbery, making sure that each member got his fair share. After that task was completed, Doolin stood and looked hard into the coyote eyes of Red Buck Weightman and famously said, "Now you get out. You're too damned low to associate with a high-class gang of train robbers," though this version has not been verified.[23]

Several months would pass before Red Buck resurfaced with all his depravity intact after his disgrace at getting the old heave-ho from Bill Doolin. On September 1, 1895, Buck, who by then had attracted the partnership of another scoundrel named Charlie Smith, came across rancher Gus Holland from D (now Dewey) County. Holland was merely tending his herd at the head of Cheyenne Creek. Red Buck and Charlie evidently saw more worth in Holland's cattle than in the man himself so they did what one would expect of Red Buck and his sort; they killed Gus and stole his cattle.[24]

Red Buck soon recruited two more like-minded fellows. One of Buck's new cronies, Joe Beckham, was the former under sheriff of Motley County, Texas, who had been under indictment for embezzling county funds and who had become a fugitive from justice. The second cohort was a Missouri cowpoke and native of Neosho whose name was

Elmer "Kid" Lewis. He worked on Bearla Bennett's T Fork Ranch near Wichita Falls before applying his horseback skills to thievery.

Although by that time Red Buck had gathered a gang of sorts, none of the gang had any clear idea on what it took to become pros at their chosen trade. A train robbery the bunch pulled off in the panhandle of Oklahoma Territory, about fourteen miles west of Woodward, netted the bunglers only a shotgun and some shells. They didn't rob any of the passengers, and when the express car's messenger couldn't be located, thanks to a crafty engineer, they left behind a safe and its contents.[25] None of them thought to ransack the mail car, which they passed through on their way to the express car.

This lack of leadership reduced Red Buck and his wolf pack to robbing general stores in Oklahoma and Texas, all with little or no success. Since they had violated the peace and dignity of both Texas and Oklahoma, a particularly hard winter wasn't the only force pressing the desperadoes. The famed Oklahoma lawman Chris Madsen and the equally renowned Texas Rangers were closing in.

Due to the harsh winter storm of stinging sleet and blinding snow, Red Buck and most of his company managed a narrow escape after an all-day gun battle with the Rangers. Sergeant W. J. L. Sullivan wrote in his autobiography that despite the terrible weather conditions and the freezing cold, he and five of his twelve-man posse fought the outlaws until, "Finally, we got so cold we couldn't pull a cartridge from our belts [or] work the levers of our Winchesters and we had to quit."[26]

The next day it was learned that one of the gang, former under sheriff Joe Beckham, may have survived the stinging cold that persisted that night, but failed to escape the hot lead the posse rained in on the bandits' hideout. Beckham's stiff, dead body lay abandoned by his comrades at the entrance to the dugout where the outlaws had loaded up. The rest managed to slither away in the night once Sergeant Sullivan made the decision to quit the barrage and head back to camp and its warm fire along the Red River.

Red Buck managed to stay holed up somewhere out of range of lawmen until the following spring. Three different dates are given on which Red Buck met his Maker, but the events are all agreed upon. The other members of his loosely constructed gang having been captured or killed, Red Buck sought the company of an old acquaintance. He left Texas and went north into Oklahoma Territory, where he came upon a dugout owned by Dolph Picklesimer, who knew Red Buck from a time when the two men lived in Texas.[27]

Picklesimer was none too wild about Red Buck's sharing his rock and earthen dugout. Even so, he allowed the fugitive to stay there while nursing a wound he had received during his encounter with the Texas Rangers in December. Eventually Red Buck and a man who was also sharing room at the Picklesimer dugout, George Miller, rode off together, making their way back to Red Buck's haunts along the Canadian River.

They would soon return to the supposed sanctuary of the Picklesimer dugout, much to the owner's consternation. He had already been visited by a posse from Arapaho, and the posse soon tracked the desperadoes back to Picklesimer's modest little place on Oak Creek.

It was still dark the morning of March 4, 1896, when the posse took position surrounding the place. They waited for Red Buck to show himself, but he failed to come outside. Then, as the sun rose, Picklesimer and Miller appeared and started to make their way to the pen, where they probably intended to feed their horses. At that moment someone in the posse hollered for the two men to throw up their hands and surrender. Picklesimer probably did as he was ordered, as no further history of his actions is mentioned, but Miller, in true idiot fashion, went for his pistol. He was badly wounded by a shot to his gun hand, making him almost useless for the rest of the fight.[28]

With Miller screaming that he had been shot and needed help and with Picklesimer cowering somewhere unable and equally unwilling to take any chances, Red Buck burst onto the scene, throwing hot lead in all directions. Two possemen had taken up positions with an unobstructed view of the dugout door, and when Red Buck ran out firing, deputies William Holcomb and Joe Ventioner shot him dead.[29]

The wounded Miller crawled back to the dugout, inspected Red Buck and saw that he was dead. Then he did what one might expect of a comrade in arms, he stole Red Buck's pocket watch and gun and began to take flight.

Again Ventioner and Holcomb would prove to be too accurate to allow the bad man to flee. The lawmen and Miller traded lead, and Ventioner was hit in the hip. Holcomb heard the thud of a bullet hit the tree stump behind which he lay prone. Undeterred, Holcomb raised his rifle, took steady aim, and fired. The bullet sliced through Miller's right arm above the wrist. A second shot exploded through the outlaw's left hand, taking three fingers with it as it passed.

Miller was too badly wounded to continue the fight and called out that he wanted to surrender. The shot had laid open his right arm, breaking it in two places, and requiring that the hand be amputated later. The watch Miller had stolen from his dead buddy, Red Buck, was the property of one Charles Noyes, whom Red Buck had robbed of it a few months earlier.[30]

George "Red Buck" Weightman, a Lone Wolf even in death, was buried without the care or concern of family or friend as no one stepped forward to claim the body. He was interred at Arapahoe Cemetery, where a common red brick was placed as a headstone with just "Red Buck" scratched into its surface.[31]

Zeke Proctor
A Crime of Not Being Able to Shoot Straight

Goingsnake District was established on November 6, 1840, by the newly settled Cherokees. The place was named for a leader of the Eastern Cherokees.[32] Having established a courthouse near present-day Flint, Oklahoma, not far from Sallisaw and not far enough from the marshals at Fort Smith, the Cherokees relished once and for all having their own jurisdiction over their own people. That sense of peaceful self-sufficiency was soon interrupted by federal marshals, intent on arresting white or mixed-blood lawbreakers of the Indian Territory, and returning them to Van Buren or Fort Smith to be tried.[33]

Ezekiel "Zeke" Proctor had a disagreement with a miller, the husband of Polly Beck. Without warning, Proctor shot a round at the miller, but the errant ball struck Polly in the head, killing her instantly. A trial was ordered, and just as the proceedings were about to commence, two U.S. deputy marshals rode up to take Proctor back to Fort Smith. The Cherokee court objected, and the citizens, seeing another abuse of power being foisted on them, revolted.

Gunfire was the result, ending in the deaths of eleven men and the wounding of the judge, one juror, and several spectators. In the end, the federal government granted Proctor a *de facto* amnesty.[34]

Ironically, Proctor later became one of those very "nosy" deputy U.S. marshals who had interrupted his own trial. He died on February 28, 1907, less than a year before Oklahoma gained statehood.

Ned Christie: A Smart and Cunning Lone Wolf

Rumor usually results from idle minds, secret jealousy, or simple hostility. It is especially insidious when it leads to someone's destruction. Such may have been the case for the Old West's most celebrated Lone Wolf: Ned Christie.

Christie's life and times inspired many a writer and historian to chronicle the cagey Cherokee's bandit career. In the course of time, Ned Christie was even introduced to Hollywood, albeit in name only and even that bastardized.

The film *True Grit* starring the epitome of modern-era portrayers of the Old West, John Wayne, contained a composite character named Lucky Ned Pepper. Pepper (as played by consummate actor Robert Duval) was a really awful badman being sought by U.S. Marshal Rooster Cogburn (John Wayne). Ned Pepper was loosely based on Indian Territory's own Ned Christie, born on December 14, 1852, not too far from Tahlequah, at a place known as Rabbit Trap Canyon.[35] The real Christie was an intelligent full-blood Cherokee who served one term on the Cherokee Council and who spoke fluent English. He was the son of blacksmith Watt Christie, widely called Uncle Watt Christie. Since his father worked in heavy metals, Ned learned the smithy's trade as well as that of gunsmith.[36]

In his teens, Christie and another Indian youth called Palone became embroiled in a quarrel that left Palone dead. Tried in Cherokee Tribal Court, Christie was acquitted of any wrongdoing, and from that point on led a rather uneventful life, except for a time when he served as bodyguard to Principal Chief Dennis Bushyhead.

No more was heard of the six-foot, four-inch smithy and proficient marksman until around May 5, 1887, when U.S. Deputy Marshal Dan Maples was murdered.

Maples was a family man out of Bentonville, Arkansas, who held his deputy marshal commission under Chief Marshal Thomas Bowles and later his successor, John Carroll.

Maples, J. M. Pile, and George Jefferson were on the trail of a man wanted in connection with the shooting death of Deputy Jim Richardson. Their quarry was a bad hombre by the name of Bill Pigeon, who had disappeared into the Flint Hills and would forever elude the lawmen.[37] Maples and company left Bentonville, on Monday, May 4, 1887, charged with the arrest and return of Pigeon. On Thursday, May 7, 1887, word reached Maples' wife that her husband was badly wounded; the victim of a sniper's bullet. A short time later, she received word that her husband was dead.[38]

It seems Christie was with an outlaw named Parris when Marshal Maples happened along the outlaws' trail that fateful night in May. Whatever the circumstances, they ended with the death of Maples, and Christie had been fingered as the triggerman.[39] Parris and his pals, Bud Trainor and Charley Bobtail, readily surrendered to lawmen when found. Christie's assumed guilt may have been the result of what happened after Maples was shot. He evidently wanted no part in facing charges in the white man's court and went on the lam to avoid that situation. Also, because Parris so eagerly gave up Christie as the shooter, he probably believed no one would believe any story he might tell of the Maples' shooting. Although he was fluent in English, when Christie learned that a warrant for his arrest had been issued in the Maples murder, from that day forward, he refused to speak another word in the white man's language.[40]

The truth as to who actually killed Deputy Marshal Dan Maples would be disputed for several years even after Christie had been gunned down by lawmen as he tried to escape arrest. The man who came forward as a witness to the murder, had, in the truest sense of the word, given the authorities a surprise ending.[41]

What is not in strict dispute is the number of times lawmen attempted to bring in Christie, and the number of their miserable failures at doing so. In fact so embarrassed by the number of failures was the U.S. Marshals Office in Fort Smith that the order was given: "Quit trying to take him alive."[42]

Nine times members of the marshal's office tried to arrest the elusive, cunning Christie, and nine times they were repelled. Christie, who gathered no group or gang to support him, fended off the officers' best attempts at capturing him for four years until his death in November 1892.

Each time an officer of the law approached Christie's home or hideout, the cagey Cherokee gave them a test by fire: marksmanship that was accurate, but humane. He only wounded his adversaries, perhaps intentionally. Sometimes, Christie would even hold his fire while the healthy posse members pulled their wounded comrades out of harm's way during a siege. The first attempt to arrest Christie only resulted in a second charge being added to his record after he shot and wounded Deputy Joe Bowers who carelessly rode into Christie's Rabbit Trap refuge. All Bowers took from that scene was a lead ball in the leg. He quickly abandoned the idea of capturing Christie alone.

Deputy John Fields, one day later, fared no better. As Fields approached the Christie home on horseback, Ned burst out the door with a Winchester in his hand, so startling Fields that he whirled on his horse and spurred furiously away from the cabin. Christie leveled his rifle at the fleeing lawman and squeezed off a single round that struck Fields in the neck. Wounded, the lawman was allowed to continue his hasty retreat without another shot from Christie.[43] With that incident, Christie gained two things: temporary relief from pesky lawmen, and a third warrant for assaulting a federal officer.

For whatever reason, Christie chose to remain at the family's Rabbit Trap home in the Goingsnake District southeast of Tahlequah, even though he was aware that every lawman in the territory knew he was there. If he was guilty of murdering Maples, his reluctance to disappear into the wild, dense forests of the Ozark foothills did little to confirm his guilt. In fact, Christie was still in the company of his wife and son when lawmen came calling again. By then, however, Ned and his son had moved some distance away from the family home, making a makeshift fortress of rocks and trees.

In one attack on his fort, a contingent of deputies boldly rode up to the place. The year is uncertain, but it may have been 1888. It wasn't until December 9, 1887, that the Fort Smith *Weekly Elevator* announced that Maples was dead and that his attackers were presumably Charley

Bobtail, John Parris, Bud Trainor, and Ned Christie.[44] This, the third attempt to arrest the fugitive, would have occurred well after that event. During this foray three deputies were wounded, none were killed, and Christie had repelled the law's long arm for a third time.

Again it was noted, surely by the possemen at the time, and repeated by historians throughout the decades, that Christie cooled his rifle's barrel while the wounded lawmen were removed. Battlefield niceties or not, Heck Thomas tired of the whole affair, which by now had painted the U.S. Marshal Service in a rather unfavorable light. It wasn't until sometime in 1889 that Thomas put together a small band of men to conduct what Thomas hoped would be the last and successful raid on Christie.

The posse included Deputies L. P. "Bones" Isbel, a man named Salmon, and Deputy Dave Rusk, who was on hand for the previous attempt to overthrow and capture Christie.[45] It took three days of skulking over craggy cliffs, quietly easing aside thousands of spindly, ensnaring, thorny branches of briar bushes, wading through swift-running creeks, and above all else, avoiding the many silent alarms that were Ned's friends and neighbors. Somehow they did it, and on the fourth day, just before dawn, the stealthy hunters closed in on their prey.

The dogs barked, and Ned jumped wide awake, kicked out a board in the upper room's gable end, took aim through the opening that had been created, and commenced to show the lawmen what they were in for. If this was going to be a turkey shoot, Ned Christie was determined that he wouldn't be the one to get plucked.

That day Ned Christie did get the worst of it, however. His gunsmith and blacksmith shop and even his home were destroyed by a fire that the marshals deliberately set, hoping to force the fugitive outside. Christie's wife and son scampered from the smoke-engulfed home, trying to make the cover and eventual safety of the trees, but deputies Salmon and Rusk put a stop to that maneuver.

On seeing a woman run from the house, they turned their attention and their guns on the male figure running beside her. Their fire hit the male in the hips and lungs. It wasn't Ned Christie but his son the two eager deputies had shot. Just before that mistake in identity occurred, Christie had felled Deputy Isbel with a shoulder wound that later caused the loss of his right arm.

During all this commotion, while the marshals tended to the injured deputy, Christie decided to make his break to freedom. That attempt didn't escape the watchful eye of Heck Thomas who took quick aim and fired one shot. Christie grabbed his forehead and stumbled into the nearby woods.

Having always been a strikingly good-looking specimen, Christie was more than a little put out with Thomas's shooting that day; so was the bridge of his nose and his right eye. The bullet left a fierce scar to Christie's classic, chiseled Native American face. That bullet inspired an incessant, fermenting hatred for whites.[46] While Ned Christie never did choose to go on the warpath against the whites, he never shied away from war that the white man brought to his doorstep.

Ned, his son, and his wife all managed to get away that day into the brush to "loyalists" or supporters who were also Cherokees weary of the white man's ways. They treated, fed, and housed the family until Ned and his son recuperated. Ned returned home when he was able. He viewed the burned-out ruins of his family's home and without hesitation began felling trees and digging corner postholes to start a new foundation for a new home.

This was no ordinary home. Even for the times it was seen as a remarkable display of ingenuity and an unwavering commitment to defy the continued onslaught against him. It was located about a mile from the old home place along Bidding Creek but up on higher ground. Christie sought to take advantage of the greater elevation for lookout purposes and the natural building materials that were available in abundance.

The future attacks, Ned knew, would be relentless. The lawmen would come again and again, and each time they would be more determined. Knowing this fact, Ned didn't just build a typical log home high upon a hill; he built a fort, a formidable stronghold on high ground that came to be called Ned's Mountain Fort.[47]

In all, Ned Christie and his "fort" withstood a series of federal lawmen and Indian posses intent on his capture. According to Art Burton in his book, *Black, Red, and Deadly,* Christie allegedly thought that by merely grazing a posseman or sending a bullet crashing into the log the pursuer was cowering behind, he would send the message to just leave him alone. Burton claims too, that Christie did not want to kill anyone.[48]

Christie built his fort with a double log wall lined with oaken two-by-fours. It had only one large opening for a door. Ned's fort was nearly impenetrable. It more than once proved its worth. On October 11, 1892, lawmen staged yet another assault on Ned's Mountain Fort. Among those participating were Rusk, Charlie Copeland, Milo Creekmore, and D. C. Dye.[49] Two of the attacking lawmen were quickly wounded but not killed by the sharp-eyed Christie. What was left of the posse regrouped in the brush at a decent distance from Ned's shooting range. They came across the wagon Ned had used during the construction of his new, improved fort and piled dried brush into it.

The posse set the contraption ablaze and shoved it toward the fort. With no one to steer the wagon, the thing zigged when it should have zagged and ran smack-dab not into Ned's fort-house but into Ned's outhouse.

The lawmen then planted enough dynamite to blow the house to smithereens. All three sticks of the stuff bounced harmlessly to the ground, however, and the ensuing explosions did little more than spook neighboring wildlife. Once again, a posse was forced to eat crow and go home.[50] Ned Christie was proving a match for the entire force of Indian Territory lawmen.

On the morning of November 2, 1892, Deputy Marshal Paden Tolbert led a sixteen-man posse, armed with a small cannon, to Ned's fort the night before the planned assault.[51] The cannon balls bounced harmlessly from Christie's fortified lair, but with the application of dynamite and fire, Ned's fort became untenable.

The fire and accompanying smoke drove out Ned and another wanted man, Arche Wolfe, plus a third accomplice, Charley Hare, a young man who had recently joined up with Christie.

Hare, badly burned by the ensuing fire, came out with hands up and was taken without any further harm to either him or the posse-men. However, Christie played a more shrewd and dangerous game. He came out of the fort and somehow fooled the lawmen into thinking he was one of them. The only light was from the burning fort, as this fourth and final assault took place just after midnight.

Christie aimed and fired at the closest deputy. The bullet passed by the face of one of the possemen, Wes Bowman, but the muzzle was close enough that it left powder burns.[52] After nearly being sent to eternity by Christie's rifle shot, Bowman spun where he stood and planted his own rifle slug just behind the fleeing outlaw's ear, killing him instantly. Young Sam Maples, the vengeful son of the slain marshal Dan Maples, then raced up to the already dead man and emptied his revolver into the body.[53]

Another account of that same incident says that several of the members of the posse took part in firing at Christie and that their shots found their mark. "In a hail of gunfire," the story goes, Christie sank to his knees, paused briefly, made a small sound, and pitched forward headfirst. Ned Christie was dead.[54] Christie's body was riddled with 115 bullet holes, but his saga was not over. Incredibly, Ned Christie was exonerated of the Maple murder some thirty years after the attack on his fort.

On July 6, 1893, just a few short months after the death of his father, James Christie was murdered, and his head was severed from his body.[55] No one ever stepped forward to claim responsibility for the assassination and mutilation of James Christie, whose only apparent crime was defending his father.

Bud Trainor, it turned out, was apparently the real killer of Maples.[56] That was, of course, before he shed his former buddies and went straight—so straight, in fact, that Trainor was a member of at least one contingent of lawmen who attempted to arrest Christie. On Christmas night 1895, Trainor was gunned down at Talala. On January 9, 1896, a *Vinita Leader* article read, "Bud Trainer, well known here, was killed at Talala on Christmas night by four negroes. It was a plot and four shotguns did the work."[57] Now, once and for all, the saga was ended. Or was it?

Many years later—either in 1918 or 1922, depending on the source—an eighty-seven-year-old former blacksmith came forward to say that he was present the night Deputy Marshal Dan Maples was killed, and it wasn't Ned Christie who killed him. At least two writers give similar accounts, although they disagree as to the year of the night Maples was murdered.

The old blacksmith, a black man by the name of Dick Humphrey, was on that same trail the night of the murder. Humphrey told his story to a since-retired deputy marshal turned freelance writer named Fred E. Sutton. Humphrey apparently had a habit of imbibing whiskey with one Jennie Schell, a regular and well-known source of the illegal drink. In fact she was so well known that Maples was on his way to arrest her when he was shot.

Humphrey, in a 1918 *Daily Oklahoman* article, said he watched Bud Trainor remove a coat from a passed-out, drunken Ned Christie and put it on himself. Humphrey suspected Trainor was up to no good and hid in the darkness. Along came the unsuspecting Maples, and Trainor opened up on him with two pistols. Maples was able to return fire four times before collapsing, dead.[58]

This evidence, if true, would have cleared Ned Christie of the murder and saved the territorial law enforcement community considerable embarrassment. With good reason, Humphrey feared Trainor, and even after Trainor's death, the old blacksmith said he feared Trainor's friends. So, for many years, the secret remained between just two men.

Chapter 12

Kidnapping, Inc.

"This is J. Edgar Hoover, Mrs. Urschel. Give me every detail you can."

No one enjoying the breeze on the front porch of the Urschel mansion the night of July 22, 1933, had ever heard of George F. Barnes or his accomplice Albert Bates. Soon, though, everyone in the nation would come to know Barnes. They would come to know him as Machine Gun Kelly.

Hearing a car coast to a stop at the foot of the Oklahoma mansion's driveway, oil magnate Charles F. Urschel, his wife, Bernice Slick Urschel, his business partner, Walter Jarrett, and his wife, thought it to be a neighbor. The mansion was an impressive affair, rising above the red dirt and flat plains just north of downtown Oklahoma City in an area called Heritage Hills. It was Saturday night just before eleven-thirty.

The foursome was playing cards on the screened-in porch when someone heard a noise just outside. Charles Urschel looked to the door. "It's me, Betty," came a call. Walter Jarrett pushed up from his chair and reached the screen door in time to unlatch it for the girl. Betty Slick ambled past the card players, offered a passing acknowledgment, and headed upstairs to bed. She was the sixteen-year-old daughter of Bernice and her late husband, Tom Slick, a one-time partner with Urschel in the oil business. Bernice married Urschel after *his* wife died so the partnership remained neatly intact. Jarrett was added later.

Outside in the quiet darkness, two men slid from the parked car and made their way surreptitiously up to the amber light of the front porch.

This time Bernice heard a noise. Charles gave the screen door a quick glance and then leaned toward the darkness, peering beyond the boundaries of the screened-in porch. The glowing light did nothing to illuminate the expanse of empty blackness outside the enclosure. Charles saw nothing, nor had he heard what Bernice had heard.

Thinking little more of it, the four continued their game, and Bernice bid two hearts just as the screen door banged open, allowing two men to step inside. Each was holding a submachine gun. "Now, which one's Urschel?" one of the men demanded.[1]

George F. Barnes Jr. was born in Chicago in 1900. Later his father, George Sr., and his mother, Elizabeth Kelly Barnes, moved with their then two-year-old son to Memphis, Tennessee, where George Sr., made a name for himself as an insurance salesman.

For most of young George's early life his future appeared to be on a high-arching trajectory. He was a glib joker who grew up in an upper-class neighborhood. Religious training he received while attending Sacred Heart Catholic School only added to the well-rounded upbringing of someone who was being groomed for higher things than many of the boys of that era.

Then young Barnes's life was ripped with tragedy when his mother died. Soon, his father found solace in the company of another woman, and little George reacted to this latest disappointment with activities far afield from the conduct approved of in catechism class. He dropped out of high school and somehow became involved in bootlegging. Barnes would buy whiskey, lots of it, in Missouri and Kentucky to resell elsewhere. Then, probably due to his father's chastisement, young Barnes entered Mississippi A&M but dropped out after only one semester. Barnes the elder had had enough of his son's ne'er-do-well tendencies and washed his hands of the whole matter. Simply put, Barnes Jr. was left with no one.

Young George then took up with the daughter of a Memphis construction millionaire who had built an empire from shrewd investments. Geneva Ramsey and George were married, and the groom was put to work at his father-in-law's company. The young couple became parents of two fine offspring, and all was right by George.

When the building mogul was killed in a construction accident, George began to unravel, in spite of the support of his mother-in-law, who purchased a parking garage and a dairy farm outright for him to operate.

Nonetheless, George turned back to his prior career of bootlegging. That bit of business acumen resulted in a number of additions to the twenty-four-year-old's somewhat tarnished resume. First of all, he was promptly arrested and sentenced to six months in a work camp. The embarrassment proved too much for his heiress wife, and she left him. Then, poor George gorged on a bottle of bichloride of mercury, apparently hoping to kill himself. That didn't work, and faced with the possibility of jail time for attempted suicide, George ran off to Kansas City, where he found work as a supermarket clerk.

Things were once again looking up for the disowned, divorced, and denounced young George. He reveled in his good fortune by embezzling enough money from his employer to buy a truck, which he promptly put to use hauling—what else—bootleg whiskey.

Barnes was a small potato and acted alone most of the time while he was illegally transporting and selling whiskey. Then he was caught bootlegging on an Indian reservation, a federal offense, and the whiskey runner—then twenty-seven—was sentenced to a stretch at Leavenworth. There he met one Frank "Jelly" Nash, who would be machine-gunned to death a few years later during the "crime of the century," the Kansas City Massacre.

Barnes even participated in an unsuccessful jailbreak attempt Nash put together. The camaraderie between Barnes and Nash was enough to warrant an introduction to some of Nash's more infamous associates, such as Harvey Bailey and Verne Miller.

It was only when Barnes married his second wife, a whiskey-guzzling, notoriety-seeking braggart named Kathryn Thorne, that he began seeing himself as more than a whiskey runner. Thorne was an Oklahoma girl who showed little remorse at sending her daughter off to be raised by her mother on the latter's Paradise, Texas, farm. She steered Kelly in the direction of unsuspecting banks instead of liquor-starved Indian reservations. She became his willing, almost giddy, accomplice.

Kathryn was a party girl, and George, who by that time had taken his mother's maiden name, Kelly, as his own, was head over heels about her. In September 1930, shortly after Kelly's parole, the couple was married.

Hoover wrote in his 1938 book, *Persons in Hiding,* that Kathryn was Kelly's Svengali. He claimed that Kathryn directed Kelly throughout his criminal career.[2] In fact, Kelly was such an inept bank robber that he was eventually shunned by Harvey Bailey, Verne

Miller, and the far more experienced and feared "yeggs" of their time. They were fed up with Kelly's amateurish behavior.

Machine Gun Kelly's fame meant little to his former confederates who, more than once, watched Kelly lose his lunch upon entering a targeted bank.

In January of 1932, Kelly decided to expand his career development program by adding kidnapping to his repertoire. His first attempt was a failure. Running her fingers through the pages of a phone book, Kathryn randomly chose Howard Woolverton as victim. Woolverton was a businessman but apparently with not much to show for it. When the family finally convinced the kidnappers that they couldn't supply the demanded ransom, Woolverton was unceremoniously released.

Seven months later Kelly and Bates would strike red pay dirt with the kidnapping of Oklahoma oilman Charles F. Urschel. Not since the Lindbergh kidnapping nearly one year earlier had the press been fueled with such a sensational, public event. With all the ingredients of a terrific crime novel in play, the nation's press devoured every morsel given them: A latenight bridge game, the mansion on the hill, the amassed fortune of an oil tycoon; it was all too much to be ignored by newspapers all across the country.

Kathryn and George finally reached the outlaw status that she at least had long foreseen and hoped for. As "Machine Gun Kelly" he was now a household name, an iconoclast who challenged the very sanctity and security of the American home. He had also been catapulted to the head of the class with his placement on Hoover's Public Enemy Number One list.

Urschel was shanghaied from the safety of his own sprawling home. Peace and tranquility had been broken, and a terrified wife left to wait. The FBI fumbled. Even before anyone heard from the kidnappers an agent told the distraught millionaire's wife, "The moment Mr. Urschel is released, we go to work."[3] That must have been reassuring. Now the machine gun-wielding young man from Memphis would get the limelight his wife Kathryn wanted. After the Urschel kidnapping and ransom demand of $200,000, nearly every newspaper in the country was salivating over any scrap of information they could find about the brazen Machine

Gun Kelly. Incidentally, $200,000 in 2006 dollars comes to just a little more than $2.7 million. That July, gangsters such as Harvey Bailey, Verne Miller, and Pretty Boy Floyd continued to rampage through rural Oklahoma, relieving banks, gas stations, and grocery stores of cash, coin, and consumer products, but the Urschel kidnapping dominated the front pages.

Hoover's FBI then focused solely on the apprehension of the persons who had the unadulterated nerve and unmitigated audacity to pluck one of Oklahoma City's most substantial citizens from his own front porch. First, however, the kidnappers had to be identified. Nothing was known about them except through a letter delivered to a Tulsa businessman and friend of Urschel's named John Catlett. The letter gave instructions as to how, where, and when the money was to be delivered and authenticated Urschel's capture with three of the kidnapped victim's business cards.

Catlett immediately drove to Oklahoma City, where he presented the ransom note to Urschel's wife, Bernice. An FBI agent was present when Catlett arrived. He was made aware of the letter, the instructions, and the amount requested for the release of Urschel. The agent, stating the obvious, said, "That's a lot of money."[4]

Still, neither Bernice Urschel, nor the FBI, nor the Jarretts had any idea who the kidnappers were. One savvy Fort Worth police detective named Ed Weatherford put clues and conversations together to formulate an opinion.

Weatherford had befriended Kathryn Kelly. She believed, through a ruse he created, that he was a "dirty" cop, more inclined to inform her of police investigations than to actually investigate her. Weatherford knew of her mother's living arrangements with an old rancher, Robert "Boss" Shannon, outside Paradise, Texas. Weatherford considered the ranch a prime location for a hideout. At one time, Kelly had been the subject of interest in the Kansas City Massacre. As such, the FBI had some interest in his whereabouts.

Eventually, however, with little or no evidence showing that Kelly was in any way involved with the Kansas City trouble, the FBI lost interest and cancelled surveillance of the ranch. Nonetheless, the time spent on and around the property gave Weatherford a pretty good feel for the place. As it happened, on July 23, one day after

Urschel was taken at gunpoint from his Oklahoma City home, the cagey detective was visiting Kathryn at her Fort Worth residence. His knowledge of the ranch and its environs of red clay dirt helped to catch the unwary moll in a lie.

The reason Weatherford was invited to visit Machine Gun Kelly's "squeeze" that Sunday morning is either not known or not talked about, but it likely had nothing to do with prayer. Weatherford made small talk with Kathryn as the two casually visited on her front porch. She had been out of town for a while, in St. Louis, she said. When it came time for the detective to bid a farewell, she accompanied him on the short walk down her driveway, passing right by her car.

As they did so, Weatherford cast a sidewise glance at the vehicle, noticing that its wheels were encrusted in red dirt, a red clay not found in St. Louis, Missouri. A harder look and Weatherford saw an Oklahoma newspaper lying on the front seat, plastered with news of the Urschel kidnapping.

Weatherford put two and two together and was convinced the Kellys were the kidnappers the FBI was looking for. He passed on his evidence to the Dallas office of the FBI. They in turn informed Special Agent in Charge Gus Jones, who had set up a command post in the Urschel home. Jones did nothing with the information, choosing instead to dismiss it as the ramblings of a city cop hoping to play with the big boys.

Undaunted, Weatherford kept a vigil on Kathryn's Fort Worth house on East Mulkey Street. The FBI did agree to place a tap on her phone, but the tap wasn't even manned by a federal agent. The monitor was a Southwestern Bell supervisor, told to call if she heard anything suspicious.

In the meantime, Bernice Urschel and the Jarretts had viewed mug shots of various criminal types, but because the only recent photo of Machine Gun Kelly had been lost at the Fort Worth Police Department, that too was an exercise in futility. The fumbling continued.

And then, even while under the watchful, familiar eye of Detective Weatherford, Kathryn disappeared. It looked as though all the suspects had outsmarted the coppers. In the meantime, Tulsa oilman John Catlett and another of Urschel's buddies, oil man E. E. Kirkpatrick, began to follow the ransom letter's instructions faithfully.

As directed, Kirkpatrick placed a bogus ad in the *Daily Oklahoman*, listing the sale of a fictitious ranch. When the kidnappers saw it they would then make further contact. A day later a letter was delivered to the newspaper with further instructions.

Kirkpatrick was told to hop a ride on the 10:10 Sooner, a Katy-Limited train, to Kansas City the upcoming Saturday night. He was to place $200,000 in a Gladstone bag. Somewhere during the journey, the letter said, Kirkpatrick would see a signal fire and then a second fire. He was to throw the bag of ransom money from the moving train as his car neared that second fire.

This rail line was the very route that had been used by such outlaws as the Dalton and Doolin gangs, Al Spencer, and the disastrous Al Jennings, who staged his last train robbery attempt along these rails. Perhaps remembering that rich tradition, Kirkpatrick wasn't taking any chances of losing the kidnappers' loot to an incidental highwayman.

He enlisted the man who first received the kidnappers' letter, John Catlett. He quickly agreed to assist in the delivery of the ransom money. The pair came up with the idea that each man would carry an identical Gladstone bag; one would contain the $200,000, the other would be filled with newspapers to be handed over in the event an untimely train robbery was to occur.

Despite all their preparation, neither Kirkpatrick nor Catlett could have prevented what happened next. It was a minor thing really, but the two couriers thought at the time that it could have resulted in serious consequences. The World's Fair, held in Chicago, was under way. So large was the list of people vying for a seat on the train going as far as Kansas City that the conductor postponed the departure time while workers connected two additional cars.

All the way to Kansas City the two men anxiously studied landscapes for any flicker of a signal fire out of the darkness. None came. Had the conductor's decision to lengthen his train by adding passenger cars unwittingly cut short the happy, rich life of Charles F. Urschel?

A provision in the ransom letter allowed for the possibility of just such a failure. The two men were to check into the Muelenbach Hotel once they arrived in Kansas City, and there they were to wait for further instructions. It was just at dawn when the two tired travelers checked into the hotel. Within minutes a knock came. Fitzpatrick walked to the door, his Colt .45 not far out of reach. He carefully opened it.

Outside in the hallway stood a young bellboy who handed the Oklahoma oilman a telegram which read, "UNAVOIDABLE INCI-DENT KEPT ME FROM WEEING [sic] YOU LAST NIGHT. WILL COMMUNICATE ABOUT 6:00 O'CLOCK [p.m.]. E. W. MOORE."⁵ E. W. Moore was the name used by Kelly when he answered the bogus ranch-for-sale ad Kirkpatrick had placed in the newspaper to initiate contact with the kidnappers.

The two men were forced to wait, all the while not knowing whether this entire incident was merely a cruel hoax or the act of some desperate criminals who might kill Urschel once having received the money. Nothing was certain. So they did the only thing left to them, wait for the kidnappers' next communiqué.

It came nearly twelve hours after the men had checked into their hotel room. At 5:40 p.m., the phone rang. A man identifying himself as Moore asked whether Kirkpatrick had received the telegram. Kirkpatrick assured the caller that he had. The caller then instructed Kirkpatrick to go to the La Salle Hotel on Linwood Boulevard, alone, where he would be approached at 6:20 p.m. Kirkpatrick packed the Gladstone bag containing the money, and his Colt .45, and took a taxi to the drop-off point. It was Sunday, July 30, 1933, nine days after Urschel was yanked from his Oklahoma City mansion.

Kirkpatrick didn't enter the La Salle but remained outside on the sidewalk with the money, smoking a cigarette. In just a few short moments, Kirkpatrick saw a squat, barrel-chested figure rapidly approaching him. The man seemed to be eyeballing the satchel and Kirkpatrick's eyes alternately. "I'll take that grip," the man said.

After a moment or so of Q & A, as Kirkpatrick stalled for time to etch a lasting mental image of the stranger's features, the deal was done. Kirkpatrick called after the man, who was now $200,000 richer, as to what message he could take back to the worried wife in Oklahoma. "Urschel will be home within twelve hours," he called back. Then the man and the money disappeared into the Kansas City traffic.⁶

Urschel was released as promised. He was dropped off at Norman, Oklahoma, and made his way, via taxi, back to his sprawling Oklahoma City residence that night. He stepped through the back door of his home where the ever anxious Bernice threw herself into his arms.

Agent Jones was notified of Urschel's return and drove to the home, arriving around 11:00 p.m. He too was anxious. He was insistent that Urschel shake off the fatigue of his ordeal and tell him everything on the spot. Urschel told the eager G-man that while he wanted to be cooperative, he had been blindfolded during the entire nightmarish process and could not possibly identify his kidnappers. Nor did he know where his captors had held him for the preceding nine days.

If Jones appeared indifferent to Detective Weatherford's persistent call for the investigation of the Kellys in the early days following the kidnapping, he did little to redeem himself later. The Dallas office's second in command, Dwight McCormack, had written an interoffice memo six days after the release, suggesting the Kellys and the bunch at Paradise as suspects; nevertheless, Jones stubbornly sought his own path.

Jones was off spying from the skies in a vain attempt to find the ranch Urschel had described to him during the interview at the Urschel home. One thing that Urschel mentioned to the persistent special agent was the rain pattern. Jones believed he was on the right track in asking the Dallas office to check the weather patterns of North Texas during the nine-day period that Urschel was held captive.

Instead, what someone at the bureau mistakenly supplied was data for the Paradise area. Eventually even the immovable Jones had to agree that that data matched Urschel's recollection perfectly. Only then did Jones, as special agent in charge, authorize the Dallas office to send men to survey the Shannon ranch. What they were looking for was a dilapidated shack where Urschel said he was held in chains during his ordeal. If the agents could identify that landmark, they would be closer to catching Kelly and his accomplices. They had to conduct the investigation in secret so as not to tip off Shannon and his wife, Kathryn Kelly's mother Ora, or anyone else who might be at the place.

On August 10, in the company of the ever-determined Fort Worth detective, Ed Weatherford, FBI agent Ed Dowd was driven to the bank at Decatur, where Boss Shannon held an account. The two officers convinced an officer of the bank that the Shannons might be mixed up in the Urschel kidnapping. The bank officer solicited the assistance of the bank's credit investigator.

The deception used was that the bank's credit investigator, along with Agent Dowd posing as a bank examiner, would have papers for Shannon's signature. The ruse worked, and while the bank investigator talked with Armon Shannon, Boss's son, Dowd casually walked about. He was able to recognize several things that Urschel had described about the place, either by partial sight or by sound. At one point, seemingly innocently enough, Dowd sauntered into the house. According to the description given, the place matched perfectly.

Convinced it was the place, Dowd raced back to Dallas to report his findings to Jones. The order was given to conduct a full-scale raid on Shannon's ranch the following day. Jones gathered a contingent of federal and local officers at Denton, north of Dallas, on Friday, August 11. That contingent also included one very determined former kidnap victim, Charles F. Urschel. If Jones had any strong reservations about Urschel participating in the raid, it was hard to tell it as the oilman was allowed to carry a sawed-off shotgun to the party.

Conditions being what they were—unpaved, rough roads, one way into the Shannon ranch and one way out, nightfall rapidly descending, and most of the posse never having laid eyes on the place—Jones decided to postpone the raid. "I've done enough shooting in my time not to want to go barging into a place where the odds are all on the other side," Jones informed his men with about twenty-six miles to go before reaching the Shannon place. "My judgment is to back off," he later said.

After spending the night in Fort Worth at the Blackstone Hotel, the lawmen once again caravanned over the narrow, potholed, dusty roads to Paradise. Once the lawmen finally arrived at the ranch house, the arrests were made without incident; however, they did produce a bit of a surprise for Special Agent Jones. With Robert, Ora, and Armon Shannon safely in custody, Jones must have been disappointed at not finding the real target of his hunt on the premises, Machine Gun Kelly. But then, that hot August morning, something a little odd caught the agents' eye. It was the figure of a person outside lying on a cot atop two sawhorses. Jones ran from the house toward the cot. As he approached he saw that the dozing figure, clad only in his underwear, had his clothes placed neatly at one end of the cot right next to a Winchester rifle and a Colt .45 pistol.

Jones cautiously approached the prone figure. Now Jones was close enough that he instantly recognized the slumbering man. Out in the backyard of a ramshackle outpost somewhere near Paradise, Texas, was the sleeping, unaware, vulnerable teacher of such outlaws as Verne Miller, Machine Gun Kelly, Alvin "Old Creepy" Karpis, and the Barker brothers. Jones had happened onto none other than Harvey Bailey, kidnapper, bank robber, and murderer, who himself had made Hoover's list of public enemies.

Despite Mama Ora's ordering her husband and his kid to remain silent, when agents took Armon aside and had what in their parlance at the time was described as a "fatherly chat," he broke. Armon told the lawmen that the Kellys had orchestrated the kidnapping. Albert Bates was also in it up to his eyebrows with them, but they had all long since left the Shannon ranch. Now it seemed the FBI's fumbling was turning to fortune.

That same Saturday police arrested Bates in a downtown Denver, Colorado, parking lot. Bates gave lawmen no leads as to where the Kellys might be. His silence only stalled the process for a short while because the Kellys, unbeknownst to them, were being dogged by the unsung hero of the Shannon raid, Detective Ed Weatherford of the Fort Worth Police Department.

Weatherford monitored the mail being sent to the Shannons. He noted the return address of each piece. The first major break in the hunt for Machine Gun Kelly came when agents found a bill at the Shannon ranch from a Cleveland, Ohio, Cadillac dealer. Agents quickly swarmed on the car dealership. The salesman said the Kellys were there just three days earlier, August 10, to make a final payment on the car they were driving. They inquired about purchasing a new one, but never did. The salesman told the agents that the Kellys said they were driving to Chicago.

From that point on, Machine Gun Kelly would be the main focus of the FBI. Hoover was tired of the bureau's past failures in the Urschel case.

Geralene Arnold was the twelve-year-old daughter of itinerant Oklahoma farmers Luther and Flossie Mae Arnold. Luther and his family had spent months since the Depression traipsing from one small Oklahoma and Texas town to another seeking any job or handout.

Like Oklahoma guineas in search of an elusive June bug, the Arnolds aimlessly wandered the dirt roads in search of sustenance of any kind. Often using gas station restrooms for shaving, sponge baths, or just a place of shelter from the sweltering Southwestern sun, life was coming down on these homeless Okies. They weren't that much different from any of the thousands of economically fragile people who had the misfortune of enduring back-to-back plagues, one man-made, the other created by the hands of nature.

It was the era of the Great Depression, and many of these unfortunates had recently lost everything because of it. To make matters intolerably worse, many of them were driven off the lands as a result of the raging dust and sandstorms that began in 1931 as a result of the longest dry spell in American history.

The drought that scorched the Midwest and Plains States' otherwise fertile soil lasted nine years until 1939, when rain finally quenched the thirsty fields. That period of devastating loss in human and agricultural terms was later dubbed the Dust Bowl era.

In those parched and sun-blistered conditions the Arnolds, like so many other farm families, were forced to humble themselves for the sake of a menial job or a crumb of sustenance. With no money, no means of transportation, and only the clothes on their backs, how does a family flee a national disaster?

Luther, Flossie Mae, and Geralene doggedly hitchhiked along one more dusty Texas road, a road that promised nothing but the certainty of disillusionment that came with the hard times that they knew lay ahead. Just outside of Hillsboro at a small town called Itasca, the pitiful hitchhikers came to a filling station and made the usual use of it.

They were all outside when a woman pulled up in a pickup truck, rolled to a gradual stop beside them, and asked, "Y'all want a ride?" She was headed north to Fort Worth some sixty-plus miles away, she said, and would be delighted to help the struggling family. The Arnolds must have cheerfully accepted the kindness of this stranger, whose intentions were a lot more self-serving than they at first realized.

The kind, attractive, redheaded stranger was in fact, Kathryn Kelly, wife of the notorious Machine Gun Kelly and daughter of Ora Shannon, arrested in connection with the Urschel kidnapping and set for trial.

Repeated attempts by Kathryn to get assurances from Sam Sayers, the Fort Worth lawyer she hired to represent her mother, were met with dismissive indifference, if not downright arrogance. At one point, Sayers chided Kathryn for calling his office, saying, "You know better than to call on this phone," then hung up.[7] Angered and frustrated, Kathryn was nonetheless a schemer, and when she happened upon the itinerant Okies she soon made known the reason for her generosity. Whatever reason it was that put lawyer Sayers in such an uncooperative state, Kathryn would circumvent the barrister's refusal to see her by sending a proxy—Luther Arnold. Kathryn and her newfound beneficiaries drove north until they reached the town of Cleburne, named for an Arkansas Confederate general from Ireland. There they stopped at a roadside tourist camp for the night.

The next day Kathryn further ingratiated herself with the family as she took Mae and the girl into Cleburne where she purchased dresses for the women. Upon returning, Kathryn approached the Arnold family patriarch with her plan.

Luther would seek out lawyer Sayers in Fort Worth and find out if there was any progress in working out a deal with the Feds in Ora's criminal case. Luther's efforts were greased with the fifty dollars Kathryn slipped him. When he returned to the anxious Kathryn, he had only bad news to report. There was no deal with the Feds, Sayers told him, and that was that.

Dejected and desperate, Kathryn turned to the wayfaring Okie and asked if he knew of an Oklahoma attorney who might take the case; since the abduction had occurred in Oklahoma and would be tried there. Sayers was a Texas attorney who, Kathryn came to realize, might not know enough Oklahoma law to help her mother. As it happened, Luther did know a man she could hire to take Mama Ora's case, an attorney in Enid, he said.

Armed with three hundred dollars of Kathryn's money and a bus ticket, Luther arrived in Oklahoma City to retrieve a Chevrolet she had left there on a previous occasion. He was then to drive to Enid, where he would use some of the money to hire the attorney he had told Kathryn about.

Luther Arnold probably had never seen three hundred dollars in his lifetime, and it is almost certain that that amount of money had never found its way inside any of his worn overalls' pockets. So when he arrived at Oklahoma City and found that the lawyer he sought to retain wasn't in, he was left to his own devices, with Kathryn's wad of cash, to find some way to kill time until he could meet up with the attorney.

An Oklahoma City police report details just exactly what farmer Arnold did do to pass the time until he could meet with the new lawyer. The report, titled UKF #732, states that Arnold took a Yellow Cab from the bus station to a bar and proceeded to quaff a brew or two. Feeling emboldened, he then asked the bartender where a man might find a little female company. The bartender strode to a telephone, dialed a number and—presto!—a young woman sidled up to the cotton-picker within minutes. Luther then bought a whole case of beer, which he and the call girl shared at her apartment.

Farm boys are not lacking in stamina. And it wasn't long before Luther found that if multiple beers were more satisfying, so too would be multiple women. Luther, having lost all signs of that awe-shucks, homespun, salt-of-the-earth quality that city women find so amusing and endearing, demanded a second woman. When she showed up at the first woman's apartment, any appearance of collaborative restraint vanished as the farmer and the belles shared beer, time, each other, and of course Kathryn's money, on a journey into a long but sordid night.

The next morning Sayers did deliver the car to Luther. He loaded the two women into the rumble seat and drove to Enid. Luther met the attorney there and hired him as agreed. That was the only part of Kathryn's plan still intact. Once he took care of business there, he and the women then drove to Oklahoma City where they rented a room at the upscale Skirvin Hotel. Before long Luther and the women picked up where they had left off the previous evening.

According to the police report, only dumb luck kept Arnold from being arrested, since a bevy of FBI men were watching the Skirvin Hotel where he and the ladies were staying. Someone had tipped Special Agent in Charge Gus Jones that an unnamed messenger of Kelly's and several lawyers Kathryn had hired were to rendezvous there. The place was put under close surveillance, but despite that fact Arnold simply wandered off out from under the G-men's noses.

The hapless agents were left holding nothing more than a convention of lawyers, two hung-over hussies, and one empty net.[8]

On that particular morning of September 11, 1933, the egg on Hoover's face was beginning to sizzle. Three days later, however, the G-men got a much-needed break in their pursuit of the Kellys. The afternoon of September 14, a fully drunken Arnold was dropped off at the Skirvin after another rousing night of fun on Kathryn's tab.

Agent Jones's men, undoubtedly feeling the heat of an angry Hoover, ramped up the pressure a bit. Using what has been called "vigorous but appropriate" methods (loosely translated that could mean they employed the old rubber hose treatment), they got Arnold to spill the beans.

Come hell or high water these agents were not about to let another opportunity slip by, thus fueling the constant call for Hoover's resignation and the disbanding of the FBI. They were going to have their kidnappers wrapped up in a neat little package before long, they promised their increasingly frustrated boss. The farmer, turned roustabout, turned philanderer, turned stool pigeon, led the Feds to Kathryn's Fort Worth home on East Mulkey Street.

A raid there, coordinated by Agent Jones, netted one very surprised yet grateful Flossie Mae Arnold. With mounting tenacity the FBI was beginning to close in on the Kellys. Flossie told the G-men that the kidnappers had left the modest house just the day before the agents swarmed in on the place and that they were headed to Cass Coleman's place, a ranch near the small town of West, Texas. She was worried, she said, because the Kellys had taken her daughter, Geralene, with them.

Cass Coleman was Kathryn's forty-three-year-old uncle, who had buried most of the Urschel ransom money on his place when Kathryn took it there, thinking it would be safe from police. With her help, Coleman had transferred the money from two suitcases Kathryn brought to the ranch and stuffed it into a water jug and a bucket, which the conspirators then buried near a willow tree behind Coleman's barn.[9]

Unfortunately for the Kellys, people can't always pick their relatives. When Kathryn and Machine Gun Kelly sent George's former brother-in-law to retrieve some of the loot sometime later, old Uncle

Coleman flatly refused, telling the courier to skedaddle since the Feds were likely watching the place. The former brother-in-law, Langford "Lang" Ramsey, left empty-handed and dejected.

Armed with the information garnered from Flossie Arnold, agents put together plans to raid Coleman's ranch with assistance from agents out of the Dallas office. The raid was of little success. Suspecting that Coleman had been under FBI surveillance for quite some time, the Kellys had left Kathryn's dear old uncle's ranch and taken up quarters at the home of a neighbor, Clarence Durham. When Durham arrived home one afternoon after work to find George, Kathryn, and their little charge, Geralene, asleep on the front porch, he ordered them off the place. They complied, and Durham went straight to the sheriff's office.

A covey of city police, deputies, state troopers, and federal agents set up roadblocks and checkpoints all across Texas, but especially in northern Texas. Lawmen feared the elusive Kellys were headed for the border and into Oklahoma. Checkpoints were established along several Red River bridges, the officers anticipating that the fleeing Kellys would pass on one of them. Their hunch was a good one, but it was one that came too late. The Kellys, with little Geralene, were already burning up the Oklahoma blacktop en route to Chicago, which they safely reached on Sunday, September 17.

The next day the kidnapping trials of those nabbed at the Shannon ranch were to begin in Oklahoma City. The suspects included Bob "Boss" Shannon; Kathryn's mother, Ora Shannon; Kellys' only true accomplice, Albert Bates; and Harvey Bailey, who had the misfortune of being at the Shannon place when it was raided but who had absolutely nothing to do with the Urschel kidnapping.

Despite the heat the FBI was turning up on the elusive couple, the Kellys remained at large. From Chicago they drove back to George's old haunts in Memphis. Once there they drove straight to a hideout used by Kelly as well as other fugitives, the bungalow of a garage attendant.

Then Kelly convinced Lang Ramsey to drive to Paradise, Texas, to retrieve some of the ransom money from Kathryn's cantankerous uncle. The long homesick Geralene was cajoled into showing Ramsey where the ranch was situated. Despondent over his lack of success with the old man, Ramsey headed out for Gainesville with a whining, complaining, homesick, twelve-year-old girl. When he reached Fort Worth, he unloaded his burdensome preteen at the train station where he bought her a ticket to Oklahoma City.

Geralene sent a telegram to her father the minute Ramsey was out of sight, telling him to meet her at 10:15 that night at the Rock Island Station. The note was signed, Gerry. Mom and Pop Arnold dutifully showed up at the station at the prescribed time. And so did the FBI.

By then the FBI had grown so resolute in its efforts to catch the Kellys that Hoover had sent Assistant Director Harold "Pop" Nathan to Oklahoma to see to things. Pop Nathan was at the train station when young Geralene disembarked. She was only too happy to share her experiences the past few weeks, while in the company of the Kellys, their cohorts and relatives. The Kellys were staying at a home in Memphis on East Raynor Street, she said.

It took some doing, but at five thirty on the morning of September 26, 1933, a National Guard plane touched down at Memphis. The cargo: Special Agent in Charge of the Birmingham, Alabama, office of the FBI, William Rorer, and another agent. They were met by the bureau's Memphis agent and six city cops he was able to muster. This contingent of officers quietly but hastily raced to one end of East Raynor Street, where other uniformed police officers stood waiting. Within minutes of Rorer's arrival all who slumbered in the house on East Raynor were in federal custody. To the FBI's long-awaited satisfaction the net had snared George "Machine Gun" Kelly and his wife Kathryn. The very next day, September 27, agents conducted a search of Cass Coleman's ranch and found $73,250 of the hidden ransom money.[10]

In October of 1933, Robert "Boss" Shannon and his wife Ora each received life sentences for their part in the Urschel abduction in the federal court at Oklahoma City. Also receiving life sentences at that trial were Alan Bates and the probably innocent Harvey Bailey. Later that same month, George and Kathryn Kelly would each receive their own life sentences. Kathryn was so outraged at her verdict and its accompanying sentence that she blurted out, "Anyone could have been convicted in this court. If they brought my dog in here he would have got a life sentence too."

Kathryn, while nonetheless guilty of at least complicity in the kidnapping of Charles Urschel, may have had a point. Not only was the handwriting evidence used against her at the trial tainted, as a later examination would prove, but the judge in the case imparted some rather remarkably biased comments to the jury before it retired for deliberation. "The court would feel it had been cowardly and derelict in duty if it had not pointed out . . . that the defendant Kathryn was not wholly truthful, the judge admonished."[11] Years later on appeal, Kathryn would be released when the FBI refused to open its records to the defense for an upcoming hearing. Her husband, George, would not be so lucky. Despite his promises to break out of one prison or another by Christmas of 1933, he spent many years housed inside the nation's most secure and austere prison: Alcatraz.

Armon Shannon, the offspring of Boss Shannon, received ten years probation for his part in the Urschel affair.

Not unlike the renowned Ma Barker, George Kelly received most of his "fame" through the efforts of his unwitting publicist: J. Edgar Hoover of the FBI. Hoover popularized the story that when cornered in the house on East Raynor Street in Memphis, Kelly famously blurted, "Don't shoot, G-men. Don't shoot."

From then on, the nickname stuck, and with it the men of the FBI had attained an unparalleled stature in crime fighting. While their early successes should not be minimized, as any seasoned cop will admit, a lot of good crime fighting is the result of crook carelessness, citizen input, and cop luck.

Hoover seemed intent on making the public view his agents as god-like figures who seemingly possessed supernatural abilities while fighting America's Depression-era War on Crime.

In his book, *Public Enemies: America's Greatest Crime Wave and the Birth of the FBI, 1933-1934,* author Bryan Burrough points to one quite convincing interview debunking the origin of the nickname. Although Burrough says the phrase "G-men" did originate at the Kelly arrest that morning in Memphis, it was Kathryn and not George who first used the term. She did so in far less dramatic circumstances than Hoover would have had the public believe.

Burrough cites a telephone interview Agent Rorer gave to a *Chicago American* reporter, shortly after the Kellys were taken into custody. Rorer told the reporter that upon her arrest Kathryn Kelly wrapped her husband in her arms, crying, and said to him, "Honey, I guess it's all up for us. The g-men won't give us a break. I've been living in dread of this."[12] Hardly the kind of stuff headlines are made of.

George "Machine Gun" Kelly spent seventeen years at Alcatraz after an initial one-year stint at Leavenworth, before being returned to Leavenworth in 1951. He died there in 1954 of a massive heart attack. Albert Bates, Kelly's partner in the late-night front-porch abduction of Oklahoma oilman Charles Urschel, died while at Alcatraz on July 4, 1948. George Kelly's former brother-in-law, Langford Ramsey, received two and half years for transporting the juvenile Geralene Arnold across state lines.

Harvey Bailey's kidnapping conviction was eventually overturned and in 1961 he was paroled. He was promptly arrested by Kansas authorities for a 1933 bank robbery, was later released from prison, and became a cabinet maker. He died in 1979.

In 1958 both Kathryn Kelly and her mother were released from prison. Kathryn later sued the FBI in an attempt to clear her name as one of the persons involved directly with the Urschel kidnapping. Ora was placed in the Oklahoma County Home and Hospital in Oklahoma City sometime after her release, and Kathryn, who was unwaveringly loyal to her mother, took a job at that hospital as a bookkeeper. Kathryn died in Oklahoma City in 1985.

In 1944, Robert "Boss" Shannon received a presidential pardon from a fellow Democrat, Franklin D. Roosevelt. Repeatedly writing to Kathryn while she was in prison, the old man said he was waiting for the discovery of oil on his property which should take place at any time. It never did.

Chapter 13

Old Creepy

We readily accept names etched on the hallowed walls of memorials or museums to extol the sacrifice, grit, and spirit of heroes, warriors, and the martyred, memorializing them for future generations.

No such halls of fame exist for prominent figures of the criminal underworld, but if they did, there are a few whose names would surely have a place there, and the subject of this chapter would certainly be among them. The name Alvin Karpis is perhaps not as commonly known as the likes of Depression-era hoodlums such as Al Capone, Machine Gun Kelly and Baby Face Nelson. However, he most certainly deserves his place among the most feared names ever placed on a police blotter or in a newspaper. Karpis had a unique talent for survival as well as for setting records, dubious as they may be, throughout his long career.

Among the dubious achievements on Karpis's criminal score card was possibly the last train robbery in the United States at a time when the head of the FBI, J. Edgar Hoover, said the nation had seen the end of its train-robbing era. Karpis had been a member in good standing of the infamous Ma Barker gang, and the only gang member not to die violently. Ma Barker, herself, died with a machine gun clutched to her bosom, according to the FBI. Karpis spent more than twenty-six years in Alcatraz, the longest of any prisoner, and was among those transferred to another facility shortly before that infamous California penal colony closed.[1]

Rather than dying in prison as many of his counterparts did, at the hands of corrupt guards, territorial prisoners, or simply old age, Karpis was paroled and finished his days basking in the sun in a small Spanish villa. He even wrote books about his experience as a gangster and an inmate of Alcatraz. Karpis made the big time in the gangster world but somehow never quite received the Hollywood billing the Capones, Kellys, or Nelsons did.

Nothing in Karpis's background could have foretold the path his life would take. Born Albin Karpowics to Lithuanian immigrants

John and Anna Karpowics in Montreal, Canada, in 1908, Albin was the second of four siblings. The eldest, a sister named Mihalin, was born in London, England. A second sister, Emily, was born in Grand Rapids, Michigan, where the family stopped on their trek south from Canada before moving on to Topeka, Kansas, where Albins' youngest sister, Clara, was born.[2]

While he was attending elementary school in Topeka, a change took place in young Albins' life. A schoolteacher, following the same sort of practice used by Ellis Island officials, simplified the boy's name to Alvin Karpis, saying the new spelling and its pronunciation would be "easier to manage." Whether that was the first act to set the high-spirited boy's jaw against authority can never be known, but he was definitely charted early for a course to infamy.

A good-looking rascal in his youth, Karpis had already managed to evolve into a petty criminal nuisance by the time he was ten years of age. By then Karpis regularly broke into stores and warehouses, obtaining not much more for his efforts than bragging rights among the local youthful offenders. This humble beginning was enough to mark his career path and encourage him to pull more daring capers in the next six or eight years. By the time Karpis reached his teens he had achieved the status of becoming more than just a nuisance to law enforcement and the good citizens of Topeka, Kansas, and surrounding cities. During one of his assaults on a building, Karpis stole a gun—the very thing he needed to set himself above the rest of the hooligans his age.

Karpis was small, standing only five feet three inches and weighing in at around 130 pounds. He grew no more, even after reaching adulthood. Despite his size, Karpis was a convincing little tough. He wasn't easy to scare, and no matter the risks, he was generally up to a job, qualities that later served him well in the seedy crime world.

Without much reason, Karpis broke from his family at an early age. Not much is mentioned of them after their move to Kansas. Alvin's idea of self-education didn't include staying on the home place, where he felt penned in by the circle of family, its responsibilities, and perhaps its greater expectations. Karpis soon began riding the rails, following the lure of the wide world pulling at his imagination.

Most of the nation's profiteering was taking place in the larger cities. Karpis was keen in intellect, and while his travels took him across the Plains States and into the Midwest, he paid strict attention to where the money was. And it was those places he later hit with expertise, hauling in a quarter of a million dollars in one heist. However, Karpis's early attempts to place his name among the underworld nobility ended rather ignobly.

One such clumsy effort resulted in his arrest and thirty-day sentence for trespassing on a Pan American Railway car. It seems Karpis broke from his usual tradition of riding the undercarriage of the train and opted instead for a room with a sky view: the roof of one of the luxury liner's cars. This humiliating beginning was Karpis's jumping-off point as a gangster. That thirty-day sentence is purportedly Alvin Karpis's first criminal conviction of record. He was just under eighteen years of age and served his sentence without incident.

Then Karpis got into real trouble. Probably because he was inexperienced, he focused on a familiar and therefore easy target in his hometown, but it didn't pan out too well for the apprentice bandit. He was caught, jailed, tried, and convicted, all without much fanfare, and given a five-to-ten year sentence in the Hutchinson, Kansas, reformatory.

His stint in the teen prison proved a great boon to Karpis's education in the ways of street crimes. Karpis spent his time in this warehouse of the underprivileged, associating with boys more experienced in the ways of his chosen career. The young tough soon held a reputation as someone not to cross. Even at his rather small size, Karpis was a pugnacious handful when angry. He quickly gained a reputation for being able to cause no small amount of damage to the person toward whom his anger was vented. He wasn't concerned that most of the men he dealt with were at least a head taller. Karpis was like a stick of dynamite. It was dangerous to set off either one.

Meanwhile, a figure that would play a major role in Karpis's story was beginning to attain her own notoriety. Twenty years before the Dalton gang met their 1892 Waterloo while trying to rob two banks simultaneously in Coffeyville, Kansas, Arizona Donnie Clark was born.[3] Arizona had a bent for the bad boys that was evident from an early age. She was reportedly thrilled with delight at hearing of the Daltons' wild disregard for the law. As a little girl growing up near

Springfield, Missouri, she was supposedly crestfallen when word of Jesse James' death reached her small town, or so the story goes. But those things were only available to her in the pages of a newspaper or by listening to the excited talk of the townsfolk. The romantic notion of being someone's bad girl was simply that, a romantic notion.

Arizona married a steady, honest man when she was about twenty. George Barker was a farm laborer who cut and baled hay in the torrid Midwestern sun. He herded Herefords and Anguses between pastures, served as midwife during calving, and did all the other things that made him a desirable fellow to have around on a farm. In 1894, George picked up what he had, including his wife of two years, and moved to Aurora, Missouri. Shortly afterward, a son, Herman, was born. Eventually, George and Arizona Barker had four sons in all.

Arizona loved and worried over her sons more than anything or anyone else in her entire life. By the time she and George were through having kids, Arizona was thirty years old, not old really even for that era, but no longer a spring chick. The boys soon began cutting their teeth on the criminal activity that would eventually become their livelihood. By the age of twelve, Herman had already been arrested for petty theft in Webb City, Missouri. He was released to his mother, who was not exactly the strictest of disciplinarians.

In fact, so lenient was Arizona Barker toward her sons, that all the boys had been arrested for one misdemeanor or another before reaching their twenty-first birthdays. Arthur was arrested first in 1910 at about the age of eleven for a string of juvenile offenses that reached into his teenage years. Herman was arrested again, this time in Joplin, and was released once again into the loving arms of his extraordinarily sympathetic mother. Society had not really noticed the beginning of what would soon enough become known as the "Ma Barker gang."

In 1915, Arizona Barker and her sons, Herman, Lloyd, Arthur, and Freddie left Webb City for a young, new state: Oklahoma. "Ma," as she was known by her boys and those she "adopted" into her nest, set her sights on Tulsa. Boys being boys as only the Barker brood could be, it wasn't long before even a relatively wild and wooly place like Oklahoma got its fill of their shenanigans. Ma kept a place in what is today downtown Tulsa, a humble abode located at 401 North Cincinnati. The Barker boys soon enlisted the help of a few locals and formed a teens-only club called the "Central Park Gang."[4]

Local Tulsa toughs like Elmer Inman and Glen Leroy Wright tagged along to make up the gang. Generally the crew did little more than make an annoyance of themselves. Their budding trouble-making consisted mainly of disturbing the peace or breaking a few storefront and warehouse windows. The Central Park gang was a nuisance to the local constabulary, but hardly a menace.

Along the way, however, Freddie, the youngest Barker, managed to land a prison sentence for his efforts. He was sentenced to a stretch of five to ten inside Kansas State Prison after robbing a bank in Winfield. At the Kansas State Penitentiary at Lansing he met a kid named Karpis, who did not look much older than sixteen. Regrettably for him, Karpis in fact had turned eighteen, just in time for the courts to consider his latest offense to be an adult crime rather than a juvenile prank. Adult court was not nearly as lax as the juvenile system where one might receive a verbal admonition and a yank on the ear by an embarrassed parent. This time Karpis found himself serving a stretch in a Kansas prison with other gangsters, rapists, thieves, and murderers, and one Freddie Barker.

From this time forward Freddie Barker and Alvin Karpis were inseparable; leading some to speculate the two may have been entangled in a homosexual relationship. About this time, the inexplicable nickname of "Old Creepy" or "Creepy" was, according to some sources, given to Karpis by police.

Alvin Karpis and Freddie Barker were paroled from Kansas State Prison in 1931 and after settling in for a time with Ma Barker, the two began a whirlwind of criminal activities. Their collaboration began with an ill-fated jewel heist from a Tulsa store. The pair were picked up and charged with the crime before their loot cooled off enough to fence. They escaped serious incarceration by returning the goods, after which they found leniency and were released. Unable to change stripes, the two embarked upon a road trip that included Kansas and Missouri towns as targets. Karpis and Barker honed their skills by hitting jewelry and clothing stores throughout both states until their joyous reunion with Ma and Lloyd back in Oklahoma.

Herman, Ma's eldest, was dead by then, and Arthur, nicknamed "Doc," was serving a life sentence for a Tulsa murder that he apparently didn't commit. Years later, a convicted thief in California confessed to the crime, and Doc was released. In the meantime, from 1926 through 1932, Karpis and Freddie Barker made headlines and earned an evil reputation. By 1932 the men were competent, notorious outlaws, and their newfound notoriety did not exactly humble them. As if in an effort to live up to the hyperbole of their reviewers, Karpis and Barker committed their first murder in 1931, gunning down Sheriff C. R. Kelly in Missouri.[5]

Karpis became a major crime figure with the Barkers, causing certain elements of the press to describe the enterprise as the Karpis-Barker Gang. In spite of impassioned arguments regarding her place in the gang and the extent of her activity or advice, it appears that Ma Barker was merely the "housemother" of the gang, providing shelter and mediocre meals. And even though the gang was officially known as the Karpis-Barker gang, it has forever been remembered as the Ma Barker gang at the whim of FBI agents desperate for her reputation to deserve the violent end they caused her.

Eventually, feeling the Oklahoma heat of its law enforcement, Ma made the decision to leave her clueless and weak husband. She moved with her boys to Kansas City, Missouri. They had not been in their new apartment long enough to decide where to hang the pictures when the FBI got their scent, closed in on them, and ultimately flushed them out.

In just three years the Barkers and other notorious gangsters were "done in" by pursuing lawmen. It was 1935 and all of the FBI's Most Wanted of the era were either dead or in prison. Major crime figures such as Machine Gun Kelly, Baby Face Nelson, and Al Capone were dead or behind bars. So far as the nation was concerned, that pretty well accounted for most everybody who made a living of robbing banks. Everybody but the diminutive and dapper Alvin Karpis, who somehow kept turning up despite the best efforts of the nation's leading crime fighters. This fact did much to embarrass the ego-driven head of the Federal Bureau of Investigation, J. Edgar Hoover. He promised the nation that he would arrest the ne'er-do-well braggart himself. From that point forward, Alvin Karpis became the object of one of the most publicized manhunts of the twentieth century, the kidnapping of the Charles Lindbergh child notwithstanding.

Karpis gained dubious fame by earning the coveted title of the FBI's Public Enemy Number One. In the 1930s only John Dillinger, Baby Face Nelson, and Pretty Boy Floyd held that distinction prior to Karpis. The previous three fellows met with a fate meted out with extreme prejudice by Hoover's G-men. Karpis then held the singular label as the last major crime figure on the FBI's list, and Hoover wanted him. The FBI was closing in on Karpis and his new companion, former Tulsan Harry Campbell. The two were hiding out in Miami, Florida, when word reached them that Ma and Freddie were killed in an FBI raid the evening of January 16, 1935.[6] Word also spread nearly as quickly that the G-men were about to commit a similar assault on Karpis and Campbell's hideout and were more than a little determined to help Hoover make good his promise to arrest Karpis personally. Instead, once again Karpis and Campbell gave their pursuers the slip. Bad intelligence, perhaps.

Karpis and Campbell beat a path to Atlantic City, New Jersey, arriving on January 20. They must have felt some sense of protection there, taking refuge with the criminal element, relying on the honor of like tradesmen not to betray their whereabouts. That reliance turned out to be misplaced. Soon Karpis and Campbell found themselves on the run again, returning to an old haunt in Ohio where Karpis had visited as a kid riding the rails not so many years earlier. But if recent history had taught him anything, Karpis knew better than to sign a long-term lease.

Toledo was first, then Youngstown, where Karpis plotted a payroll robbery. His plan was intricate, and he knew he needed help. The old gang, however, was not inclined to lend their diverse talents to the enterprise for a number of reasons, so Karpis headed back to Tulsa. Would-be cronies were reluctant to sign on because he was simply too hot. Lawmen everywhere kept a vigil for Karpis. He was lucky to be able to crisscross the country as blithely as he did, thought the boys in the back rooms. Down but not out, he and Campbell returned to Youngstown to ponder their next move.[7] There, Karpis decided that if he couldn't get the gang he wanted he would get the gang available. In April he, Campbell, and a band of

Youngstown locals robbed Youngstown Steel and Tube of a $75,000 payroll. Campbell was in hoodlum heaven and shared the spoils of his gangster activities with an eighteen-year-old Tulsa girl. The two found a preacher and became husband and wife.

By June of 1935, Alvin had had enough of the Great Lakes region. He threw off the frigid, snowy climes of the North for the balm of warm summer days and the relaxation of the hot springs of Arkansas. While in Hot Springs, Karpis met a recent parolee from Oklahoma State Penitentiary named Sam Coker, who maintained a close relationship with two known gangsters he had met on the inside, Volney Davis and Arthur "Doc" Barker. This crew consisting of Coker, Davis, Barker, and Karpis would form a gang of successful bandits that would operate with impunity for years to come.

The relentless J. Edgar Hoover was still dogging Karpis's trail and, like any old bloodhound, the director did a lot of baying before treeing his prey. By early that September Hoover learned too late that Karpis had holed up in Hot Springs. By then, Alvin had left for points north, where he scoffed at Hoover and his great proclamation that the close of the era of the train robber was at hand. Karpis's response to Hoover's declaration was to do the only thing a self-respecting thief could do... he robbed a train. This prompted ridicule from some highly placed statesmen, resulting in Hoover's becoming the object of a little "heat" himself. One politician of the day called Hoover nothing more than a "desk cop" who "never made an arrest in his life." That was the moment Hoover vowed that when his G-men cornered Karpis, he, personally, would be the one to make the arrest.

Karpis thought that Hoover's calling him a hoodlum was demeaning. After his arrest, Karpis told of an opportunity he once had to go to work for a Chicago syndicate as a machine-gunner, but he had turned down that position, saying he only killed when necessary and not for the joy of it. Karpis, oddly enough, never considered himself a violent man, even though in the six-year run of the Barker-Karpis gang ten men were killed in the commission of their other crimes. "I'm no hoodlum, and I don't like to be called a hood," Karpis told Hoover. "I'm a thief," he added with righteous indignation.

The train robbery that Karpis and gang had executed was at Garrettsville, Ohio. Known participants in the heist were the ever-present Harry Campbell and Burrhead Keady, both Tulsa residents. Another T-Town boy, John Brock, a bartender by trade, probably fast-talked his way into a tryout with the gang and was given a chance to debut his talents. Evidently Brock contracted stage fright and failed to show up for the first act. Milton Lett, a native of Oklahoma City, and Sam Coker rounded out the gang. The job was a success, as the train came into Garrettsville on time but about $35,000 underweight.

Not satisfied, Karpis and the Barkers developed a lucrative sideline: kidnapping. In a span of one year the gang picked up $300,000 for the safe return of its hapless victims. The first, in 1933, was William A. Hamm of the Hamm Brewery, headquartered in St. Paul, Minnesota. Hamm was released after three days in captivity.[8] He told the FBI, the press, and anybody else who would listen that he was treated well, ate decent food, and, in all, felt the experience had left him none the worse for wear. In fact, he said upon his release that one of his captors helped him carefully from the car and told him, "[I]f there's anything we can do for you in the future, let us know." Authorities found that benevolence somewhat less than sincere, as the gang failed to provide Hamm with a forwarding address.

Karpis's second kidnap victim was Edward G. Bremer, an enormously wealthy Minneapolis banker.[9] He reappeared after a few days as had Hamm. Bremer was touched for a whopping $200,000, which his family paid.

Karpis and the Barkers proceeded to commit acts that reminded all that they were indeed worthy of their reputations as ruthless killers. In 1931, just two days after the armed robbery of a West Plains, Missouri, store, a car matching the description of the one used by Karpis and Freddie Barker was spotted by a suspicious county sheriff, C. R. Kelly. Sheriff Kelly sidled up to the car to get a better look, but what he got instead was a blast of deadly gunfire from Karpis and Barker. That same year the terrible two shot and killed Pocahontas, Arkansas, police chief Albert Manley Jackson, who died after receiving five rounds in the back.

A year later Karpis was involved with two of the Barker boys and four others in the robbery of Minneapolis's Third Northwestern Bank where they realized a take-home pay amount of $112,000. To get it, they gunned down two police officers and wounded a passerby, with no apparent regard for the innocent or the unarmed. In 1933 Karpis, aided by some of the participants in the Northwestern gig, raided the bank in Fairbury, Nebraska, where they successfully got $151,350. In the process, the bank president and a bank guard were wounded, but they wounded one of the holdup men during an exchange of gunfire.

Karpis was either responsible for, or knowledgeable of, other homicides as well. Gang member Fred Goetz, who had been with the outfit for at least two years, was murdered after a vote of "no confidence." Fearing the authorities might be able to hone in on their trail by identifying the corpse, they took the precaution of repeatedly firing shotguns into the dead man's face so as to make it unidentifiable.

Another acquaintance of Karpis and the Barkers, underworld contact William Harrison, was lured to a barn near Ontarioville, Illinois, where he was shot for being a suspected stool pigeon. The body was then doused in gasoline and ignited, and once on fire it set the barn ablaze. No useful explanation exists for that particular event unless it was to snuff out any sign of their whereabouts. Ironically, the deed probably served more as a clue than anything else.

These were the types of crimes that commonly impassioned law enforcement to kill rather than capture notorious gangsters. By 1935, the ranks of Karpis's close friends were rapidly diminishing by death or imprisonment. Ma Barker and her "favorite boy," Freddie, were riddled with bullets during an FBI raid at their Florida cottage. Baby Face Nelson was killed during a chance encounter with some of Hoover's Oklahoma-based G-men on a lonely county road. Alvin Karpis, who had cajoled, conned, schemed, bitten, and battled his way to prominence, became, in law enforcement parlance, "the last man standing." With every other major crime figure behind bars or buried, Karpis rose to the highest spot on a list of self-made celebrities. By 1935, the same year Ma Barker and Freddie Barker's names were crossed off J. Edgar Hoover's list with machine guns, Alvin Karpis was named Public Enemy Number One. ·

Hoover had promised the nation that he would wipe out gangster activity, and in fact he had accomplished a rather thorough job of it. By 1935, most all the larger-than-life figures were no longer considered threats, and only one man remained to be a reminder to the director that the promise had not been fulfilled. Both public and private scrutiny was increasing.

A Tennessee senator, Kenneth McKellar, ridiculed Hoover for not having made any significant arrests personally. Hoover was then at a point where he was convinced that the best end to this cops and robbers undertaking was to take out Karpis in a very public grandstanding of good versus evil. Hoover stipulated that a key factor had to be that he be present at the end. Hoover had no compunction about expressing hatred for Karpis, probably brought on by Karpis's dismissive, go-to-hell attitude toward the nation's Top Cop.

Following the Garrettsville train robbery in November of 1935, which gave the boys a payday of $35,000, the gang split up. Karpis eventually found comfortable surroundings in New Orleans, where he lived in relative anonymity and peace for about a year, all the while sharing the wealth of his exploits with local diners, clubs, and a host of entertainment enterprises. On one fine day in 1936, that life of ease in The Big Easy came to an end.

Karpis had been living in a downtown apartment for some time. As not all criminals are known for their loyalty, it wasn't too long before the FBI got wind of where to find him. The agents quickly relayed the hot news to Hoover, who instructed his G-men to do nothing until he could get there. A contingent of twenty-eight agents reportedly kept watch on Karpis until the director arrived. Hoover flew to New Orleans as soon as he got word of Karpis's imminent capture. With Hoover in the commander's seat on the scene, he ordered his men to storm the building, killing any and all inside the Karpis apartment. Instead of pulling off an incredibly showy arrest replete with charging G-men, smoke, and gunfire in a firestorm of righteousness, Karpis was taken without a single shot fired.

He was spotted leaving the building on his way out for the day with no particular chore in mind. Karpis had no idea the FBI had him under surveillance with apparent plans to execute him inside his own home when he strolled to his 1936 Plymouth coupe. Realizing they couldn't open fire while their prey was on a busy street, the federal agents instead frantically scrambled to their government vehicles and sped with much clamor to Karpis's coupe, still sitting idle.

There are two versions of Karpis's capture. One was the official version distributed by the FBI at that time. In that version, "The FBI Story: A Report to the People," Hoover indeed single-handedly made the historic arrest of the last Public Enemy Number One. "Hoover ran to one side of Karpis' car immediately after he had entered it and reached into the car and grabbed Karpis before he could reach for a rifle on the back seat." A second, and even a third, version from two independent sources differ just enough to render Hoover's "official version" doubtful. Hoover was present for the arrest but not nearly as active in it as the "official version" portrayed.

Karpis later told interviewers that he noticed someone peering around the corner of a building as the officers rushed his car. He said that when the agents had completely surrounded him, one of them called out to the secreted figure, saying, "Come on Chief! We got him! You can come out now."[10]

According to historian Patterson Smith in *Literature of the American Gangster*, Hoover rushed up to the captured Karpis, who was completely surrounded by lawman, and commanded his men to "put the cuffs on him." But because nobody had thought to bring handcuffs, they were reduced to borrowing one agent's necktie and using it to bind the hands of the latest Public Enemy Number One.[11]

Even though the arrest of Karpis secured Hoover's reputation, the details were nonetheless in dispute. Karpis was fond of giving himself credit for Hoover's newfound celebrity by saying, "I made that son of a bitch."

One especially glaring detail Hoover chose to include in the events of his alleged arrest of Karpis was that he was able to keep Karpis from reaching into the back seat of his 1936 Plymouth coupe, thus preventing him from grabbing a rifle stashed there. Nice work, but it so happens that a 1936 Plymouth coupe had no back seat. Regardless of how it went down it was a sufficient piece of police work as police work went in the 1930s, and it certainly served to end Karpis's long-running career. He later wrote, "My profession was robbing banks, knocking off payrolls and kidnapping rich men. I was good at it. Maybe the best in North America for five years, from 1931 to 1936."

Karpis received a life sentence on one of his kidnapping charges and was sentenced to serve his time at the recently opened super-prison located in San Francisco Bay: Alcatraz. He spent twenty-six years on The Rock before being transferred to a federal prison at McNeil Island in Washington in 1962. He spent seven years there and met a young inmate named Charles Manson who, some say, cajoled the aging gangster to teach him to play the guitar.

Karpis wrote a book on his experiences in prison. *On the Rock* was published in 1980, one year after his death by overdose in 1979 while living in Spain. Depending on who tells the story, Karpis (1) was poisoned by jealous cronies, (2) committed suicide, or (3) was introduced to prescription pills by a current girlfriend and mixed them with alcohol. Not previously having been exposed to such recipes, Karpis may have accidentally overdosed himself.[12] Reader's choice.

Chapter 14

Just Passing Through

Even before the Twin Territories joined together and became a state on November 16, 1907, Oklahoma hosted its share of gangsters, outlaws, and lawmen, sometimes for only a short while. Forces of good, such as the Three Guardsmen—Deputy U.S. Marshals Chris Madsen, Heck Thomas, and Bill Tilghman—and famed FBI agent Melvin Purvis, and purveyors of evil such as the likes of Deacon Jim "Killer" Miller and James Wesley Hardin spent significant time in what came to be known as the Sooner State. This chapter presents some of these men and others and their various connections with Oklahoma.

Wyatt Earp

Wyatt Earp was a frontier marshal whose name was enshrined on the altar of law and order long ago, as the leader of the men who did battle with the cowboys at the OK Corral in Tombstone, Arizona. Although few knew it, he had a somewhat sullied past before gaining fame and an indelible place in history as a lawman. He was born Wyatt Berry Sharp Earp on March 19, 1848. Wyatt had a hankering for law enforcement, and in 1870 he narrowly defeated his half-brother Newton Earp and was elected constable of Lamar, Missouri. Wyatt soon married a Miss Sutherland, who after only three and half months died, presumably of typhoid.

The despondent Wyatt sulked about for a while before feuding with his dead wife's two brothers, Fred and Bert Sutherland. Wyatt wasn't alone, however, as he enlisted the help of his brothers, James, Morgan, and Virgil, to deal with the Sutherlands. Reinforced by the Brummet brothers, Ganville, Lloyd, and Garden, the Sutherlands commenced a "20-minute street fight" with the Earps.

History does little to explain any reason for the altercation and even whether the fight involved guns or what the outcome was. It is known that shortly after going head to head with the Sutherlands, et al., the Earp brothers left Missouri and made for Kansas.[1]

Wyatt then wandered the Kansas prairies hunting the seemingly endless supply of buffalo. At some point, he hooked up with two men, Edward Kennedy and another flatland wanderer whose name is lost to history. These three allegedly set about the prairies in search of an easier prey—horses—anybody's horses.

Eventually federal officers corralled the accused rustlers in Indian Territory and jailed them until bond was set. Earp came up with the $500 needed to post bond and was released. He immediately lit out of Indian Territory back into Kansas. There he apparently lived the life of a law-abiding citizen, turned serious about returning to a career in law enforcement, and became one of the most famous lawmen of the Old West.[2]

Wild Bill Hickok

James Butler Hickok wasn't called "Wild Bill" until he was nearly forty years old, just after the Civil War started. The year was 1861, and Hickok was employed by the Union Army, serving under Gen. Samuel P. Curtis. It is said that he backed down a lynch mob in Missouri. A woman spectator to the event called out, "Good for you, Wild Bill," and the name stuck, or so the legend goes.

During his tenure as scout and spy for the Union Army, Hickok led a troop of soldiers into what is now Texas County in the Oklahoma Panhandle. However, a raging snowstorm developed, and the famous scout, along with the cavalry, got hopelessly lost until the weather cleared.

A legend in his own life, Hickok was murdered by Jack McCall on August 2, 1876, at Deadwood, in Dakota Territory. A drifter, McCall had allegedly lost $110 to Hickok in a poker game the day before. Hickok was inside Saloon No. 10 seated at a poker table, when McCall walked up behind him and shot him in the back of the head. Another scenario was that local enemies of Wild Bill hired McCall for $200 to kill him. Either way, the once renowned buffalo hunter, army scout, performer, gambler, and lawman, died a pauper. An auction of his personal belongings was conducted to offset funeral expenses.[3]

James P. Masterson
You Know His Brother, Bat

Like Hickok, James P. Masterson was an Illinois native who migrated to the Southwest. The youngest of three brothers, his best-known sibling was William "Bat" Masterson. James followed his older brothers to Dodge City, Kansas, where he became a policeman and later joined the Ford County Sheriff's Office as a deputy.

James Masterson participated in the Oklahoma Land Run of 1889, and became one of the first white settlers of Guthrie. In 1893, he was appointed deputy with the U.S. Marshals Service. He spent many years pursuing many of Oklahoma's bad men and was present at Ingalls during the raid on the Doolin gang in 1893. Two years after that historic gun battle, James Masterson was dead of what was called "galloping consumption." He died in Guthrie on March 31, 1895, at around forty years of age.[4]

John Wesley Hardin

He was born at Bonham, Texas, on May 26, 1853, to a Methodist circuit preacher who named him John Wesley, fully expecting the boy to follow in his father's footsteps and become a minister. Hardin the elder was to be badly disappointed. Wesley's father might have done well to take notice of his son's tendency toward violence. Young Wesley could be often observed honing his marksmanship by shooting at effigies of President Abraham Lincoln during the Civil War.[5]

By age eleven, John Wesley, known more by his middle name, had already stabbed a fellow youth several times in the chest and back during a fight. The victim lived, but Wesley showed no signs of slowing down his killer instincts. By fifteen, Wesley shot and killed a former slave who refused to give him right of way on a road where the two men met.

During Reconstruction, three bluecoats came to arrest Hardin for killing a freedman. Hardin got word of the impending arrest and lay in wait for them at a creek. When the soldiers started to cross, Hardin fired a shotgun at them, killing two. Then Hardin shot and killed the third soldier with his pistol.

Since it was carpetbaggers and soldiers who held political sway over Texas at the time of these killings, most Texans saw no crime in killing either of the likes of them. Most citizens were, after all, Southern sympathizers, who just four years earlier had lost a terribly bitter, costly war. Some of those sympathizers hid the bodies while Hardin made good his escape.[6] Perhaps Hardin believed he was merely continuing the fight against Northern aggression, as had Missouri guerrillas such as the James-Younger gang, who branched into bank and train robbery after the Civil War.

Hardin was educated until he was fifteen, and came from a family with deep Texas roots. Kountze, Texas, along present-day State Highway 69, is in Hardin County, which is named for Judge William B. Hardin, a presumed relative of Wes's. Supposedly, another of his relatives fought at the battle of San Jacinto and yet another signed the Texas Declaration of Independence.[7]

This was not the typical background for such a violent young man. After all, Hardin went to his grave having been involved in nineteen *reported* scrapes, most ending with someone losing the conflict to the quick draw and deadly aim for which he was noted. Most of Hardin's killings occurred in Texas, and involved everyone from disgruntled gamblers to policemen and deputies attempting to serve arrest warrants for his past crimes.

He even killed a grifter who thought to rob him with the help of a young woman. Hardin, then about eighteen, was traveling through Kosse, Texas, in January of 1870, as the story goes, when he met a girl whose charms were irresistible. She apparently led the eager lad to a barn with a kiss and a promise. Once inside the darkened barn, Hardin found the lass was not an intended paramour at all but half of a strong-armed robbery duo. The femme fatale's boyfriend suddenly appeared, and he had the drop on Hardin. A demand to hand over all his money was obeyed, but Hardin had a trick up his own sleeve. As he produced a wad of bills in his outstretched hand, he "accidentally" dropped some of it on the barn's floor. Obviously fatally inexperienced, the gunman stooped to pick up the fallen cash. Once he did so, Hardin smoothly drew his own six-gun and neatly placed a single round between the bandit's eyes. Hardin then picked up the cash, mounted his steed, and galloped into the night.[8]

Although he had killed five people between 1868 and 1870, Hardin nevertheless remained a free man until January 1871, when he was captured by two Texas peace officers. While waiting in the Marshall, Texas, jail for transfer to Waco, Hardin somehow obtained a pistol. As one of the lawmen went to feed their horses, Hardin shot the remaining guard and escaped. Soon he was captured at his parents' place, but while at a camp one evening Hardin blasted his way free, this time with a shotgun, killing one man.

Hardin then made for Mexico, but ran into some "shirt-tail" relatives near Gonzales, Texas. The Clements bunch discouraged their murderous cousin from heading to virtual freedom south of the border: They urged him to join them in a cattle drive into Kansas. That enterprise, they said, would take Wesley out of Texas long enough for his troubles to "die down." Unfortunately for Hardin, his cousins were dead wrong.

Driving the herd north from Texas along the Chisholm Trail into Kansas, the cowboys entered Indian Territory. Before the crew had a chance to enjoy the scenery, Hardin shot and killed two Indians who were supposedly attempting to impose a ten-cent-per-head tax on the bovines.[9] Abetted by his cousin Jim Clements, he would kill six more men up the road from the spot where he slew the Indian "tax" collectors.

A second herd came up the Chisholm Trail, according to one source, as did Hardin and the Clements party, and as they attempted to push through, the two herds became one. During subsequent attempts to unscramble the two brands, some of the cowboys became frustrated.

Words were exchanged between Hardin and the trail boss of the other herd, and a duel was agreed on. Hardin, however, didn't expect the gunfight to involve the small posse of cowboys his opponent brought with him. Hardin had with him only Cousin Jim. Everybody met at the agreed place at a bend along the Arkansas River. When Hardin and Clements realized they were outnumbered three to one, they simply leaned forward in the saddle, gave a wild hoop and holler, and charged the six challengers. When the smoke cleared Wes and Jim looked around and saw that they were the only survivors. From this battle Hardin would take the nickname "Little Arkansas."

Hardin would go on to kill six more times in Texas, twice more in Kansas, and once in Florida before an assassin's bullet tore through the back of his head in a saloon in El Paso on August 19, 1895, forever silencing the quick-tempered killer, who had become of all things, a lawyer.

Hardin was shooting dice in the Acme Saloon with H. S. Brown, while his back was to the door. At around 11:00 p.m., John Selman Sr. entered the saloon and walked up behind him. Selman pulled a pistol and without a word placed it point blank at the back of Hardin's head and fired once.

Hardin was said to have told Brown seconds before a bullet crashed through his skull, "You have four sixes to beat."[10] Hardin was dead before he hit the floor, but the assailant walked around the corpse and fired twice more. One bullet hit Hardin in the arm; the other pierced his chest on the right side.[11]

Lawman and veteran gunfighter John Selman Sr. was said to have had words with Hardin earlier in the day. At that time Hardin allegedly threatened to kill Selman's son, John Jr.[12] Instead, John Wesley Hardin was dead at the age of forty-two.

Tom Horn
A Job to Die For

Tom Horn was born on November 21, 1860, in Memphis, Missouri. He died in Cheyenne, Wyoming, nearly forty-three years later, almost to the day, on November 20, 1903.

After leaving school at the age of fourteen, Horn held a number of jobs, most of which were on the right side of the law. One of the first jobs Horn took once he arrived in Newton, Kansas, was as a railroad employee. According to Bill O'Neal in his book, *Encyclopedia of Western Gunfighters,* Horn's career path was a mixed bag, but usually didn't involve anything illegal until 1894, when he became a paid assassin for the Swan Land and Cattle Company.

He was once a freight man, driving wagons up the Santa Fe Trail. Later he worked as a cowboy, teamster, army scout, law officer, miner, Pinkerton detective, cattle company range detective, and soldier. Altogether wholesome and worthwhile pursuits, none of those jobs were necessarily the Job to Die For. None, that is, but the last job, a professional endeavor that he held for a good many years, but one that would see him hanged.

In 1890, while working as a Pinkerton detective, Horn, accompanied by a fellow detective, C. W. "Doc" Shores, was hot on the trail of a pair of train robbers thought to be headed toward Indian Territory from Colorado. Shores was also sheriff of Gunnison County. The pursued pair committed a train robbery the last day of August. The suspects, Thomas Eskridge—alias Peg Leg Watson, alias McCoy—and Burt "Red" Curtis, were reputedly former members of Butch Cassidy's Wild Bunch.

The hunt for the desperadoes took the detectives through the Rocky Mountains of Colorado, south through New Mexico, and into the Chickasaw Nation. Finally Horn and Shores caught up with the bandits at Pauls Valley, Indian Territory. There Peg Leg and Red were apprehended without incident. That put an end to their life as criminals for the time being, but it also was at about that same time that Horn tired of his work as a detective with the famous agency.

His next employment, in 1894, would be with the Swan Land and Cattle Company out of Wyoming. Horn's employers listed him as a horse breaker. Even so, though Horn did spend a little time atop the backs of some bucking broncos, he was really a hired gun.

When Horn was not breaking horses he was breaking the spirit of varmints such as rustlers, or worse, those pesky homesteaders. The cattle company execs would identify potential or perceived nuisances, and sic Tom Horn on them. He apparently took great pride in his work. Once he garnered all the necessary information, Horn would ambush his troublesome victim.

Horn apparently thought of himself as a real pro, and wanted everyone else to recognize his work by laying the body out straight and then placing the dead man's head on two stones.[13] No other traces were left behind. He even carried all empty cartridges from the scene. Neatness counted even then.

Sometime in 1901, Horn found employment with a Wyoming rancher named John Coble, who maintained a large spread north of Laramie. Soon he fell in love with a local schoolteacher named Glendolene Kimmel. Nearby, a bunch of pesky homesteaders was becoming bothersome to the schoolteacher's family. The Kels P. Nickell family might have simply remained an annoying thorn in the side of the Kimmels if the nesters hadn't irritated Horn's employer as well. When the head of the family was earmarked by the powerful rancher for elimination, Horn got the job.

Somehow, instead of sniping Kels Nickell, Horn plugged his fourteen-year-old son by accident, killing him on the spot. The incident outraged the entire community, and Horn soon found himself behind bars awaiting his hanging. Despite one escape attempt, the pleadings of Miss Kimmel, and the lobbying of several large cattle operations, Horn was hanged on November 20, 1903, one day before his forty-third birthday.[14]

John Dillinger

John Dillinger's criminal career path probably didn't carry him into the Southwest very often. His Oklahoma connection comes in the curvaceous form of a Tulsa girl, a college aspirant turned Chicago chanteuse. Patricia Long was born in Arkansas to William Long and Goldie Jacquas on September 26, 1903. The Longs later lived in Chickasha and then in Tulsa where the proud parents hoped to enroll their daughter in college one day. Alas, during her terrible teen years, Patricia turned from scholar to romantic, became pregnant, and married Art Cherrington. With her collegiate career and marriage somewhat on hold, Patricia Cherrington left Tulsa and used her knowledge of poetry and musical talent to fetch a respectable salary performing in the many Prohibition-era speakeasies of Chicago. Throughout all this time, she maintained contact with her husband, Art, back in Tulsa.

Patricia was diagnosed with a seriously failing gall bladder at age thirty. With no medical insurance, she turned to the dandies and high rollers who frequented the clubs she sang in. One such dandy fell for her, and she instantly became the moll of one Harry Copeland, a member of the John Dillinger gang.[15]

After Copeland's arrest in 1933, Patricia set her sights on another of Dillinger's gang members, John "Red" Hamilton, who became her next sugar daddy and supported her through the lonely times without Harry. Brimming with affection, Patricia even managed to keep a romantic correspondence with her time-serving husband Art's cell mate, Welton Sparks, who had been a confederate of his.

She did all this and still continued to visit Copeland while he was doing time at Indiana State Prison at Michigan City. During one of these visitations to Copeland, John Dillinger wrote to her, informing her of the untimely death of Red Hamilton. Shortly after Hamilton's death, Patricia was thrown into jail. The authorities accused her of harboring Hamilton and the ever-elusive Dillinger at the Little Bohemia Lodge in Wisconsin, scene of the famed gunfight on Sunday, April 23, 1934.

With a lengthy prison sentence of her own and the death of Hamilton, Patricia's life as a gang moll was effectively over. After her release, she led a relatively uneventful life until her death of natural causes in 1949 at the age of forty-five. Her body was discovered in a room of a Chicago flophouse where she had quietly spent her remaining years.

Patricia Cherrington has been described as the quintessential moll. She was perky, vivacious, and a former chorus-line dancer who possessed all the skills necessary to become a hit with gangster desperadoes. She is remembered mostly for her quip about Dillinger after his death, "He was a good piece of company."[16]

Baby Face Nelson

He was born Lester Joseph Gillis on December 6, 1908, at 942 North California, in Chicago. He often used aliases to keep his identity hidden from the federal agents tracking him. One alias he used was Jimmy Williams. Another, which did little to hide his identity and in fact probably highlighted the gangster's bloody career, was the one that made history: George "Baby Face" Nelson.

Although Nelson was never reported to have been in Oklahoma, he had significant connections to the state. One such connection was a long-time Oklahoma gangster, Alvin Karpis, whom he met while chauffeuring noted Reno, Nevada, bootlegger Bill Graham in the fall of 1932. Karpis was the Tulsa gangster who at an early age was a member of that city's Central Park gang, through his association with Ma Barker and her brood of bandits.

Nelson died on November 27, 1934, after a running gun battle with FBI agents, which leads to his other, less amiable Oklahoma connection. Two of the agents involved in that gun battle were Inspector Samuel Cowley and Special Agent Herman Hollis, both of the Oklahoma City office of the FBI. Cowley and Hollis were both killed on that bloody day in November, but not before Cowley blasted Baby Face with a charge from his shotgun. Nelson died a few hours later. His corpse was discovered wrapped in a blanket and laid out in a corner of St. Paul's Cemetery near what was then Niles Center, now Skokie, Illinois.[17]

Al Capone

The man who terrorized Chicago and much of the Midwest for nearly a decade became the first major criminal to be sent to prison for tax evasion and one of the earliest inmates of Alcatraz. He also went a little nutty from the effects of an untreated venereal disease. During the summer of 1932, he also negotiated for a prize piece of Oklahoma real estate through a mob intermediary.

Al Capone was feared as one of the country's leading bad men. So far-reaching was his influence that unholy alliances were established among other crime factions in order to maintain a semblance of peace. The nation's first crime syndicate was the result, and its power was broad among punks and politicians alike.

Through this and other alliances Capone established a web of gambling houses, speakeasies, and illegal liquor distributorships over a wide section of the country. He likely dabbled in every other form of turpitude before his empire collapsed in 1931.

While serving an eleven-year prison sentence for tax evasion at an Atlanta facility—before being transferred to Alcatraz—Capone sought to purchase the legendary 101 Ranch near Ponca City, Oklahoma.[18] Fallen into disrepair, it had once been a reputable destination attracting celebrities from across the country. Capone sent his intermediary Louis "Diamond Jack" Alterie to do the bidding. The deal was never finalized.

Capone was paroled on November 16, 1939. He died at his palatial estate at Palm Island, Florida, on January 25, 1947, just eight days before his forty-eighth birthday.[19]

Profiles of Oklahoma Outlaws, Gangsters, and Lawmen 1839-1939

BY
LAURENCE YADON

Aliases, nicknames, and epithets have been inserted in parentheses after the names. In some entries, locations have been inserted to distinguish similar names. Where possible, approximate life dates have also been inserted in parentheses. Some entries are places or gun battles rather than personal names. All references are abbreviations of resources that can be found in the bibliography.

Harry Aurandt (d. 1921)

Secretary (modern term Administrative Sergeant) to the Tulsa Police and Fire Commissioner, Aurandt was mortally wounded in a 1921 gun battle with two suspects near the present-day intersection of Admiral and Delaware. Detective Ike Wilkinson, with whom Aurandt had been hunting for squirrel, was seriously injured but survived. The perpetrators, Alvin Fears and Tom Cook, received life sentences. During the course of the citywide search for the assailants, two innocent citizens were killed accidentally. Aurandt's son is radio commentator Paul Harvey.

Trekell, 58-59.

Harvey Bailey (1887-1979)

Felled by kidney failure on March 1, 1979, at Joplin, Missouri, after a dangerous life of crime, Bailey was born on August 23, 1887, to a Union veteran and his wife in West Virginia. The family moved to Green City, Missouri, in about 1900. Bailey's criminal life began in earnest in about 1918, when he began to run whiskey. During the Roaring Twenties, his partners reportedly included Oklahomans Frank "Jelly" Nash and Al Spencer. Other suspected Oklahoma associates included Fred Barker, Alvin Karpis, and George Barnes

(Machine Gun Kelly). Most of his bank robberies occurred in Minnesota, Iowa, Ohio, and Indiana. His body of work included theft of about $500,000 in bills from the Denver Mint (1922) (2005 value $15,175,703) and a one-million-dollar heist at the Lincoln National Bank, Lincoln, Nebraska. Released from prison in 1964, he returned to his father's occupation, cabinetry.

Kohn, 19.

Thurman Baldwin (Skeeter) (b. 1867)
Member of the Cook gang, Baldwin was captured in the fall of 1895, near Wichita Falls, Texas. Possibly from Ohio, he earned the moniker Skeeter from fighting off mosquitoes on ranches near Sapulpa and the Verdigris River.

Shirley, *Marauders,* 16, 32, 42-43, 64-66, 74, 77-78; Drago, 168.

Arizona Donnie Clark Barker (Ma, Kate, Arrie) (1872-1935)
Mother of four criminals and the protector of many others, Arrie was born near Springfield, Missouri. Married to George Barker of Lebanon, Missouri, in 1892, the couple resided in Aurora, then Webb City, Missouri, raising sons Herman, Lloyd, Fred, and Arthur (Doc or Dock), all of whom died by the gun.

Upset with the way Missouri law enforcement "messed with" her boys, she moved the entire family to Tulsa in 1910. Fred, Lloyd, and Herman immediately helped found the East Side gang, specializing in house burglary, which by 1918 became the Central Park gang, with world headquarters at the Sixth and Peoria green space for which the organization was named. The Barkers and some twenty associates, half of whom reportedly died violently, branched into car theft, strongarm robbery, and murder, with Arrie providing moral support, perhaps innocently. Along the way husband George Barker returned to Missouri and was replaced, romantically if not legally, by Tulsan Arthur V. Dunlop. Through the ensuing years, which saw the formation of the Gang of Eight (Terrell-Barker-Inman gang), Arrie played a nurturing role, without necessarily knowing the details of the crimes her sons committed.

Herman died in 1927 after a robbery gone wrong. Young Fred

picked up the banner and, with Alvin "Creepy" Karpis, moved the gang into the big time, forming the Barker-Karpis gang in 1931. Following the killing of Arthur Dunlop for discussing gang activities—with Arrie's apparent concurrence—Fred, Alvin, and associates perpetrated two of the most notorious kidnappings in American history, holding two Minnesota capitalists for ransoms totaling $300,000.

Hiding at Lake Weir, Florida, Arrie and Fred were killed by the FBI on January 16, 1935. Whether Arrie was an active member of her sons' various gangs is still a subject of much debate. While Alvin Karpis and other gang members were insistent that her criminal contributions were minimal, the criminologists perhaps will decide some day whether the lethal tendencies of the Barker boys were due to nature or nurture.

Kohn, 22-23; Winter, 1-6, 78.

Arthur Barker (Doc or Dock) (1899-1939)

Born in 1899 in Aurora, Missouri, Doc came to Tulsa with his family in 1915, and worked in 1917 as a glassblower. He stole a federal vehicle in 1918, while working as a common laborer. Convicted of bank robbery, he was released from prison in June 1921. In 1922 he was convicted of murdering a guard at St. Johns hospital, then under construction, with Volney Davis. In 1932 he was paroled from Leavenworth from a conviction for robbing the Third Northwest Bank of Minneapolis, in which two guards and a bystander were killed.

A participant in the 1933 kidnapping of St. Paul brewer William Hamm ($100,000 ransom), in 1934 he was involved in the kidnapping of St. Paul banker Edward Bremer ($200,000 ransom) and killed plastic surgeon Joseph P. Moran of Toledo, Ohio. Convicted in the Bremer kidnapping in 1935, he died attempting to escape from Alcatraz in 1939.

Winter, 2, 7, 19-28; Poulsen, 171, 174, 198, 255, 258, 374, 375.

Fred Barker (Freddie) (1902-35)

Fred launched the family into national notoriety with two high-profile kidnappings, those of beer magnate William A. Hamm in 1933 and Edward Bremer in 1934. Fame has its price, which Fred perhaps learned by experience when he and Arrie "Ma" Barker were mortally ventilated in a bloody but necessary FBI assault on January 16, 1935, in sunny Florida.

Kohn, 23; Winter, 2, 6, 34-37, 50, 54, 61, 78, 106, 111.

Herman Barker (1893-1927)

Born on October 30, 1893, in Missouri, Herman was instrumental in the formation of Tulsa's East Side gang and its successor, the Central Park gang. Regrettably for Arrie, his operational skills were less developed. He committed suicide while being pursued by police at Wichita, Kansas, on August 29, 1927, following the botched robbery of an ice plant in nearby Newton, Kansas.

Kohn 23; Winter 49, 53, 61, 73-76, 81, 91-95.

Barker-Karpis Gang (prom. 1930s)

During 1931-35, the Barker-Karpis gang reputedly consisted of Fred Barker, Doc Barker, Alvin Karpis, Harvey Bailey, and others. Karpis and Freddie Barker were the core of the gang, which was planned when both were in the Kansas State Prison.

Selected Robberies and Gunfights

Mountain View, Missouri, October 7, 1931
Fred Barker, Alvin Karpis, and Bill Weaver were suspected of robbing the Peoples Bank. Amount taken unknown.

West Plains, Missouri, December 19, 1931
Two days after a clothing store robbery in West Plains, Fred Barker, accompanied by Alvin Karpis, killed Sheriff C. Roy Kelly in a commercial garage.

St. Paul, Minnesota, 1932
Fred Barker, Alvin Karpis, Arrie, and her love interest, Tulsan Art Dunlop, lived on South Robert Street, St. Paul, Minnesota. A police raid apparently prompted the execution of Dunlop, who was suspected

of verbal indiscretions about the gang. Other residents from time to time included Frank "Jelly" Nash, Verne Miller, and Harvey Bailey.

Youngs' Orchard, near Brookline, Missouri, January 2, 1932

In this, the single most deadly incident of officers killed in U.S. history to that date, Greene County sheriff Marcel Hendrix and others arrived to arrest Harry and Jennings Young. The sheriff, two deputies, and three Springfield police officers were surprised and killed, with two others wounded. The brothers were trapped three days later in Houston and committed suicide. Fred Barker and Alvin Karpis were spotted by law enforcement officials on the outskirts of Springfield on New Years Day, and suspected of participating in the shoot-out because of the volume of outlaw fire.

Fort Scott, Kansas, June 17, 1932

The gang was suspected of a bank robbery.

St. Paul, Minnesota, June 15, 1933

Beer magnate William A. Hamm Jr. was kidnapped by the Barker-Karpis gang, then consisting of Dock and Fred Barker, Alvin Karpis, and others, who extracted $100,000. Tulsans Harry Campbell and Volney Davis later joined the group.

Union Station, Kansas City, Missouri, June 17, 1933

Barker gang associate Frank "Jelly" Nash, three police officers, including Otto Reed, police chief of McAlester, Oklahoma, and an FBI agent, were killed by three assailants. The FBI identified Verne Miller and Oklahomans Charles Arthur Floyd, and Adam Richetti as the perpetrators. All three died violently, but only Richetti was convicted of the crime and executed on October 7, 1938.

St. Paul, Minnesota, January 17, 1934

The Barker-Karpis gang kidnapped businessman Edward G. Bremer and released him for the paltry sum of $200,000.

Perrin, "Trail of Slain Officers"; Edge, 20, 22, 158, 187-88, 195-96, 218-19; Burrough, 488.

Lloyd Barker (1896-1949)

Less notorious than his brothers, Lloyd initiated his career in Tulsa around 1910, as a founder of the East Side gang, later known as the Central Park gang. He was first arrested for vagrancy, then used as a general purpose charge against criminal suspects. Participating in a 1922 mail robbery near Baxter Springs, Kansas, on the Oklahoma border with fellow Tulsan Will Green, he found asylum at Leavenworth Prison, from which he was released in 1945. He married and moved to Colorado. There, while serving as assistant manager of a snack shop, he was gunned down by his wife in 1949 for reasons unknown.

Kohn, 23.

George Barnes (Machine Gun Kelly) (1900-1954)

Born in Chicago in 1900, George moved with his family to Memphis, Tennessee, where his father was an insurance executive. He attended Mississippi A& M, married a wealthy debutante, and tried a number of legitimate businesses, including goat farming, before turning to a life of crime. In the 1920s he was involved in bootlegging operations in Oklahoma and other states, drawing a 1927 liquor arrest in New Mexico and a vagrancy arrest in Tulsa. Arrested for liquor sales in the Osage Nation, he was sentenced to three years at Leavenworth, where he met Frank "Jelly" Nash of Kansas City Massacre fame.

His associates included Harvey Bailey and Wilbur Underhill, who escaped on May 30, 1933, from the Kansas State Prison at Lansing and regrouped in the Cookson Hills. They allegedly conducted several bank robberies. Barnes masterminded the first nationally prominent kidnapping since the Lindbergh tragedy, the July 22, 1933, abduction of oil magnate Charles F. Urschel in Oklahoma City.

The once famous plea "Don't Shoot, G-men" was attributed to Barnes (or his wife). George died of a heart attack in prison in 1954, and his wife, who worked in an Oklahoma hospital, died in 1958. The federal judge in the Urschel kidnapping trial paid for the college education of Kelly's stepdaughter and was reimbursed by the kidnapping victim.

Hamilton, *Machine Gun Kelly's Last Stand,* 68-179; Burrough, 545.

Blanche Caldwell Barrow (1911-88)

Born on January 1, 1911, at Garvin, Oklahoma, to Matthew and Lillian Fountain, Blanche married Marvin Ivan "Buck" Barrow in 1931 at America, Oklahoma, and died on December 24, 1988, at Tyler, Texas. Her biography, published in 2004, states that she and Buck met Bonnie and Clyde "in Oklahoma" on March 29, 1933. However, her active life of crime with the Barrows was apparently founded on June 13, 1933, at a Joplin, Missouri, shoot-out in which two law officers were killed. She also claimed that in June 1933, the Barrows and Bonnie traveled to the Floyd farm in Sallisaw, in a futile effort to team up with Charles Arthur Floyd. During her last illness, Blanche refused to see her ninety-three-year-old mother, who later attended her funeral anyway.

Barrow, 33-34, 40, 73, 195, 214, 261.

Clyde Chestnut Barrow (1909-34)

Born on March 24, 1909, Clyde was first arrested for turkey rustling in Dallas at Christmastime. Big brother Buck helpfully claimed Clyde "didn't know the turkeys were stolen." Clyde Barrow, Bonnie Parker, and Oklahoman Raymond Hamilton were involved in the shooting of two officers at Stringtown, Oklahoma, on August 5, 1932; Deputy E. C. Moore was killed when the officers challenged gang members for drinking moonshine at an open-air dance. About October 12 of that year, the gang again crossed the Red River to engage in a series of Oklahoma robberies. They reportedly stole a physician's bag and car at Enid, on June 24, 1933, returning two days later to rob an armory then located at what would become Phillips University.

Their work required frequent commutes through Oklahoma. On April 5, 1934, they engaged in a gunfight with authorities at Commerce, resulting in the death of Constable Cal Campbell. Five days later, Clyde, or someone using his name, mailed an endorsement of the Ford V-8, his favorite car, to Henry Ford from the Tulsa post office. On May 23, 1934, Bonnie and Clyde were killed in Louisiana.

Milner, 60-160.

Marvin Ivan Barrow (Buck) (1905-33)

Born on March 14, 1905, at Jones Prairie, Texas, Buck married Margaret Heneger and was eventually convicted of theft and sentenced to a five-year prison term. He walked away from a work detail to freedom and married Blanche Caldwell on July 3, 1930, at America, Oklahoma. She soon convinced him to surrender. When he was paroled in 1933, Buck, Blanche, Bonnie, and Clyde rented an apartment at 3347½ 34th Street in Joplin, soon drawing the suspicion of local authorities. A shoot-out at the residence on April (or June) 13 left two law officers dead.

Following forays into Enid on June 24 and Oklahoma City on June 26, Buck and the others arrived at the less-than-luxurious Red Crown Tourist Court in Platte City, Missouri, on July 18, drawing local authorities like moths to a flame. The ensuing shoot-out left Buck mortally wounded, and he died on July 29, 1933, in a Perry, Iowa, hospital.

Steele, *Bonnie and Clyde,* 29, 33, 46, 104, 108, 114.

Sam Bass (1851-78)

This Texas gunman founded his criminal career at Fort Sill by seizing a herd of horses he "won" from a Native American. He was born near Mitchell, Indiana, on July 21, 1851, one of seven children. Orphaned young, he moved west and joined the Collins gang operating in the Black Hills of South Dakota about 1876.

Selected Robberies and Gunfights

South Dakota, March 25, 1877
The gang robbed the Cheyenne and Black Hills stage, killing driver John Slaughter.

Round Rock, Texas, July 20, 1878
Bass and three gang members cased out the local bank, not knowing that associate Jim Murphy had made "arrangements" with local authorities. A gunfight erupted when Deputy Sheriffs Grimes and Moore attempted to arrest Seaborn Barnes, who fatally wounded

Grimes. Bass was mortally wounded in the ensuing battle and died on Sunday, July 21, 1878.

O'Neal, 35.

George Birdwell (1894-1932)

Born on February 19, 1894, in Texas, Birdwell partnered with Charles Arthur Floyd for about two years in the bank robbing business. Early in life, he worked with his honest father James Birdwell in ranching and farming operations. However, by 1913 he was apparently on the wayward trail. He was accused of philandering with the wife of a local farmer, but dodged an untimely end at the hands of the unhappy husband.

Birdwell met Floyd when both were oil field workers in the Earlsboro field of Pottawatomie County. He married and became responsible for a family that eventually grew to eleven, just in time for the Depression. Seeking resources nearby, Floyd and Birdwell robbed the Bank of Earlsboro on March 9, 1931, taking $3,000. Later robberies that year included The Citizens Bank of Shamrock ($300), The Morris State Bank ($743), and First National Bank of Maud ($3,850).

He reportedly attended his father's funeral in Earlsboro, on October 15, 1931, in the company of Floyd and a hostage, Pottawatomie County Deputy Sheriff Franks.

Unlike Floyd, who favored cities and towns such as Kansas City, Tulsa, and Fort Smith between jobs, Birdwell stayed close to home in the Seminole area. On November 23, 1932, accompanied by accomplices C. C. Patterson and Charley Glass, he attempted to rob the Bank of Boley and was killed, along with bank president D. J. Turner.

Butler, "George Birdwell"; Wallis, *Pretty Boy,* 221-25, 251, 283-87.

William Blake (Tulsa Jack) (ca. 1862-95)

Thought to be from Kansas, Blake joined the Doolin gang after working as a cowboy. He was killed on April 4, 1895, in Major County, Oklahoma Territory, by Deputy U.S. Marshals Banks, Prather, and others. Bill Tilghman stated that Blake earned his moniker by being well known in Tulsa gambling dens.

Shirley, *Guardian of the Law,* 204.

Richard L. Broadwell (Texas Jack) (d. 1892)

A Dalton gang member, Broadwell was also known as John Moore and "Jack of Diamonds" for continuously singing that tune. Reputedly robbed and dumped by his betrothed, he turned to robbery as a consequence. He was killed by citizens in the Coffeyville Raid on October 5, 1892.

Shirley, *Daltons,* 50.

Henry Brown (1857-84)

Reportedly born near Rolla, Missouri, Henry moved west early and served with Billy the Kid as a Regulator during the Lincoln County War. According to some, he drove a wagon out of Vinita, Indian Territory, for a period of time. Later he became a Kansas lawman with a strong side interest in robbing banks, ultimately being shot to pieces trying to escape a lynch party at Medicine Lodge, Kansas, on April 30, 1884.

O'Neal, 48.

William Bruner (Billy) (1862-1952)

Bruner was the Tulsa-area bandito who shattered Grat Dalton's arm on or about March 15, 1889, during a gunfight at present-day Berryhill in Tulsa County. Lawman William Moody was also fatally shot in the chest. Bruner died on April 18, 1952, in Tulsa County.

Samuelson, *Dalton Gang Story,* 78.

Charles Bryant (Blackface Charlie) (d. 1891)

The pocked victim of a gunfight opponent's muzzle blast, Charlie reputedly participated in several Dalton raids. Following the "Battle of Twin Mounds" he checked into the Rock Island Hotel at Hennessey, Oklahoma, where Deputy U.S. Marshal Ed Short arrested him. Subsequently, they shot and killed each other on August 23, 1891, when Charlie made an escape attempt near Waukomis, some thirteen miles north of Hennessey. Short, an Indiana native, had been a deputy sheriff at Caldwell, Kansas, and city marshal at Woodsdale, Kansas, in prior years.

O'Neal, 53.

Ernest Burkhart (b. 1892)

A native of Greenville, Texas, and a taxi driver, Ernest pled guilty to the murder of W. E. Smith in an explosion at Smith's residence in Fairfax on March 10, 1923, at about 4:00 a.m. Also killed were Smith's wife Rita and Nettie Brookshire, a servant. Burkhart was paroled in 1926, later returned to prison, and died in Cleveland, Oklahoma.

Hogan, *Osage Indian Murders,* 267.

Cattle Annie and Little Britches

Two Oklahoma teenagers, Annie McDoulet (McDougal, ca. 1879), known in legend as Cattle Annie, and Jennie Stevenson (Stevens, ca. 1879), called "Little Britches," were long reputed to be associates of the Bill Doolin gang. While this makes good copy, there is little to suggest that the pair were involved in anything more than theft and bootlegging, although these offenses were enough to warrant jail time.

Standard works regularly recite that both were imprisoned in a Framingham, Massachusetts, institution, that Jennie "settled down," and that Annie ultimately died of consumption. Others claim that Annie died a grandmother in 1978 in Oklahoma City. Jennie is said by some to have died in Tulsa. However, according to one distinguished authority, Jennie Stevens Midkiff was last heard from in 1896 though some individuals, including the widow of Bill Tilghman, protected her anonymity in later years.

Samuelson, *Shoot from the Lip,* 115; O'Neal, 325.

Patricia Cherrington (1903-49)

Born Patricia Long on September 26, 1903, to an Arkansas farming family that migrated to Texas, then Chickasha, Oklahoma, she moved on to Tulsa. There she married in 1920, deserted her husband,

and moved to Chicago with a daughter in 1922. Following a dancing career, which may have been exotic, she became associated with the Dillinger gang through Dillinger's love interest Evelyn "Billy" Frechette. Cherrington was present during the Little Bohemia Lodge gun battle and was eventually convicted of harboring fugitives. She was released and died on May 3, 1949, in Chicago.

Poulsen, 8, 75, 405.

Ned Christie (1852-92)

Born on December 14, 1852, in Rabbit Trap Canyon near Tahlequah and well educated, Christie served as a member of the Cherokee national council and legislature, in spite of a penchant for occasionally overindulging in alcoholic beverages. Ned was taught the gunsmith trade by his father. The death at Tahlequah of Deputy U.S. Marshal Dan Maples was attributed to Ned, perhaps unfairly, with some claiming at the time, and even today, that one Bud Trainor actually killed Maples while Ned dozed in an alcoholic slumber nearby. Ned ultimately succumbed to lead poisoning during a shoot-out with authorities in which he held out until his self-constructed fort was set afire and he made a futile break for freedom on November 3, 1892.

Steele, *Last Cherokee Warrior,* 69-108; Speer, *Ned Christie,* 72-131.

Dan Clifton (Dynamite Dick) (d. 1897)

A Doolin gang stalwart, Dan Clifton escaped with Bill Doolin and twelve others from the Guthrie jail on July 5, 1896, only to be killed a little more than a year later near Checotah, Indian Territory. He initiated the "West-Clifton" gang with Little Dick West in September 1896, allegedly committing two robberies in October of that year. The first effort, at Carney, northwest of Chandler, was hardly successful, netting two pairs of shoes and $150. A more successful day was had at the Sac and Fox agency on October 27, 1896, where $500, two gold watches, and some promissory notes were collected. Regrettably for the new gang, $46,000 in tribal payments would have been available had the job been done a week earlier.

Apparently because of disappointing financial performance, the West-Clifton gang "merged" in June 1897 with the even less successful Al Jennings gang, the Titanic of Oklahoma criminal organizations. Dan was killed about ten miles west of Checotah by Deputy U.S. Marshals Lawson and Bussey.

Shirley, *Heck Thomas,* 244; Shirley, *Guardian of the Law,* 268.

Bill Coe (Captain Coe) (prom. 1860s)

An elusive figure who entered the Black Mesa area of Western Oklahoma during the Civil War years, Coe posted himself at Lookout Point in order to prey on Santa Fe travelers on the way west. Coe and his gang reportedly built a fort on Lookout Point called "Robbers Roost." Gang activity was initially hampered by the proximity of Fort Nichols, some twelve miles away in Colorado, but business expanded dramatically when that installation closed in 1865. Gang depredations continued until 1867 when soldiers from Fort Lyons used cannon to terminate the roost and hang those Coe associates unlucky enough to be available. Coe himself reportedly escaped to the west, only to be hanged impromptu, while awaiting trial in Pueblo, Colorado.

Smith, "Badmen in No Man's Land," 30-36; Farris, 15-25.

Charles Francis Colcord (1859-1934)

Colcord enjoyed a remarkably varied and colorful life, even by frontier standards, as a cowboy, policeman, county sheriff, deputy U.S. marshal, oilman, and large-scale real estate investor. Although an honest lawman, his early occupations in Kansas and Oklahoma gave him personal familiarity with notorious outlaws. (See **Wells, Frank.**)

He was born on August 18, 1859, near Paris, Kentucky, the son of a Civil War veteran who had raised a Confederate battalion. He moved with his family to Texas and later to Kansas in about 1877. While there and associated with the huge Comanche Pool ranching operation, he observed and later met Pat Garrett, Henry McCarty (Billy the Kid), McCarty associates Jim French, John Middleton, and others. Although not entirely free from doubt, an early draft of Colcord's memoirs still in existence strongly indicates that his sister, Maria "Birdie" Colcord, was briefly married to the outlaw John Middleton after the Lincoln County War.

Colcord joined the 1889 Oklahoma Land Run, and became a policeman under the provisional Oklahoma City government that year. After arresting notorious bad man Clyde Mattox, who had murdered the city marshal of South Oklahoma (City), and J. C. Adams, who had mortally wounded popular Mayor Couch, Colcord was appointed a deputy U.S. marshal. He then served as the first territorial sheriff of Oklahoma County from 1890 until 1893. Appointed by U.S. Marshal E. D. Nix as deputy in charge of the Fourth District, he supervised Frank N. Canton, Bill Tilghman, Wiley G. Haines, and other deputy U.S. marshals. Colcord worked with Bill Tilghman to maintain order in the notoriously dangerous Hell's Acre section of Wharton (now Perry), Oklahoma Territory.

Although never involved in a recorded gunfight, during his law enforcement career Colcord pursued Little Bill Raidler, Red Buck Weightman, Charley Pierce, and Bitter Creek Newcomb, all of whom he knew personally. Present on May 3, 1895, when the bodies of Bitter Creek Newcomb and Charley Pierce were brought in by the notorious Dunn brothers for reward money, Colcord observed what others perhaps chose to ignore: bullet holes in the soles of the bandits' feet, suggestingf that they had been shot while asleep and denied the chance to "die game." He also observed the shoot-out in which Frank Canton killed Bee Dunn on November 6, 1896.

Hardly missing a beat, Colcord became one of the most successful oilmen in Oklahoma at the closing of the frontier. Among other ventures, he participated in the Glenn Pool near Tulsa and other oil exploration with Charles Page, founder of Sand Springs. His real estate developments included many housing additions and the recently refurbished Colcord building in downtown Oklahoma City. Perhaps he was equally proud of his long association with the Oklahoma Historical Society, which he served as president. Colcord died in December 1934.

Colcord, 1, 146, 156, 170, 196, 198, 202, 225.

Peter Conser (Peter Coinson) (1852)

Born near Eagletown, and originally named Coinson, he became a deputy sheriff of Sugar Loaf County, and eventually joined the Choctaw Light Horse police.

Milligan, *Choctaw of Oklahoma*, 98.

William Tuttle Cook ("Bill") (1873-1900)

William Tuttle Cook was born on December 19, 1873, the son of a Union soldier of Southern origins. Bill grew up on the Grand River some four miles north of Fort Gibson and organized a horse theft ring that worked between Wagoner and Muskogee. His crime spree began in June 1894 and concluded on January 11, 1895. According to some historians, his associates included Crawford Goldsby (Cherokee Bill), Jim French, George Sanders, and the Verdigris Kid (Sam McWilliams). Some authorities include Thurman "Skeeter" Baldwin, Elmer "Chicken" Lewis, and even Henry Starr in the Cook crew.

He began in a shoot-out with the Cherokee Light Horse on June 4, 1894, about fifteen miles from Tahlequah on 14 Mile Creek, continued with a robbery of the Muskogee-Fort Gibson stage in the Arkansas River bottoms on July 14, a train robbery at Red Fork near Tulsa on July 16, a robbery of the Lincoln County Bank on July 31, and an attempted robbery of a Kansas City and Missouri Pacific train near Wagoner on October 20.

On October 22, 1894, Cook and three others attempted to rob the Arkansas Flyer at Watonga, but watched helplessly as the train rumbled safely by, covering the gang with dust. Cook concluded his criminal career symbolically enough with his capture at or near the place (and according to some the very house) where death met Billy the Kid, old Fort Sumner, New Mexico, on January 11, 1895. Upon his return to Fort Smith he was sentenced to forty-five years imprisonment at Albany, New York, and died in prison on February 7, 1900, of the prisoner's ailment, consumption. Thurman "Skeeter" Baldwin's sentence was commuted by Theodore Roosevelt in 1903, while Lucas, Dayson, Snyder, and Farris served their terms and left the Twin Territories for good.

Selected Robberies and Gunfights

Nowata Station, July 5, 1894
Goldsby and Munson robbed the Kansas-Arkansas Valley Railroad station, killing Al Richards.

Halfway House, between Tahlequah and Fort Gibson, July 17, 1894
Sequoyah Houston, a Light Horseman, was killed by Cook and Goldsby.

Bill Province house, near Sapulpa, August 2, 1894
Approximately fourteen miles west of Sapulpa, gang members Munson and Gordon were killed by a posse led by Creek Lighthorse and tracker Tiger Jim. Baldwin, Cook, and Goldsby escaped. Curtis Dayson was captured.

Near Fort Sumner, New Mexico, January 12, 1895
Cook was arrested by Sheriff C. C. Perry of Chaves County, New Mexico, and Sheriff Thomas D. Love of Burden County, Texas. Cook admitted only to the Red Fork job.

Shirley, *Marauders,* 1-8, 17, 21, 25-30, 32-33, 37-39, 42-44, 52-53, 73-75, 77-78, 82-94, 111-12, 151.

Mont Cookson (prom. 1920s)
A nephew of the pioneer for whom Oklahoma's Cookson Hills are named, Mont apparently participated in a 1922 bank robbery in Gore, Oklahoma, with others, but died peacefully in Tulsa in the 1950s.

Morgan, *Bandit Kings of the Cookson Hills,* 182.

Rev. Phillip W. Coughlan
Coughlan was a priest who allegedly scouted jobs for psychopathic Lester J. Gillis (Baby Face Nelson), voluntarily or otherwise. A longtime friend of Gillis's parents, he was persuaded by the Nelson gang to find refuge for Gillis after he was mortally wounded in a gunfight with Oklahoma-based FBI agents and others. Coughlan left Chicago on March 1, 1935, and reportedly resided at Holy Family Church, in Canute, Oklahoma, where he was served with a subpoena by the Federal Bureau of Investigation. He reportedly died in Oklahoma.

Poulsen, 408.

Roy Daugherty (Arkansas Tom Jones) (1870-1924)

Born in Missouri, Roy was a member of the Doolin gang who killed three lawmen during the Ingalls battle. Ultimately, he served a fifteen-year sentence, operated a restaurant briefly at Drumright, and then, following a brief movie career, was killed resisting arrest on bank robbery charges at Joplin, Missouri, while babysitting for friends, August 16, 1924.

O'Neal, 88.

Larry DeVol (Larry O'Keefe, Chopper) (d. 1936)

A Tulsa associate of Alvin Karpis of the Barker-Karpis gang, DeVol was incarcerated at Pauls Valley at a young age; upon release he began burglarizing homes in Kansas City and elsewhere. While incarcerated in Kansas, he taught safecracking to Alvin Karpis. He supposedly became known as "Chopper" for his willingness to use weapons in robberies, particularly against the police. He escaped from the Kansas State Prison in 1929.

DeVol and Karpis were captured in Kansas City in March 1930 and promptly jumped bail. Returning to Oklahoma, he was suspected in a double homicide on April 26, 1930, at the Severs Hotel in Muskogee. Incarcerated in the Muskogee jail, he escaped on August 1. DeVol killed Kirksville, Missouri, policeman John Rose on November 17, 1930. He then fled to Omaha, where he is said to have worked as an enforcer for local gangsters before joining the Barkers and Karpis in St. Paul, Minnesota.

Engaging in a series of bank robberies, he was captured and incarcerated in the Minnesota Hospital for the Insane. Escaping from captivity again, he was involved in gunfights resulting in the death of three policemen and was killed at Enid, Oklahoma, on July 8, 1936. During his last gunfight, DeVol killed Enid police officer Cal Palmer.

Morgan, "Severs Hotel Murder Mystery."

Dillinger Gang (prom. 1930s)

The story of John Dillinger (1903-34), perhaps the most famous of the Depression-era gangsters, has many Oklahoma connections.

Patricia Long Cherrington, who became associated with the gang in about 1933, grew up in Chickasha, then worked and married in Tulsa. Ed Hollis, Sam Cowley, Melvin Purvis, and Clarence Hurt all served as FBI agents in Oklahoma before participating in the pursuit and killing of Dillinger. Later, Clarence Hurt served two terms as sheriff of Pittsburg County, Oklahoma. He died in 1974.

Matera, *John Dillinger,* 367.

Bill Doolin (1858-96)

Doolin worked near Tulsa on the Turkey Track Ranch and was reportedly a semi-resident of that town. Born about 1858 in Johnson County, Arkansas, he was killed on August 24, 1896, near Lawton, Oklahoma, by Deputy U.S. Marshal Heck Thomas. His first criminal foray may have been a dispute with Coffeyville, Kansas, authorities regarding illegal beer sales on July 4, 1891, which turned into a shoot-out. One tale, perhaps mythical, states that Bill was saved from almost certain death at the Coffeyville disaster when his horse went lame and he fell behind the gang.

Following a train robbery at Dover, Oklahoma Territory, and his ultimate bathhouse arrest at Eureka Springs, Arkansas (which, according to some contemporaries and modern authorities, was arranged), he was killed on August 26, 1896, near Lawton, Oklahoma Territory. His gang members may have included Bill Dalton, Red Buck Weightman, Dan Clifton (Dynamite Dick), Little Dick West, Roy Daugherty (Arkansas Tom Jones), Little Bill Raidler, William Blake (Tulsa Jack), and Bitter Creek Newcomb. Occasional members included Alf Sohn, Bob Grounds, and Ben Howell.

An alternative, and improbable, version of his death has Heck Thomas firing a shotgun into the body of already-dead Bill, a victim of consumption, to help his widow collect part of the reward money. Adding to the controversy, Doolin's death also highlighted conflicts between the territory's better-known marshals. Both Tilghman and Canton were reportedly quite unhappy about losing a share of the $5,000 reward on Doolin's head.

Outlaw lore says that in 1893 Bill assisted Payne County sheriff Bob Andrews to arrest "Ragged Bill" and "Long Tom," who had stolen forty dollars from an elderly man.

Probable robberies involving Doolin include a Caney, Kansas, bank, on October 14, 1892; a Katy train; a Ford County, Kansas, bank (date uncertain); the Spearville, Kansas, bank, on November 1, 1892; a Santa Fe train at Cimarron, Kansas, on June 10, 1893; and the Farmer's and Citizen's Bank at Pawnee, Oklahoma Territory, on January 23, 1894.

Doolin led the May 10, 1894, raid on the Southwest City, Missouri, bank in which J. C. Seaborn, former Missouri State auditor, was mortally wounded. His favorite hideouts included the headwaters of Turkey Creek and the Cimarron River south of Yale in Payne County.

Shirley, *Heck Thomas,* 218; Shirley, *Guardian of the Law,* 268; Samuelson, *Shoot from the Lip,* 68; Hanes, 65, 107, 144; Smith, *Daltons,* 194.

Bluford Duck (Blue Duck) (1859-95)

Reputed but highly unlikely lover of Belle Starr, Blue Duck had his picture taken with Belle at Fort Smith, at his lawyer's request to promote a possible pardon. He grew up west of Oologah on Rogers Creek. On or about June 23, 1884, with one William Christie, he killed a young white farmer named Wyrick in the Flint District of the Cherokee Nation.

Arrested by Deputy U.S. Marshal Frank Cochran, convicted on July 23, 1886, and sentenced to hang, Duck eventually received a commutation of sentence to life. He entered Menard Penitentiary on October 16, 1886, and was released for reasons undocumented but probably related to his health. He is reputed to have died of consumption on May 7, 1895, and is buried near Catoosa.

Shirley, *Belle Starr and Her Times,* 133, 171, 195.

Charles Arthur Floyd (Choc, Pretty Boy) (1904-34)

Born on February 3, 1904, in Adairsville, Georgia, Floyd migrated with his parents to Hanson, Sequoyah County, Oklahoma, as a child. His first heist was a box of cookies taken from a Sallisaw grocer at age ten. Floyd developed an early taste for "Choc" beer, earning him the nickname most often used by friends and family. His adolescent criminal career was launched with a theft from the Akins, Oklahoma, post office in May 1922 followed by a St. Louis robbery gone bad that earned him serious time at the Missouri State Prison at Jefferson City.

Selected Oklahoma Bank Robberies and Gunfights

Earlsboro, March 9, 1931
With Bill Miller and George Birdwell, Floyd stole $300.

Shamrock, August 4, 1931
Birdwell and Floyd collected $300.

Morris, September 8, 1931
Birdwell and Floyd scored $743.

Maud, September 29, 1931
Floyd and Birdwell increased the pot to $3,850.

Earlsboro, October 14, 1931
Returning to the same bank, Floyd and Birdwell recovered $2,498 of other people's money.

First National Bank of Conawa, November 5, 1931
Floyd and Birdwell treated themselves to $2,500.

Morris State Bank, December 17, 1931
Floyd and Birdwell returned for another $1,162.

Castle, January 14, 1932
Birdwell and Floyd liberated $2,600.

Tulsa, near the Intersection of Peoria and Apache, February 7, 1932
During the evening hours, Tulsa police officers converged on a sedan occupied by Birdwell and Floyd, who opened fire with tommy guns, escaped, and were later confronted again near Fifth and Utica. Later the bandit car was found abandoned at the intersection of

Thirteenth Street and the Katy tracks (near Lewis). The pair was also spotted on Fifth Street near Harvard.

Tulsa, 513 E. Young, February 11, 1931
Police converged on the Floyd residence, but he and accomplice Birdwell escaped out the back door.

Meeker, March 23, 1931
Floyd relieved the Meeker bank of $500.

Near Bixby, April 9, 1932
Some three miles south of the present-day White Hawk golf course, Tulsa law enforcement laid an ambush for Floyd at his in-laws' place, but he killed former officer Irv Kelley and eventually escaped.

Stonewall, April 21, 1932
Floyd and Birdwell relieved the Stonewall bank of $800.

Sallisaw, November 1, 1932
Floyd greeted old friends as he, George Birdwell, and Aussie Elliott robbed his hometown bank, taking away $2,350.

Marlow, November 7, 1932
In his last undisputed Oklahoma bank robbery, Floyd netted only $278.

Wewoka dance hall, late 1932
Floyd supposedly spoiled the festivities by bagging $291. (Disputed)

Near East Liverpool, Ohio, October 22, 1934
Floyd was killed by a group of FBI agents and local officers led by Melvin Purvis about 4:25 p.m. between the farming communities of Clarkson and Calcutta.

Big Jim French (New Mexico)

According to Lincoln County War participant Frank Coe, Big Jim French was a drifter from Indian Territory who was brought to Lincoln County in the 1870s by rancher John Chisum. Apparently, Chisum sometimes purchased horses in Indian Territory and may have met French on such a trip.

Eventually French joined the McSween faction of the Lincoln County War, participating with Henry McCarty (Billy the Kid) in the killings of Frank Baker and Buck Morton on March 9, 1878, as well as the killing of Lincoln County sheriff Brady and his deputy, George Hindman on April 1. Some claim Big Jim sailed for "South America," although Frank Coe insisted that French returned to Indian Territory, where he lived until at least 1905 and perhaps until 1924.

Bartholomew, "Myths of the Lincoln County War"; Bartholomew, *Biographical Album of Western Gunfighters,* 31.

Jim French (d. 1895)

According to one historian, this Jim French was half Cherokee and was raised in the Fort Gibson area by his father Tom. He graduated *cum laude* from the Male Seminary at Tahlequah, Oklahoma, but killed a man in or near Fort Gibson in either 1889 or 1891. He is said to have married Belle Starr in Catoosa (a myth), and to have ridden with the Cook gang (1894). He was eventually mortally wounded on February 7, 1895, at Catoosa during the robbery of the W. C. Patton store, after killing a manager named Sam Irvin.

Shirley, *Law West of Fort Smith,* 120-21; Shirley, *Marauders,* 102.

Dick Glass (d. 1885)

Dick Glass was described by some authorities as a black Creek and a freed slave. One authority states that the Glass gang was Tulsa's first. When caught with horses of questionable ownership by local citizens just north of present-day downtown Tulsa, Glass and his gang beat a hasty retreat. Glass also was a whiskey trader, having a regular route that began with liquor purchased in or near Denison, Texas, and bartered for horses in Indian Territory. Some authorities place him at the head of a raid into the Cherokee Nation in the vicinity of Marshalltown on July 27, 1880, conducted by black Creeks who considered themselves to be victimized by Cherokee mixed-bloods. Some authorities also place him in a shoot-out with Creek Lighthorse in 1882. Glass may have made one major contribution to criminality. He developed a rudimentary bulletproof vest, which, on one occasion, allowed him to fake death and eventually kill two law officers.

In October 1884, he was reported illegally selling whiskey near Sacred Heart Mission, then passed through Weleaka Mission (present-day Leonard) with stolen horses on November 20 and established a base seven miles north of Muskogee in early April 1885. Glass was killed by Deputy U.S. Marshal Sam Sixkiller and two other deputies (some authorities say Indian police) while carrying a load of whiskey near Post Oak, thirty miles west of Colbert on June 11, 1885.

Trekell, 16; *Chicago Sun Times,* December 12, 1993; Burton, 17-28; Katz, 157-58.

John and Mack Glass (prom. 1880s)

According to the July 22, 1893, *Cherokee Advocate,* John and Mack were arrested in July 1893 for the 1887 murder of Walter Scott in Indian Territory near Fort Smith. The Glasses had been on the scout (run) since the murder and were arrested by Deputy U.S. Marshals J. C. Rogers and Howell C. Rogers. The outcome of their trial, if any, has not been determined.

Cherokee Advocate, July 22, 1893.

Crawford Goldsby (Cherokee Bill) (1876-96)

Reportedly, Crawford once worked north of Tulsa for the Turley family, for whom the town of Turley is named. He really preferred a life of crime. An inventory of his murder victims includes one "Richards" (first name not reported), a railroad agent at Nowata; his brother-in-law George "Mose" Brown at Nowata, whom Crawford killed in a fight over a pig or pigs; Ernest Melton, a curious housepainter who unluckily observed a robbery in progress at Lenapah; and, finally, turnkey Lawrence Keating, whom Crawford killed in a jailbreak attempt at Fort Smith.

Crawford was executed for the murder of Ernest Melton. Robberies in 1894 to his "credit" include the Scales Store at Wetumka; a train at Red Fork (a job that may be falsely attributed, since he is known to have engaged U.S. marshals in a gunfight on 14 Mile Creek near Tahlequah that evening); the Parkinson Store at Okmulgee; an express office at Chouteau; and A. F. Donaldson at an unidentified locale in the Cherokee Nation. Following the killing of Ernest Melton, Lenapah reportedly passed an ordinance forbidding the harassment of Goldsby within town limits. According to lore, he also killed train conductor Sam Collins for requesting train fare.

Selected Oklahoma Robberies and Gunfights

Watonga, October 22, 1894
Six miles south of Nowata, Goldsby and three others took $400 from two stores and a post office.

Lenapah, November 9, 1894
Goldsby and Sam McWilliams (the Verdigris Kid) robbed the Shufeldt store and post office of $700. In the process, fatally curious housepainter Ernest Melton, who observed the heist from the building next door, was shot in the face and killed. Goldsby and McWilliams fled to the vicinity of present-day Leonard and eventually Tulsa.

Nowata, December 24, 1894
At about 7:00 p.m., the Kansas-Arkansas Valley Railroad depot was robbed of $190 by four individuals believed to be Goldsby, Jim French, George Sanders, and Sam "Verdigris Kid" McWilliams.

Talala, December 30, 1894
The Christmas pleasantries over, Goldsby killed his brother-in-law Mose Brown, allegedly in a dispute over a herd of pigs or, according to others, in order to eliminate an informant.

Nowata, December 30, 1894
Goldsby allegedly robbed George Bristow, station agent at

Nowata, who had turned in his resignation following the Christmas Eve robbery described above.

Near Nowata, January 29, 1895

Goldsby was enticed to the residence of ex-Deputy U.S. Marshal Ike Rogers by the allure of Maggie Glass, knocked over the head with a piece of firewood, and arrested.

May, 277; Shirley, *Marauders,* 13.

Alonzo Gordon (Lon) (d. 1894)

Gordon, a Cook gang member, was intercepted and mortally wounded by authorities on August 2, 1894, west of Sapulpa with Henry Munson, who was also killed. A third gang member, Curtis Dayson, was captured. Curiously, Cook had earlier served as a posseman under a deputy U.S. marshal hunting for Gordon, whose family lived on Polecat Creek, south of Sapulpa.

Shirley, *Marauders,* 6, 32, 39, 42.

William K. Hale (Bill) (1874-1962)

Kale was convicted with John Ramsay for the murder of Henry Roan, who was discovered dead with Roan's cousin Anna Brown about three miles from Fairfax on May 27, 1921. Hale was also suspected of participating with Ernest Burkhart in the bombing death of Bill and Rita Smith, who were murdered in March 1923 with Nettie Brookshire. Hale had allegedly asked Al Spencer and Spencer gang member Dick Gregg to kill the Smiths for $5,000. Hale received a life sentence from which he was paroled on July 31, 1947. He died on August 15, 1962, in Phoenix, Arizona, at age eighty-eight.

Hogan, *Osage Indian Murders,* 154, 267-69.

Frank Hamer (1884-1955)

Hamer was the Texas lawman, who, with sheriff's deputies Bob Alcorn and Ted Hinton, tracked Bonnie and Clyde to Durant on

April 3, 1934. Hamer eventually laid the ambush in which the deadly duo was killed in Louisiana.

Burrough, 279.

Harry and William Hart (ca. 1894-1917)

The twins were sons of English immigrant George W. Hart, who initially settled in Labette County, Kansas, but migrated to Centralia, halfway between Vinita and Nowata, in Indian Territory. After George died of a heart attack, the twins fell in with horse thief Pony Poe, whom they reportedly met at the Muskogee State Fair in 1915. The Poes and Harts upgraded their operation to include bank robberies, being among the first to use automobiles in such endeavors. They ultimately were engaged by law enforcement in a gunfight on January 20, 1917, at Nuyaka Mission near Okmulgee in which Oscar Poe and the Hart twins were killed.

Morgan, *Desperadoes,* 14-15, 69-86.

Herman Hollis (Ed) (d. 1934)

A Tulsa resident agent sent by J. Edgar Hoover to supplement the Dillinger squad managed by Melvin Purvis in May 1934, Hollis participated in the Chicago Biograph shooting of Dillinger on July 22, 1934. Hollis was also present for the shooting of Charles Arthur "Pretty Boy" Floyd and was himself killed by Lester Gillis (Baby Face Nelson) at Lake Geneva, Wisconsin, on November 27, 1934. Agent Samuel P. Cowley was killed, and Gillis was mortally wounded.

Burrough, 409, 476.

J. Edgar Hoover (1895-1972)

Born on January 1, 1895, in Washington, D.C., Hoover had several little-known connections to Oklahoma. First, Hoover's uncle, Laban J. Miles of Pawhuska, was a Quaker Indian agent to the Osage in 1889. Second, the FBI was a little-known federal agency until the "War on Crime" was launched in 1933-34, partially to solve several crimes which were planned by Oklahomans or which occurred in the state. Notable among such crimes was the Urschel kidnapping in Oklahoma City, the Barker-Karpis kidnappings of prominent St. Paul businessmen Bremer and Hamm, and according to some, the Kansas City Massacre.

Mattix, "Southwestern Lawmen," 15.

Ingalls Battle, September 1, 1893

Second in Western lore only to the Gunfight at the OK Corral is the conflict at Ingalls, in present-day Payne County, Oklahoma. The battle, which occurred on September 1, 1893, between federal officers and the Doolin gang, resulted in the death of three lawmen and the injury of two bystanders, one of whom later died. All of the outlaws save one rode away.

However ill conceived the plan, the bravery of the law enforcement officers involved has never been disputed. Two federally led posses, posing as homesteaders, converged the previous evening on the small community, known in law enforcement circles, fairly or unfairly, as an outlaw town. The first wagon, occupied by Deputy U.S. Marshals Dick Speed, Hamilton B. "Ham" Hueston, Henry Keller, George Cox, M. A. Iason, and Hi Thompson, left Stillwater at nightfall on August 31. The second group, including Deputy U.S. Marshals Jim Masterson (brother of Bat), Doc Roberts, Isaac A. Steel, J. S. Burke, Lafe Shadley, and John Hixon, left Guthrie that same evening. A request for reinforcements brought a posse of eleven to the scene the next day, too late for the gunfight, but in time to join in the futile search for the gang after the battle.

Upon arrival the previous evening, the two federal posses sealed off the small town, taking into custody a young boy serving as a lookout for Doolin.

When the gunfight began Friday morning, according to traditional accounts, Arkansas Tom Jones was recuperating from an undisclosed illness on the second floor of the OK Hotel, while Bill Doolin, Bill Dalton, Dan "Dynamite Dick" Clifton, and Tulsa Jack Blake were playing poker in the Ransom Saloon as Bitter Creek Newcomb looked on. When Bitter Creek left the saloon to look after a horse, he overheard young Del Simmons identify him to Deputy U.S. Marshall Dick Speed.

Speed immediately fired at the outlaw, who returned fire. Speed injured Newcomb, but was apparently himself killed by Arkansas Tom, firing from his second-story hotel window. Tom also killed Del Simmons, whom he mistook for a marshal. The general mêlée that followed left officers Thomas J. "T. J." Hueston, brother of Ham Hueston, Lafe Shadley, and a traveler identified only as Mr. Walker dead. Arkansas Tom was captured after a brief standoff. The other outlaws rode away, however, to enjoy temporary freedom and eventually meet violent deaths.

O'Neal, 92; Samuelson, *Shoot from the Lip,* 57; Shirley, *Gunfight at Ingalls,* 68-86.

Alexander Franklin James (Frank) (1843-1915)

Born on January 10, 1843, in Clay County, Missouri, Frank James participated in the Civil War Battle of Wilson's Creek on August 10, 1861, as a Confederate, was captured and paroled, then joined a band of guerillas led by William Quantrill. Frank participated in the August 21, 1863, raid on Lawrence, Kansas, and the October 6, 1863, raid near present-day Baxter Springs, Kansas, on the Indian Territory border. One hundred Union soldiers, including about ten unarmed band members and a newspaper correspondent, were killed. His "banking and railroad" career, which began about 1866, sometimes involved commutes through the Indian Territory to Texas. He is also said to have worked at Colbert's Ferry on the Red River.

One source has Frank moving to Denison, Texas, in early June 1881, and into Indian Territory in July. He owned a farm at Fletcher, Oklahoma, from 1907 to 1911. His mother, Zerelda James Samuel, died February 10, 1911, on an eastbound train near Yukon, Oklahoma, while returning to Kansas City from a visit with Frank. He died on February 15, 1915, on the James farm in Missouri.

Smith, *James-Younger Gang,* 7, 10, 14, 22, 205, 207; *Daily Oklahoman,* February 11, 1911; O'Neal, 164-66; Milligan, *Choctaw of Oklahoma,* 129.

Jesse Woodson James (Dingus) (1847-82)

Born on September 5, 1847, in Clay County, Missouri, in 1864 he joined Confederate guerillas led by Bloody Bill Anderson. Jesse once stated he was in Indian Territory in February 1871, meeting Oscar Thomason at Perryville. According to Myra Belle Shirley (Belle Starr), Jesse visited Younger's Bend in 1880 or 1881 and stayed several weeks, identifying himself as Mr. Williams from Texas.

Some also claim that Jesse and his brother Frank stayed at Robbers Cave near Younger's Bend on trips through Indian Territory to and from Texas. The *Dallas Herald* reported in May 1876 that the Jameses were conducting robberies in Arkansas, Missouri, and Indian Territory. However, research has produced no hard evidence of any criminal activity by Frank or Jesse James in Indian Territory, although they may have participated with Quantrill or Anderson on unreported Civil War raids. One source states that Jesse James once killed an escaped outlaw being pursued by a Texas posse on the Choctaw Nation side of the Red River.

Smith, *James-Younger Gang,* 35, 44, 52, 181; Shirley, *Belle Starr and Her Times,* 85, 148, 151; Yeatman, *Frank and Jesse James,* 99; Milligan, *Choctaw of Oklahoma,* 129.

Alphonso Jennings (Al) (1861–1961)

One-time cellmate of author Sidney Porter (O. Henry), Al Jenings was born in Virginia, the son of a prominent jurist who moved his family to Oklahoma. Al served as prosecuting attorney, but eventually turned to crime after his brother Ed was killed in a shoot-out with fellow counsel Temple Houston, son of Sam Houston in 1895 Woodward. While working as a ranch hand near Bixby, he joined an outlaw band and embarked on an unsuccessful outlaw career. He parlayed his outlaw career into Hollywood income, after a brief imprisonment. He died at age one hundred near Hollywood, California.

Shirley, *Temple Houston,* 223-26; Adams, *Burs under the Saddle,* 42-43.

Matthew Kimes (1908-45)

Mathew Edward Kimes was born about 1908, and his older brother George, about 1907, at or near Beggs. They were involved in theft from an early age, first being accused of car and merchandise theft near Holdenville in April 1924. Gradually their robberies escalated toward banks and then resulted in the killing of Deputy Perry Chuculate of

Sallisaw, Oklahoma, while resisting arrest on August 26, 1926.

Suspected in an attempted triple bank robbery at Beggs in 1927, they were eventually captured with two hostages at the residence of some relatives some thirty miles from Van Buren, Arkansas. George was paroled from prison in 1957. After years in prison, Matt was released on parole in 1945. He died in Little Rock, Arkansas, when he was struck by a chicken truck.

Koch, 3, 4, 91, 113, 371-75, 387-88; Winter, 43-47; Morgan, *Bandit Kings of the Cookson Hills,* 185.

Elmer Lucas (Chicken) (prom. 1890s)

Elmer rode with the Bill Cook gang in the 1890s. Ultimately arrested following the robbery of the Lincoln County Bank at Chandler on July 31, 1894, he served fifteen years in a Michigan prison.

Shirley, *Marauders,* 32, 37, 39, 54-56, 107, 151.

Christian Madsen (Chris) (1851-1944)

Born on February 25, 1851, on the island of Funen in Denmark, Madsen apparently engaged in a series of petty crimes as a youth before immigrating to New York, where, according to claims he prepared, he enlisted in the United States Army on January 21, 1876. Madsen served in the Fifth Cavalry through 1891, in campaigns against the Sioux, with a brief November 1881 time-out in the Wyoming Territorial Prison for larceny.

Participating in the 1889 Oklahoma Land Run, he settled at El Reno and was appointed a deputy U.S. marshal in 1891. He left federal service in 1916, having been chief deputy and acting U.S. marshal, with a brief break in service for duty with the Rough Riders during the Spanish American War. By August 1917, he was serving as the chief bookkeeper of the Tulsa Police Department. He died in Guthrie on January 9, 1944.

Selected Oklahoma Gunfights

Orlando, November 29, 1892
Deputies Chris Madsen, Heck Thomas, and Tom Houston tracked

Ol Yantis to his sister's home where the bandit was mortally wounded resisting arrest.

Beaver City, 1893
Madsen confronted three cowboys in the street who were disturbing the evening slumber of Judge Buford in a second-story hotel room. When they resisted his request for silence, Madsen knocked one over the head with a pistol. The sorehead filed charges against Madsen the next day but withdrew his complaint when he realized which judge the case had been assigned to. When the pummeled cowpoke was first confronted he exclaimed: "I'm a son of a bitch from Cripple Creek" to which Madsen cleverly retorted "I knew who you were, but didn't know where you were from," or so the story goes.

El Reno, May 12, 1894
Madsen confronted train robber Felix Young, whose attempt to escape was thwarted when Madsen killed his horse.

Near Cheyenne, March 5, 1896
Doolin gang member George "Red Buck" Weightman was surrounded by a Madsen-led posse and killed by Madsen himself.

O'Neal, 211, 213.

Annie Maledon (d. 1895)
Annie was the daughter of George Maledon, the Fort Smith hangman. Annie met a tragic and violent end on March 25, 1895, dying at St. John's hospital, in Fort Smith, after being shot by Frank Carver, whom she met while he was on trial for bootlegging. Carver abandoned his wife and two children, taking Annie to Muskogee. Later, in Frank's absence, Annie reportedly had shown her gratitude by taking up with Frank Walker. Carver was not amused.

Harrington, 132, 151.

George Maledon (1830-1911)
Called the "Prince of Hangmen," Maledon served as a deputy and hangman at Fort Smith from 1875 until his retirement in 1894. His

first multiple hanging was on September 3, 1875, at which he hanged six convicted murderers. Maledon was a Union veteran who had run a small mill in Indian Territory, eventually becoming a guard at Fort Smith. He reportedly shot a number of men who attempted to escape.

Harrington, 31-32; Shirley, *Law West of Fort Smith,* 80-81.

Henry McCarty (William H. Bonney, Henry Antrim, Kid Antrim, Billy the Kid) (ca. 1859-81)
Overshadowed in Western lore only by Jesse James, if anyone, McCarty had at least two significant associations with Indian Territory. Moreover, he probably spent part of his youth on the Kansas frontier near Oklahoma. The remote possibility even exists that he lived at the site of present-day Coffeyville (earlier called Possumtown) on the Indian Territory border.

Although his traditional birth date of November 23 is most certainly a fabrication, he was probably born around 1859 to Irish-American parents. The place of his birth was most likely New York City, the impression of a customs official who interviewed him at Santa Fe in early 1881 and noted his Manhattan street dialect. He may have been baptized Patrick Henry McCarty at the Church of St. Peter in lower Manhattan, possibly the church portrayed in the film *Gangs of New York.*

Military pension records, city directories, and real estate records are persuasive that by about 1868, Henry and his widowed mother and brother were living in Indianapolis, where they met William Henry Antrim, with whom Mrs. McCarty purchased Wichita real estate in 1871. She married Antrim in Santa Fe in 1873, with Henry and his brother serving as witnesses, eventually journeying to Silver City, New Mexico.

Using the name Antrim and William H. Bonney, Henry (now called Billy) eventually found himself in the Lincoln County War, a mercantile affair pitting Scotsman Alexander McSween and Englishman William Tunstall against Irishmen Lawrence "Larry" Murphy, James "Jimmy" Dolan, Johnny Riley and others whose retail establishment dominated Lincoln County affairs.

Forsaking heritage for friendship, Billy joined Tunstall's

Regulators, whose ranks included Frederick T. Waite, from the vicinity of present-day Pauls Valley, Oklahoma, and Big Jim French, most likely a native of the Choctaw Nation. Another Regulator, John Middleton, according to at least one authority, died in 1885, the very year a John Middleton associated with Belle Starr drowned, or was murdered in the Choctaw Nation.

Waite was, according to some scholars, Billy's closest friend, with whom he dreamed of starting a farming operation. Some evidence exists that at the conclusion of the Lincoln County War, Waite offered to help Billy establish himself in the Chickasaw Nation. Instead, the young man known today as Billy the Kid chose to stay in New Mexico. He was killed by Pat Garrett, on July 14, 1881, at Fort Sumner, and thus became a legend.

Rasch, 4-5, 10, 15, 153-56; Adams, *More Burs under the Saddle,* 72; Utley, *High Noon in Lincoln,* 43, 143, 166; Metz, *Lawmen,* 21; Tower, 190.

Elmer McCurdy (c. 1880-1911)

A native of Maine and an army veteran, McCurdy's criminal career began after 1907 and was distinguished by misfortune. For example, on March 30, 1911, at Lenapah, Oklahoma, McCurdy, Walter, Lee, and Glenn Jarrett attempted to rob the Iron Mountain Railroad, but they overestimated the amount of nitroglycerin required and destroyed the train safe and all its contents.

On October 4, 1911, McCurdy robbed a Katy train near Okesa, Osage County, obtaining only forty-six dollars and two demijohns of whiskey, while an express train carrying the payroll he was seeking rumbled safely by a few minutes later. Killed three days later, his greatest adventures were all ahead. After years of service as a mummified carnival display, his remains were sold to a California funhouse and apparently presumed to be a mannequin. His true nature was discovered during a filming of an episode of the television series *The Six Million Dollar Man.* Then he was returned to a place of honor next to the Bill Doolin grave in Guthrie.

Farris, 105-10.

Sam McWilliams (Verdigris Kid) (d. 1891)

The Verdigris Kid was killed on March 28, 1891, at Braggs, Indian Territory, while robbing the T. J. Madden store with Cook gang member George Sanders (also killed) by Indian deputies John Manning and Hiram Stevens. Young "trainee" Sam Butler, who was also on the Madden job, was later killed on August 1, 1895, near the Island Ford of the Verdigris River by Deputy John David, who was also killed.

Shirley, *Law West of Fort Smith*, 121-22; Shirley, *Marauders*, 108.

John Middleton (Indian Territory) (d. 1885)

Allegedly a cousin of Jim Reed, in 1883 Middleton murdered J. H. Black, the sheriff of Lamar County, Texas, and may have become a lover of Belle Starr in about 1884. He was found dead near Keota on the banks of the Poteau River in the Choctaw Nation. Sam Starr was his suspected killer.

Harman, 586; Shirley, *Belle Starr and Her Times*, 175-76, 180, 247-48, 256.

John Middleton (New Mexico) (ca. 1854)

Little is known of the John Middleton who rode with Henry McCarty during the Lincoln County War. One historian (Ramon Adams) states that after separating from McCarty at Tascosa, Texas, in 1878, the John Middleton of New Mexico went to Barber County, where he ran a grocery store. Another authority (Robert M. Utley) states, however, that the John Middleton of New Mexico died in 1885, the very year that a John Middleton associated with Belle Starr died in the Choctaw Nation, Indian Territory.

Adams, *More Burs under the Saddle*, 72; Utley, *High Noon in Lincoln*, 166.

Eugenia Moore (ca. 1868-ca. 1892)

An 1889 photograph illustrates to all with romantic experience that fair Eugenia was a sweetheart of Bob Dalton. Beyond this fact, not much verifiable evidence about the lass is available. Lack of solid documentation has never impeded a good story where the Old West is concerned, and the life of Eugenia Moore is no exception. First, examining the best things said about her, Emmett Dalton, whose recollections have often been faulted, wrote that he met Eugenia, approximate age twenty-two, in Silver City (in about 1890) and that she was a schoolteacher and of a good Missouri family.

Emmett also stated that Eugenia was a member of the gang who rode from Parsons, Kansas, to Denison, Texas, seeking information for raids. Emmett further claimed she was a telegraph operator who frequently eavesdropped in railroad depots to learn of money shipments. He attributed the success of the train robbery at Leliaetta, on September 15, 1891, to her skills.

Another writer states that she facilitated the July 1, 1892, Santa Fe train robbery near Red Rock in the Cherokee Strip in which the gang collected $11,000. This version of her life, relatively mild and charming though it is, does not make much sense when one considers the practicalities that she would have faced in riding such a circuit.

Worse still, other early writers contended without proof that Moore was a harlot, that she was Daisy Bryant, the love interest (or sister) of Blackface Charlie Bryant. Others contend that in reality she was Flora Quick Mundis (aka Tom King). One need not be a forensic anthropologist to see from the photographs of the two women that such assertions are raw fiction. It is known with relative confidence that she died of cancer before the Coffeyville Raid of October 5, 1892.

Shirley, *Daltons,* 52-53; O'Neal, 81; Nash, 95, 97; Shirley, *West of Hell's Fringe,* 53, 69.

Frank Nash (Jelly) (d. 1933)

Nash was an Oklahoma-born gangster who participated in the last Oklahoma train robbery on August 8, 1923, at Okesa, Oklahoma, with horseback outlaw Al Spencer. Nash died during the Kansas City Massacre, along with Police Chief Otto Reed of McAlester and other lawmen at about 7:15 a.m. on June 17, 1933. Verne Miller and Charles Arthur Floyd were among the attackers according to some authorities, now doubted by some, and afterward drove to the Kansas City residence of fellow Oklahoman Adam Richetti.

Edge, 2-9, 22, 27, 30, 41.

Ed Newcome

Associate of Henry Starr, Newcome was tracked with Starr and Jesse Jackson the evening of January 20, 1893, to a hideout near Bartlesville, where Deputy U.S. Marshals Ike Rogers and Rufus Cannon shot Jackson's right arm off. Newcome was captured the next month at his mother's home on California Creek near Nowata, was imprisoned, and reportedly went straight after serving in the Spanish American War. Jackson killed himself in the Guthrie jail.

Shirley, *Henry Starr,* 37-39.

George Newcomb (Bitter Creek) (ca. 1860-95)

George Newcomb, born about 1860 near Fort Scott, Kansas, was also known as Slaughter's Kid, because he worked as a youth for rancher Charlie Slaughter. The name "Bitter Creek" came from a trail song of the time. He participated in the Ingalls shoot-out of September 1, 1893, was wounded at Sacred Heart in a holdup, and was killed on May 1, 1895, by the Dunn brothers at their ranch for reward money.

Bitter Creek either died inside the house while entertaining a young lady or outside the Dunn house at the gate, as Frank Canton contended.

Shirley, *Guardian of the Law,* 250; O'Neal, 242.

Robert A. Olinger (Big Indian) (1841-81)

Born in Ohio, Bob moved with his family to Indian Territory and then on to New Mexico about 1876, where he was killed by Henry McCarty (Billy the Kid) on April 28, 1881. His brother, John Wallace Olinger, also a gunfighter, was employed during the Lincoln County War. Bob's disposition may have been the result of maternal conflict. His own mother once stated he was a murderer at heart.

O'Neal, 246; Adams, *More Burs under the Saddle,* 87; Klasner, 183-84.

O'Malley Brothers (prom. 1890s)

Bit players in the comedy known as the Al Jennings gang, Morris and Pat O'Malley were Tecumseh toughs whom Al Jennings characterized as mere "Wild Irish Boys." Remarkably, they started their careers in law enforcement. Morris served as a deputy U.S. marshal who was discharged for financial indiscretions. Pat had served as a posseman in 1894 and 1895.

Midnight, October 29, 1897, found the boys at the Crozier and Nutter store in Cushing with the famously unlucky lawyer-bandit Al Jennings, Doolin alumni Richard "Little Dick" West, and Dan "Dynamite Dick" Clifton. Relieving the proprietor of fifteen dollars and carefully selected apparel, yet dissatisfied with the take, West and Clifton submitted their resignations.

Earlier, the O'Malleys had participated in a series of ineffective train robbery attempts, notably including one at Bond Switch. There, the gang watched helplessly as a quick-thinking engineer sped through a barricade the banditos had carefully constructed from railroad ties. Eventually, the O'Malleys pled guilty to robbing the U.S. mails.

Shirley, *West of Hells' Fringe,* 384, 390-91, 393, 406, 408, 410-11; Johnson, 140-41, 143.

Bonnie Parker (1910-34)

Born in Rowena, Texas, Bonnie was, according to family stories, a bright and happy child. She became a study in divided loyalties, contradictions, and an American tragedy during hard times in tough West Dallas, Texas, when the Depression started in the twenties. She married Roy Thornton, an alumnus of the juvenile reform school at El Reno, Oklahoma, in 1926, and was faithful to him in her own way. Although he was in prison during her years on the criminal road with Clyde Barrow, she refused to divorce Thornton and was wearing his wedding ring when she died. Even though she had no problem associating with trigger-happy Clyde Barrow, Oklahoma's Ray Hamilton, and other stone-cold killers, she was kind to children, pets, family members, and hostages. Loyal to Barrow to the end, she refused his entreaties to turn herself in, sharing his death as she had predicted in a fabled poem. Her first known criminal act was bringing a weapon to Clyde Barrow in prison to aid an escape. She committed her first robbery with Barrow at Kaufman, Texas, east of Dallas, on April 19, 1932. She participated in numerous holdups thereafter, but always waited in cars while Clyde and others collected the cash. Perhaps her fate was sealed when a press report incorrectly portrayed her as the killer of two motorcycle patrolmen shot by Henry Methvin and Clyde Barrow at Grapevine, Texas, on Easter Sunday, April 1, 1934. She died with Clyde on May 23, 1934, in a Louisiana ambush. Her family and some 10,000 curious onlookers participated in her funeral ceremonials in Dallas, Texas.

Steele, *Bonnie and Clyde,* 37, 50; Milner, 17, 31; Knight, 3, 142, 147, 194.

Charley Pierce (Cockeye Charlie) (d. 1895)
Doolin gang member Pierce was ambushed with Bitter Creek Newcomb for a $5,000 reward at the Dunn Brothers Ranch near Ingalls and killed on May 2, 1895.

O'Neal, 255; Metz, *Lawmen,* 60, 66, 101-2, 181.

Wiley Hardeman Post (1898-1935)
Today, few Oklahomans know that the world-renowned aviator and friend of Will Rogers had an earlier, less admirable career. He was born on November 22, 1898, at Grand Saline, Texas, to Irish-American Mae Quinlan Post and William Francis Post, a Scot. The family had lived in Oklahoma earlier and migrated to Rush Springs in 1907. Trained as an automobile mechanic and employed as an oil-field roughneck, Wiley eventually tried his hand at highway banditry. In early April 1921, the *Chickasha Star* reported his capture. He had been hijacking cars near Ninnekah that spring. Arrested, brought to Chickasha, and convicted of robbery on April 21, 1921, he was sentenced to ten years in the state reformatory at Granite.

Paroled by Governor J. B. A. Robertson on June 3, 1922, he went on to become a renowned aircraft pioneer, associating with such aviation pioneers as oilman Frank Phillips, aviatrix Amelia Earhart, and others involved in the fledgling industry. Within ten years of his parole, his exploits setting records aboard the *Winnie Mae* won him worldwide acclaim. He met two presidents and numerous other luminaries before his tragic death with Will Rogers near Point Barrow, Alaska, on August 15, 1935, brought to a close perhaps the most prominent story of personal redemption in Oklahoma history.

Burke, 19-25, 186.

William Tod Power (Bill Powers, Tom Evans) (d. 1892)
Apparently born in Missouri, this Dalton gang associate was killed at Coffeyville on October 5, 1892.

Smith, *Daltons,* 48.

Ezekiel Proctor (1831-1907)
Born on July 4, 1831, the Georgia son of a white man and a full blood Cherokee, Zeke came to Oklahoma on the Trail of Tears and was reportedly one of the few Cherokee citizens of his locale to fight for the Union. In 1872, he accidentally killed Polly Beck at Becks Mill. The ensuing Cherokee Nation trial was interrupted and ten killed when U.S. marshals attempted to arrest Proctor for a trial under federal jurisdiction.

Reports indicated that Zeke had killed twenty-three men by 1889, but there is no dispute that the United States government granted *de facto* amnesty to Proctor in 1873, the only such agreement known to this day. He later served as a deputy United States marshal. He died on February 28, 1907.

Speer, *Ned Christie,* 78; Steele, *Last Cherokee Warrior,* 15-60.

Moman Pruiett (1872-1945)
Born on July 12, 1872, at Alton, Illinois, the son of a Confederate veteran, Pruiett knew much about criminality first hand. Convicted

of forgery in December 1887, he served eight months of a two-year sentence. In Paris, Texas, he was convicted of robbery, serving two years on this offense. He swore that he would return and defeat the judicial system, or so the story goes. After parole, he returned to Paris, Texas, where he worked in a cotton warehouse by day and studied law by night, gaining admittance to the Texas bar in 1895.

He then established his practice at Pauls Valley, Oklahoma Territory, and was known for exonerating clients at any cost. Possessing a violent streak, he once shot a man for borrowing his father's dress coat without permission. On another occasion, Pruiett and a client brawled during jury deliberations. Pruiett later stood proudly by his bandaged client as the jury foreman intoned "not guilty."

Oklahoma City, October 1921
Pruiett killed Oklahoma City bootlegger and gambler Joe Patterson in a gunfight at Patterson's home. A coroner's jury decided the killing was justified.

Pruiett won acquittals in 303 of the 343 death penalty cases he tried, often with dubitable evidence. His reputation for success at any cost was so potent that four men, including notorious assassin Jim Miller, were lynched at Ada on the rumor that Pruiett would defend them on murder charges. Pruiett died on December 12, 1945, in Oklahoma City.

Butler, *Oklahoma Renegades,* 142-50.

Melvin Purvis (1903-60)
Melvin Purvis was responsible more than anyone else for successfully tracking down and killing John Dillinger. In January 1932, he headed the Division of Investigation office in Oklahoma City.

Burrough, 126, 128-29, 147, 331, 544.

Bill Raidler (Little Bill) (1865-ca. 1905)
Perhaps a Pennsylvania native and the only member of the Doolin gang who lived to tell the tale, he died a respectable citizen sometime after 1905, possibly in Yale, Oklahoma. He had been incarcerated

with Al Jennings and the novelist O. Henry while in an Ohio federal prison. Raidler's survival was itself an amazing story. Raidler was
shot-gunned at close range in a hen house by Bill Tilghman about
eighteen miles south of Elgin, Kansas, and was not expected to survive. Raidler calmly swigged cold beer while he waited for the end,
but instead he survived and found himself in federal prison.

O'Neal, 258; Nix, 214; Shirley, *Guardian of the Law,* 253.

Nathan Reed (Texas Jack) (d. 1950)

Born on March 23, 1862, in Madison County, Arkansas, Reed was
orphaned and went west at a young age, working in Colorado,
Wyoming, Idaho, and Texas. Eventually he became a ranch hand in
Oklahoma. He claimed to have committed seven robberies between
1885 and 1892, none of which have been verified. It is known for certain that by the summer of 1895, Reed was living at federal expense
in Fort Smith, courtesy of Judge Parker, having participated in the
robbery of a Katy train at Blackstone Switch, Indian Territory, on
November 13, 1894, with Tom Root, Buss Luckey, and Will Smith.

Blackstone Switch, November 13, 1894
Reed, with Tom Root, Buss Luckey, and Will Smith robbed a
train at about 10:00 p.m., collecting $460 and eight watches, miss-
ing $60,000 protected by guards.

Shot and captured by Deputy U. S Marshal Ledbetter in the
Boston Mountains of Northwest Arkansas, he used his time "in stir"
to plot the downfall of informant Jim Dyer, who was convicted, but
later shown to be at a horse race in Wagoner at the time of the robbery. Reed was allegedly the last robber to face Judge Parker. His
second career was that of outlaw exhibitionist and evangelist. He
died peacefully in downtown Tulsa on January 7, 1950.

Shirley, *The Fourth Guardsman,* 25-33, 35-41, 43, 171; Reed, 3-66.

Bass Reeves (ca. 1838-1910)

Reeves is believed to be the first black deputy U.S. marshal
commissioned west of the Mississippi. A controversial figure, he

once was accused of murdering his own trail cook. In fact, the cook was accidentally killed when a weapon misfired. Some accounts state that Reeves was born a slave in July 1840 in Lamar County, Texas, and ran away after fighting with his owner, going through Indian Territory to Van Buren, Arkansas. Some have speculated that blacks were recruited for deputy U.S. marshal positions because whites were not ordinarily welcome in 1874 Indian Territory.

Reportedly required to kill some fourteen people in his career, he was never convicted of a wrongful killing. In 1884, he was dismissed from the marshals service. One Fort Smith newspaper published allegations that he had been involved in cattle rustling with a former posseman. Bass once arrested his own son, Benjamin, for killing an unfaithful wife. Later in his career he served with the Muskogee Police Department and died in that city of Bright's disease.

Williams, 154; Burton, 202.

Adam Richetti (d. 1938)

Associate of Charles Arthur Floyd from near Krebs, Oklahoma, Richetti was convicted of participating in the Kansas City Massacre and was executed on October 7, 1938. His Oklahoma record included a 1932 arrest for a bank robbery, time at the state penitentiary in 1935, and allegedly a Tishomingo robbery.

Mill Creek, Johnson County, March 9, 1932

An automobile with three men pulled up in front of Mill Creek State Bank. A former deputy sheriff, Fred Hemner, and L. C. "Blackie" Smalley robbed the bank of $800. Hemner was killed, and Blackie seriously wounded by well-armed and suspicious citizens as the robbers emerged from the establishment. Richetti, the getaway driver, was wounded, then abandoned the vehicle south of town, only to be captured in a barn. Following conviction and a few months of imprisonment, he was released on August 24, 1932, and soon joined Charles Arthur Floyd in a series of robberies.

Burrough, 520; King, 200.

Bob Rogers (1874-95)

Hailed by some as "copycats" of the Daltons, Bob and his gang apparently began their crime career as early as the fall of 1891. Bob himself was arrested on November 10, 1891, for assault with intent to kill by Deputy U.S. Marshal Colbert, taken to Fort Smith, and released on bond. His gang consisted of Bob Stiteler, Willis Brown (of the Chelsea area), Dynamite Jack Turner of the Eureka, Kansas, area, and his brother Kiowa Turner.

Reportedly, the gang stole some twelve horses in Indian Territory for resale in Arkansas in the summer of 1892. Arrested by Heck Bruner, Bob was given a light first-offense sentence by Judge Parker. He then killed Jess W. Elliott at Catoosa on November 3, 1892. Following train robberies at Kelso and Seminole, and some horse thefts in 1894, Bob was killed at Horseshoe Mound, twenty miles south of Coffeyville, Kansas, on March 13, 1895. His raids included the robbery of a Katy train at Adair in the fall of 1895. Later, according to some, he arranged for the arrest of four partners to avoid his own arrest.

Selected Robberies and Gunfights

Near Catoosa, November 3, 1892

Forty-year-old constable Jess W. Elliott of the Cherokee Indian Police and a lawyer of ten years experience was ambushed after quarreling with Bob Rogers in a pool hall. Rogers slit his throat in three places and later returned to stomp on the body in the presence of a Dr. Warren and others. Rogers took some legal papers and a hat, then removed to Sapulpa.

Near Vinita, July 29, 1893

A Heck Bruner-led ambush planned for Rogers at the George Harlan farm west of Vinita instead netted his brother Sam who was wounded. Ralph Halleck was also killed, upsetting his wife so badly she never picked up the body.

Kelso Switch, December 22, 1893

Five miles north of Vinita, the Rogers gang cleverly reset a switch to divert a Katy train to an alternative track for looting purposes. An observant train engineer foiled the plot by "highballing" through the barrier, leaving the banditos swearing in the dust. One outlaw managed to shoot train fireman Charles Milne in the jaw, and his grateful employer sent Charles to New York City for facial reconstruction.

Lenapah area (Seminole Springs), December 22, 1893
Learning from mistakes earlier that day, the gang diverted a Kansas-Arkansas Valley train onto a track blocked by empty freight cars and robbed it. The amount taken is unknown.

Cherokee Nation, January 1894
Curiously, Bob assisted Deputy U.S. Marshal Will C. Smith by handing over gang member Bob Stiteler at Rogers' brother-in-law's place on January 8. Fifteen days later, Bob and his gang were discovered at Bob's father's home. Kiowa Turner was killed during the ensuing gunfight. Rogers, Brown, and Dynamite Jack were taken to Fort Smith, and Brown succumbed to gunshot wounds. According to some, Bob got some of the reward money.

Horseshoe Mound, south of Coffeyville, March 15, 1895
Deputy U.S. Marshal Mayes and members of the Anti-Horse Theft Association, undaunted by a lack of a warrant, shot some two hundred rounds of ammunition into the home of Bob's father at dawn. After posse member W. D. McDaniel was fatally wounded, Bob agreed to surrender, then changed his mind and died in a hail of bullets on the front porch.

Shirley, *Law West of Fort Smith*, 105, 109; Butler, "Outlaw Career of Bob Rogers."

Myra Belle Shirley (Belle Starr) (1848-89)
Born about 1848 near Carthage, Missouri, Myra Belle married Jim Reed in Texas on November 1, 1866. Upon his death, she may have married Bruce Younger, an uncle of the outlaw Younger brothers, on May 15, 1880. She reputedly married Sam Starr on June 5,

1880, at Catoosa, then known as the hellhole of Indian Territory. She moved with him to the Starr place at Hi-Early Mountain in the Bend of the Canadian, which ultimately became known as Younger's Bend.

Sam was killed during Christmas week 1886, in a gunfight with Frank West near Whitefield, Indian Territory. Belle herself was killed on February 2, 1889, near Younger's Bend. One authority (Ramon Adams) states that she was visited about 1881 by Jesse James at Younger's Bend. The records do show that she was convicted of horse theft at Fort Smith in February 1883, her only fully documented crime.

Shirley, *Belle Starr and Her Times,* 31, 34, 35, 51-52, 63, 135-37, 148-49, 152, 161; Adams, *Burs under the Saddle,* 361, 370.

Ed Short (d. 1891)

Lawman, veteran of the Kansas County Seat Wars, and deputy U.S. marshal, Short was born in Indiana (date unknown), moved west at the age of seventeen, and settled briefly in Emporia, Kansas, before beginning work as a cowboy.

The year 1888 found Ed serving as city marshal of Woodsdale, a new community in Western Kansas directly north of "no man's land," striving to supplant nearby Hugoton, which had been named interim county seat of Stevens County. Woodsdale was founded by Samuel N. Wood and I. C. Price, who were once kidnapped by Hugoton partisans then rescued by some twenty-four Woodsdale men. Prominent among Hugoton boosters was Kentuckian and reputed troublemaker Sam Robinson.

In July 1888, Robinson is said to have led a posse of Hugotons who massacred Stevens County sheriff John Cross and three other Woodsdalians approximately twelve miles west of present-day Hooker, Oklahoma, a locale known then as Wild Horse Lake. The murderers inadvertently left one seriously wounded survivor alive to testify, but no one was ever convicted. Samuel N. Wood was subsequently murdered, and Hugoton became the permanent county seat of Stevens County.

Ed Short avoided this effusion of blood and became a deputy U.S. marshal in Oklahoma Territory, but was killed in the line of duty on August 23, 1891, near Waukomis by outlaw Charles "Black Face

Charlie" Bryant, whom he had arrested earlier. Bryant was also killed in the gunfight. (See **Bryant, Charles.**) Woodsdale eventually blew away in the Kansas wind.

O'Neal, 53; Smith, "Murder by Moonlight"; Butler, "Kansas Blood Spilled in Oklahoma."

Al Spencer (1887-1923)

Known to the press as "King of the Osage," the "Phantom of Terror," and the "Wild Rider of Oklahoma," Al conducted the last train robbery in Oklahoma, on August 20, 1923, at Okesa, obtaining some $20,000 in Liberty bonds and $65 in cash. Jailed and subsequently on the run, he was killed by a posse led by Deputy U.S. Marshal Alva McDonald near Bartlesville on September 15, 1923. Fittingly, he is buried at Ball Cemetery, several miles northeast of Nowata near the last Spencer gang member killed, Dick Gregg.

Selected Robberies and Gunfights

Pawhuska, last week of February, 1922
Spencer, Frank Wells, and others robbed the American National Bank at Pawhuska.

Lenapah, September 22, 1922
Spencer, Wells, and others conducted a nostalgic horseback robbery of the Lenapah Bank and robbed the Centralia Bank two days later.

Okesa, August 20, 1923
The "new" Spencer gang, which included Frank "Jelly" Nash, Grover C. Durrill, and Earl Thayer, conducted the last train robbery in Oklahoma history, taking $65 in cash and $20,000 in bonds from the Missouri, Kansas and Texas (Katy) Railroad.

Wallis, *Frank Phillips,* 81-82, 100, 115, 131, 140, 357-58; Johnson, 132-37; Morgan, *Desperadoes,* 134; Winter, 41-43.

Henry Starr (1873-1921)

Born in 1873 near Fort Gibson, Henry was the grandson of Tom

Starr, and the cousin (or brother) of Belle Starr's husband Sam. Henry began his criminal career in June 1890, peddling whiskey near Nowata, for which he was arrested. He killed Deputy U.S. Marshal Floyd Wilson on Wolf Creek, Indian Territory, on December 13, 1892, then engaged in a series of robberies in Chelsea, Pryor Creek, Nowata, and Chouteau. Eventually, he was mortally wounded during a bank robbery in Harrison, Arkansas, in 1921. Starr had been an intermittent resident of Tulsa, selling real estate and insurance. His 1893 gang reportedly consisted of Link Complin, Frank Cheney, Hank Watt, Kid Wilson, Bud Tyler, and Happy Jack, all but one of whom met unhappy endings.

Happy Jack and Cheney were reportedly killed by deputy marshals. Watt was killed by a posse while stealing horses; Wilson reportedly died as a bandit; Complin was reported killed in Alaska. Surprisingly, Bud Tyler died in bed. In 1914, while engaged in banditry, Henry resided at 1534 East Second, Tulsa, about two blocks from the home of the county sheriff and four blocks from the mayor, each of whom he knew, or so the story goes.

His 1915 gang for a double bank robbery at Stroud on March 27, 1915, reportedly consisted of Lew Estes, Bud Maxfield (captured), Claude Spencer (fate unknown), and Al Spencer, who was killed in 1922. Although Henry Starr was shot and captured, four members of the gang escaped, even though their horseback getaway was followed by a posse using automobiles.

His 1921 gang for the Harrison robbery included Charlie Brackett, Rufus Rollen, and Ed Lockhart. He is believed by some to have robbed more banks than the Dalton gang and James-Younger gang combined.

Drago, 294; Shirley, *Henry Starr,* 147, 166; Morgan, *Bandit Kings of the Cookson Hills,* 20; Shirley, *Law West of Fort Smith,* 175-76.

James Starr (d. 1845)

The father of Tom Starr, James was reportedly involved in the Cherokee dispute between the Old Settlers, who signed treaties with the United States, and those who opposed the treaties. Some theorize that James was involved in the murder of Benjamin Vore (Vere) and his wife and son on September 15, 1843, at the Vore trading post some thirty miles from Fort Gibson. James himself was reportedly murdered on November 9, 1845. Ironically, the violent Starrs and their many non-violent relatives were the descendants of a peace-loving Quaker, Caleb Starr of Pennsylvania, who migrated to the Cherokee country about 1790.

Shirley, *Belle Starr and Her Times,* 79-82; Gibson, "More Like Comets Than Starrs."

Sam Starr (d. 1886)

Sam is said to have married Myra Belle Shirley at Catoosa and moved to the Bend of the Canadian, sometimes called Younger's Bend. Killed by Frank West near Whitefield, Sam was suspected of murdering John Middleton, who was found dead near Keota in the Choctaw Nation on the banks of the Poteau River.

Shirley, *Law West of Fort Smith,* 91.

Tom Starr (Old Tom)

A Cherokee rebel opposed to the Ross faction, Starr took land between Briartown and Eufala on the Bend of the Canadian River, sired Sam Starr, and reportedly entertained such notable crime figures as Jim Reed, Jack Spaniard, Felix Griffin, Jim French, the Jameses, and the Youngers. He reportedly named Younger's Bend for Cole Younger and occasionally sheltered the James brothers following the Civil War. Starr killed his own brother-in-law, reaping a $2,000 reward after presenting the severed head to the Cherokee chief and treasurer as proof of death.

Shirley, *Law West of Fort Smith,* 88, 314.

Ray Terill (Rob Dale)

Ray Terill (sometimes spelled Terell), nominal head of the Terrell, Barker, Inman gang, was Oklahoma born in 1899, finding himself in the state prison at age nineteen on a grand larceny charge. Later he was convicted of a series of crimes, including the robbery of a florist in Ardmore on Mother's Day.

Winters, 10, 20, 49, 58, 70, 101-5.

Texas Jack (1862-1950)

"Texas Jack" was shot out of the saddle on Main Street, downtown Tulsa, in 1881 (or 1883) by Tom Stufflebeam, after threatening Stufflebeam, described in some reports as an officer appointed by a vigilance committee. Another version states that Tom made a disparaging remark about Jack's horse, prompting him to dismount and point a pistol at Tom, who promptly ventilated him with a shotgun. Although he lived almost a week, Texas Jack refused to reveal his name and reportedly slumbered for years beneath that part of Second Street that was formerly the paupers' section, not relocated with the rest of Tulsa's first cemetery in 1910, or so the story goes. His remains may have been among those discovered beneath Second Street in October 2005, during construction of the BOK Center.

Stufflebeam was a former deputy U.S. marshal living in Tulsa at the time. Henry Munson, a member of the Bill Cook gang killed near Sapulpa in August 1894, favored a similar moniker, "Texas Jack Starr." These individuals are not to be confused with Dick Broadwell of the Dalton gang, Nathaniel Reed, impresario Texas Jack Omohundro, or his adopted son, "Texas Jack, Jr." who discovered Will Rogers.

Hall, 55; Trekell, 15; Rogers, 559.

Henry Andrew Thomas (Heck) (1850-1912)

Perhaps the most distinguished and authentically heroic of the deputy U.S. marshals riding for Judge Parker in Indian Territory, Thomas was born on January 6, 1850, at or near Oxford, Georgia. Following Confederate war service as a boy, he migrated to Texas, worked as a railroad guard and detective, then became a deputy U.S. marshal stationed at Fort Smith. His wife left him shortly thereafter, and he married Mattie Mowbray, daughter of the pastor of the First Methodist Church in Tulsa. Thomas worked with Bill Tilghman and others in Wharton (now Perry), Oklahoma Territory, a place that seemingly had as many saloons as houses. He died on August 11, 1912, at Lawton, where he had been police chief.

Selected Oklahoma Gunfights

Snake Creek, south of Red Fork, June 27, 1888
A Thomas-led posse located Aaron Purdy and others at a still while in search of train robbers. Purdy was killed resisting arrest.

Orlando, OklahomaTerritory, January 29, 1892
Fellow deputies Chris Madsen and Tom Houston killed Ol Yantis when Yantis attempted to shoot Thomas

Near Bartlesville, July, 1895
Little Bill Raider left behind parts of two fingers compliments of Deputy Thomas in a shoot-out.

Near Lawton, August 25, 1896
Thomas and a posse killed Bill Doolin, who was resisting arrest.

Near Sapulpa, November, 1896
Dynamite Dick Clifton eluded Thomas after a brief gun battle.

O'Neal, 312-15; Shirley, *Heck Thomas,* 324.

Irvin Thompson (Blackie) (1893-1933)
A shoemaker born to parents from Wheeler County, Texas, Thompson may have been born in Arkansas or Oklahoma. He was a key witness in the Osage Indian murder trials. He testified against Ernest Burkhart on June 4, 1926, in the murder of W. E. Smith.

A 1920 automobile theft in Osage County had earned him a five-year sentence, but he was paroled in 1922. Suspected of a Grady County bank robbery, he was captured on December 22, 1923, in Joplin, Missouri, convicted, and sentenced. He was paroled to work as an informant for federal agents investigating the Osage Indian murders, but his work proved unsatisfactory to say the least. He organized the "Thompson gang," which ambushed and killed Drumright police officer U. S. Lenox, on July 2, 1924, following a $1,500 robbery of the First State Bank of Avery.

Selected Robberies and Gunfights

Skedee, Oklahoma, August 22, 1924

Henry Cornett, "Buster" Holland, and Blackie Thompson robbed the bank. During the holdup Blackie managed to shoot Holland four times.

Hoffman, Oklahoma, December 19, 1924

Blackie, Jeff Duree, and others were suspected of robbing the Security State Bank of $3,000 in currency and $5,000 in county bonds, by simply loading the 2,600-pound safe into a stolen truck.

Bartlesville, December 25, 1924

Thompson was surrounded by a posse led by U.S. Marshal Alva McDonald and surrendered without incident.

McAlester, Oklahoma, August 30, 1933

After convincing an incredibly gullible guard he just wanted to go fishing at the prison farm lake, Thompson escaped the McAlester State Prison with two other prisoners. Recaptured in 1934 following several Texas bank robberies, he escaped Huntsville Prison with R. A. Hamilton, who would soon join the Barrow gang.

Amarillo, Texas, December 6, 1934

Observed and charged by Police Chief W. R. McDowell in a stolen car, Blackie sped eastward on Route 66, but was forced off the highway by gunfire and killed at point blank range by Deputy Sheriff Roy Brewer.

Koch, 12, 15, 334-35; Cordry, *Alive If Possible,* 87.

Three Fingered Jack (d. 1893)

Shot early one morning in 1893 by bartender Bill Haney at the Buckhorn Saloon in "Hell's Half Acre," Wharton (now Perry). Haney had discovered his best girl, "Lady Lou" on the victim's lap. Later, Haney and Lady Lou married, bought a farm in Noble County, and presumably lived happily ever after. Ironically, a second "Three

Fingered Jack" was also mortally wounded elsewhere in the Half Acre that night.

Shirley, *Guardian of the Law,* 222.

William Tilghman (Bill) (1854-1924)

Bill Tilghman was a deputy U.S. marshal, who, with Chris Madsen and Heck Thomas comprised the "Three Guardsman" of Indian Territory days. He was born to a sutler at Fort Dodge, Iowa, on July 4, 1854. Bill's parents migrated to the Atchinson, Kansas, area about 1856. Bill became a buffalo hunter. He had several scrapes with the law after becoming the deputy sheriff of Ford County, Kansas, seated at Dodge City. Serving in law enforcement while running a saloon, he participated in two bitter County Seat wars, becoming acquainted with the Earp brothers and Doc Holliday along the way.

He made the 1889 Oklahoma Land Run with Jim Masterson (brother of Bat), settling at Guthrie, and helped tame "Hell's Half Acre" at Wharton (now Perry). He became a deputy U.S. marshal in 1892, then served as Lincoln County sheriff, Oklahoma City police chief, and a state senator. One authority states that Tilghman met Wild Bill Hickock at an early age and emulated his gun style.

While at Guthrie, Tilghman was reportedly targeted for death by Fido, his own hunting dog, who retrieved a stick of dynamite Bill had thrown into a farm pond to catch dinner the easy way. Bill, the story goes, outran Fido, but being the sentimental type, kept some of Fido's hair—found in a tree—in a golden locket the rest of his days.

Selected Oklahoma Gunfights

Petrie, Indian Territory June 25, 1874

Tilghman and fellow buffalo hunters, including Hurricane Bill, confronted "Blue Tooth" (known by no other name) and others who were holding the dead body of fellow buffalo hunter Pat Conger. Shots were exchanged, and the hunters retrieved the body for burial.

Near Pawnee, 1894

Tilghman and law officer Steve Burke found Cattle Annie (Annie

McDougal) and Little Britches (Jennie Stevens) at a farmhouse. Stevens attempted to escape, and Tilghman pursued her, shooting her horse to end the chase, or so the story goes.

Cromwell, November 1, 1924

Tilghman was killed attempting to arrest Wiley Lynn, a federal prohibition officer, whom Tilghman perceived to be intoxicated. Earlier, according to some, Tilghman had caught some Lynn associates with a plane load of narcotics near Cromwell.

Cordry, "Deadly Business," 254; Shirley, *Guardian of the Law,* 79, 294; Samuelson, *Shoot from the Lip,* 30-40, 117-27; O'Neal, 323-26.

Bud Trainor (d. 1895)

A Cherokee, Bud (sometimes Bubb or Bub) Trainor was the son of a curiously matched Bostonian father and a mother who served as a Confederate courier. He operated a gang in 1887, consisting of himself, John Leach, Joseph Miller, and William Chuis (*sic*). On September 25, 1887, the Trainors fought the Vann gang on 14 Mile Creek. Less than a month later, on October 8 the gang harassed the town of Oaks north of Tahlequah. Bud's curriculum vitae included suspicion of the Dan Maples murder, introducing liquor, and assault with intent to kill.

Nevertheless, in the flexible environment of Indian Territory, Bud found himself fully qualified to become a deputy U.S. marshal on December 31, 1888, with Clem Rogers, father of entertainer Will Rogers, serving as bondsman for the position. Bud participated in the September 26, 1889, assault on Ned Christie at Rabbit Trap. January 23, 1890, found Bud assisting Deputy U.S. Marshal Bob Hutchins in the killing of Jim July Starr, then a suspect in the killing of his wife Belle Starr.

Later, Hutchins claimed Bud's assistance consisted of passing out drunk on the ground during the gun battle, but his involvement was sufficient to get him indicted for murder, for which he posted bond and returned to his gang. Bud completed his checkered career mortally wounded in a messy shotgun ambush on Christmas evening 1895, near Talala.

Speer, *Ned Christie,* 74-93, 126; Shirley, *Belle Starr and Her Times,* 248, 250.

George Weightman (Red Buck) (d. 1896)

Red Buck was a member of the Doolin Gang. He was killed on March 4, 1896, near Arapahoe, Oklahoma Territory, by D County deputy Joe Ventioner, assisted by officers Womble, Shahan, Duckworth, and Lewis Williams of Washita County. Contrary to some reports, Chris Madsen was not involved. Red Buck's crimes reportedly included killing Fred Hoffman, both the treasurer of Dewey County, Texas, and a U.S. commissioner, who had been assisting in the pursuit of parties attempting to swindle an express company. Rumored by some to be willing to kill for $150, he was unpopular with the Doolin gang members.

Farris, 51; Shirley, *Temple Houston,* 256-58; Samuelson, *Shoot from the Lip,* 77; Hanes, 62.

Richard West (Little Dick) (ca. 1865-98)

Perhaps born in Texas, Dick was reputedly an orphan who preferred to always sleep and dine "al fresco," that is to say, outdoors. He was said to have been "discovered" washing dishes in Decatur, Texas, in 1881, then worked at the H. H. Ranch in Oklahoma Territory.

Dick joined the Doolin gang, participated in their Southwest City, Missouri, robbery, a robbery at Dover, Oklahoma Territory, and perhaps others. Late in his career, he joined the spectacularly unsuccessful Al Jennings gang, only to be killed on April 13 (or April 7), 1898, near Guthrie, Oklahoma, by a posse led by Deputy U.S. Marshals Bill Tilghman and Heck Thomas. Bat Masterson reportedly considered him the worst criminal in the territory other than Doolin.

Nix, 58; Hanes, 63-64.

Nathaniel Ellsworth Wyatt (Zip Wyatt) (1870-95)

Wyatt (alias Dick Yeager) was born in Indiana, the son of a Civil War veteran and brother of professional gambler "Six Shooter Jack" Wyatt. Zip, whose nickname came from his uncanny ability to stay ahead of the law, migrated with his family to the Guthrie area in about 1889. He began his criminal career on July 4, 1891, killing Deputy Sheriff Andrew W. Balfour at Pryors Grove, Kansas, reputedly during a circus.

The "Great Gamboni," who observed the murder from the high wire, was so disturbed he fell to the ground, never to perform again. Zip later quipped upon arrest "Guess I'm the only badman who ever brought down a bicycle rider."

New Years Eve of 1892 found him breaking out of the Guthrie jail during a Salvation Army prayer service. Known for his romantic prowess rather than religiosity, he became notorious in outlaw circles for stealing the wife of an associate, Matt Freeman. Some writers attribute robberies at Fairview on June 3, 1895, and Oxley on July 23, 1895, to Zip.

He was fatally wounded by an Enid posse on August 4, 1895, and died the following month of blood poisoning in the Enid jail. His associates included Isaac "Ike" Black (killed in July 1895) and Matt Freeman, the unhappy husband (disposition unknown). Efforts of the authorities to eliminate Wyatt were quite intense, as farmhand William Willet discovered when a Garfield County posse fatally wounded him in a case of mistaken identity in early August 1895. Willet, who died confined in the Enid jail on September 7, 1895, was exhumed twice before authorities admitted their mistake.

Selected Robberies and Gunfights

Woods-Blaine County Line, June 4, 1895
Zip, Ike Black, and their women were surprised by a posse, which captured the ladies.

Blaine County, July 27, 1895
Wyatt and Black surveyed the Guthrie jail on July 23 and found the Bastille too heavily guarded to attempt breaking out their women. Wyatt and Black then robbed the post office at Oxley and camped about six miles to the northwest. Rudely interrupted at dawn by a posse, which surrounded them, they shot their way out, retreating down a creek bed. Two days later on July 29, the duo was bottled up

in a canyon by a posse, yet escaped again. Later, one of the posse observed that Wyatt was apparently wearing a bulletproof vest, in that he was struck in the center of the breast and in the back, yet rode away.

Cabin near Cainville, August 2, 1895

Ike Black and Wyatt were surrounded by Deputy Sheriff Marion Hildreth and posse while arguing about a plug of tobacco. Black was shot in the head and killed instantly. Wyatt was shot in the chest, escaped to a doctor's home for treatment, and was eventually found on August 4, 1895, southwest of Marshal in Logan County. Zip was mortally wounded on Skeleton Creek about five miles south of Marshal and captured while the pitiless murderer begged, "For God's sake don't kill me!" Transported to the jail in Enid, he died unrepentant on September 7, 1895, at about 12:06 a.m.

Samuelson, *Shoot from the Lip,* 65-66; Shirley, *Toughest of Them All,* 34-36, 53-108; Hanes, 60, 65-66, 149-50.

Oliver Yantis (Ol) (d. 1892)

Shot while feeding his horse by Sheriff Beeson of Dodge City or members of his posse, who split a $450 reward, Yantis died at about 1:00 p.m. on November 30, 1892, at Orlando, Oklahoma Territory. Reportedly he had joined the Doolin gang about three years prior to his death. Some authorities state that he participated in a train robbery at Wharton Station and a robbery of the Ford County, Kansas, bank at Dodge City in October and November of 1892, respectively, earning the fatal attraction of Sheriff Beeson. Described by one observer as a tall, sallow Kentuckian with buckteeth, he reportedly farmed about three miles southeast of Orlando.

Farris, 25-30; Hanes, 60, 64.

Bruce Younger (prom. 1880s)

A half-brother to the Younger brother's father, Bruce reportedly lived with Belle Starr in Galena, Kansas, during the 1878-79 time frame and may have married her on May 15, 1880, before Justice of the Peace John P. Shields. The marriage is said by one authority to have lasted about three weeks. Bruce was then replaced by Sam Starr.

Shirley, *Belle Starr and Her Times,* 133-37, 161.

James Younger (Jim) (1848-1902)

Born on January 15, 1848, in Lee's Summit, Missouri, he followed his brother Cole into the Quantrill irregulars in the spring of 1864, working first as a scout. Present when Quantrill was mortally wounded near Louisville, Kentucky, in May 1865, he was captured and transported to the military prison at Alton, Illinois. Released at the conclusion of the war, he returned to farming on the home place in Jackson County, Missouri.

Joining Cole and the James brothers in the April 1872 robbery of a Columbia, Kentucky, bank and perhaps two prior robberies, he joined Brother John in a gunfight on March 16, 1874, with Pinkerton agents at Monegaw Springs, Missouri, following a train robbery. John Younger and Pinkerton agent Louis J. Lull were killed, but Jim Younger and Agent John Boyle rode away.

Later, Jim was not so fortunate. On September 21, 1876, he received a disfiguring and disabling wound while pursued and cap tured following the ill-fated Northfield, Minnesota, raid. Restricted to a near-liquid diet during his prison term, he was paroled in 1901, then partnered with Brother Cole in the tombstone business. After falling in love with journalist Alice "Alix" Miller, he became despondent when parole restrictions kept him from marrying or even selling valid life insurance policies. Jim killed himself in a St. Paul hotel on October 19, 1902.

Smith, *James-Younger Gang,* 31, 37, 209-10; O'Neal, 341-43.

John Younger (1851-74)

Born in 1851, in Lees Summit, Missouri, and younger brother of James-Younger gang leader Cole Younger, John reputedly fled to the Indian Territory on January 20, 1887, and then Missouri after killing Col. Charles H. Nichols, acting sheriff of Dallas County, Texas. Following his January 1874 participation in a train robbery at Gads Hill, some hundred miles south of St. Louis, John and Jim

Younger were hiding out with friends at Monegaw Springs, Missouri. Pinkerton agent Louis J. Lull and Deputy Sheriff Ed Daniels stopped at the residence to ask directions on March 16, 1874. When Jim and John followed the pair, a gunfight ensued. Lull shot John in the throat before Jim mortally wounded Lull. Before falling to the ground dead, John fired at Deputy Sheriff Ed Daniels, who escaped.

Shirley, *Belle Starr and Her Times,* 92; O'Neal, 343-44.

Robert Younger (Bob) (1853-89)

Baby brother to the deadly Youngers, Robert was born in October 1853 at Lee's Summit, Missouri, too late to participate in the Civil War. By July 1873, he had joined the James-Younger gang in the derailment and robbery of a Chicago, Rock Island and Pacific Railroad train near Adair, Iowa. Although his brother Jim was troubled by the accidental death of hapless engineer John Rafferty during the derailment, Bob had no problem dividing Jim's share with the rest of the gang, or so the story goes. Although the trail is far from clear, one authority places Bob in a James-Younger stagecoach robbery between Malvern and Hot Springs, Arkansas, in mid-January 1874. During that robbery, the perpetrators exempted Confederate soldiers from the pilfering, then lectured the passengers on the perfidy of Northern interests. Bob may have been with John Younger and others during a train robbery at Gad's Hill, Missouri, on January 31, 1874.

Clever use of the "border shift" when wounded during the Northfield, Minnesota, raid, on September 7, 1876, allowed Bob to escape the town, only to be captured two weeks later near Madelia, Minnesota. Left to their fate by the James boys, Bob, Cole, and Jim were shot up and captured by a posse. Samuel Wells (aka Charlie Pitts) was killed on the spot.

During his sojourn at Stillwater Prison, Bob studied medicine, but succumbed to the prisoner's curse, tuberculosis, on September 16, 1889.

Smith, *James-Younger Gang,* 208-9; O'Neal, 345-46.

Scout Younger (prom. 1920s)

The *Oklahoma Leader* reported on April 18, 1917, that one week earlier, "Scout" Younger had led an expedition to "lost mountain," approximately six miles west of Tulsa, where Cole had supposedly buried $63,000 about forty years earlier. "Scout" claimed to be a cousin of the famous bank robber.

Oklahoma Leader, April 18, 1917.

Thomas Coleman Younger (Cole) (1844-1916)

Born on January 15, 1884, in Lee's Summit, Missouri, Cole was the son of Henry Washington Younger, a self-made dry goods merchant and farmer with property in Jackson and Cass Counties, Missouri. Like many Missourians, Charles was a slaveholder, but against secession. He was robbed of a large sum of money and murdered near Lee's Summit in July 1862. Cole immediately assumed the worst and joined Confederate irregulars. Within months, it was discovered that the atrocity had been carried out by one "Captain Walley" and Federal militia he commanded. Walley was arrested by regular Federal forces, who reported that Walley confessed to the crime. A court martial had been disbanded in spite of the confession because corroborating Federal militia witnesses had been ambushed on the way to the trial by Confederate irregulars presumably led by Cole Younger.

Cole Younger was an effective guerilla who participated in the Lawrence, Kansas, massacre, yet later decried the wanton murder that occurred there. However, Younger denied participation in the murders of unarmed Union forces at Centralia in which he was supposed to have fired through a file of fifteen Union soldiers. He saw service as a bushwacker in Arkansas, Louisiana, and Texas. Returning home after the surrender, he participated with his wartime colleague Frank James in the first recorded daylight bank robbery of record, at Liberty, Missouri, on Tuesday, February 13, 1866.

The generally accepted James-Younger body of work included at least four train robberies, two stagecoach robberies, eleven bank robberies, and a profitable raid on the Kansas City State Fair. There is credible evidence that Cole and other gang members periodically hid in Indian Territory between jobs, but apparently committed no overt crimes there.

The good times came to an end in Northern climes, perhaps providing federal interests a measure of poetic justice. Following his 1876 capture in the aftermath of the disastrous Northfield, Minnesota, raid, Cole founded the first prison newspaper in the United States, the *Prison Mirror,* at Stillwater, Minnesota, in 1887. Ironically enough, Cole was first employed following his release from prison selling tombstones. Then he took a job selling coal oil burners in Muskogee and other Indian Territory venues.

Later, during his career giving testimonials against the life of crime, his wallet was once stolen while he was giving a lecture. During his final years in Lees Summit, he delighted in lecturing young people, including this writer's great aunt, about the benefits of clean living. He died peacefully in Lees Summit, Missouri, on February 21, 1916.

Smith, *James-Younger Gang,* 29-33, 210-13.

Notes

Chapter 1

1. Burton, 88.
2. Shirk, 252.
3. Shirley, *Thirteen Days of Terror,* 16.
4. Ibid.
5. Burton, 90.
6. Shirley, *Thirteen Days of Terror,* 21.
7. Archives, *Muskogee Phoenix,* August 15, 1895.
8. Burton, 89-90.
9. Shirley, *Thirteen Days of Terror,* 24-25.
10. Burton, 90.
11. Jones, "Memories of a Marshal."
12. Ibid.
13. Shirley, *Thirteen Days of Terror,* 33.
14. Burton, 99.
15. Harman, page number not specified.
16. Burton, 101.
17. Harman, as cited in Burton, 101.
18. Burton, 101.
19. Harman, as cited in Burton, 102.
20. Shirley, *Thirteen Days of Terror,* 40-42.
21. Ibid., 44.
22. Burton, 104.
23. Ibid., 106.
24. Shirley, 69.

Chapter 2

1. Cordry, "Outlaws and Lawmen," 1-9.
2. Ibid.
3. Ibid.

4. Ibid.

5. Ibid.

6. Ibid.

7. Ibid.

8. Ibid.

9. Yeatman, *Frank and Jesse James,* 266, 278, 292.

10. Cloud, "Dead," 6-11.

11. Ibid.

12. Ibid.

13. Ibid.

14.Ibid.

15.Ibid.

16. Yeatman, *Frank and Jesse James,* 266, 278, 292.

17. Cloud, "Dead," 6-11.

18. Ibid.

19. Ibid.

20. O'Neal, 231.

21. Ibid.

22. Ibid.

23. Ibid.

24. Ibid.

25. Ibid.

26. Ibid.

27. Ibid.

28. Metz, *Pat Garrett,* 288.

29. Ibid., 289.

30. Ibid., 288.

31. Ibid., 289.

32. Ibid.

33. Ibid., 293.

34. Shirley, *Shotgun for Hire,* 77.

35. Ibid., 77.

36. Ibid., 79.

37. Wallis, *Pretty Boy,* 312.

38. Ibid., 315.

39. Ibid., 316.

Chapter 3

1. Faust, 606.
2. Ibid.
3. O'Neal, 346.
4. Yeatmen, *Frank and Jesse James,* 44.
5. Ibid., 49.
6. Faust, 51.
7. Fugate and Fugate, 20.
8. Ibid.
9. Faust, 807.
10. Ibid., 808.

Chapter 4

1. Gumprecht, 15.
2. Ibid.,16.
3. Ibid.
4. Ibid., 2.
5. Ibid.
6. Ibid.
7. Ibid., 5.
8. Ibid.
9. Kirkwood, 4.
10. Gumprecht, 9.
11. Kirkwood, 4.
12. Gumprecht, 9.
13. Ibid., 6.
14. Ibid., 7.
15. Ibid.
16. Ibid., 8.
17. Ibid.
18. Rucker, "Newly Opened Pott County."
19. Ibid.
20. Ibid.
21. Gumprecht, 8.

22. Ibid., 11.
23. Shirk, 239.
24. Gumprecht, 16.
25. Ibid., 17.
26. Ibid., 14.
27. Ibid., 17-18.
28. Ibid., 18.
29. Ibid.
30. Ibid., 19.
31. Ibid.
32. Ibid.
33. Ibid., 20.

Chapter 5

1. Metz, *The Shooters,* 20.
2. O'Neal, 228.
3. Bartholomew, "Myths of the Lincoln County War."
4. Shirley, *Law West of Fort Smith,* 120-21.
5. Tower, "Fred Tecumseh Waite."
6. Adams, *Burs under the Saddle,* 423.
7. Utley, *High Noon in Lincoln,* 166.
8. Shirley, *Belle Starr and Her Times,* 178.
9. O'Neal, 228.
10. Shirley, *Belle Starr and Her Times,* 175-76, 180.
11. O'Neal, 49-50.
12. Ibid., 52.
13. Ibid.
14. Ibid.

Chapter 6

1. Harrington, 102.
2. Ibid., 103.
3. Ibid., 104.
4. Ibid.
5. Ibid., 106.

6. Ibid., 108.

7. "Outlaws, Gamblers and Lawmen in Colorado," www.ellens place.net.

8. "El Buscaderos—Cowboys Action Shooting—Feature," www.netw.com/cowboy.

9. Ibid.

10. Ibid.

11. Shirley, *Hell's Fringe,* 306.

12. "Cattle Annie and Little Britches," 1, Theoutlaws.com.

13. Shirley, *Hell's Fringe,* 305-6.

14. "An Outlaw Life," Graham Leader Online.

15. Ibid.

16. Shirley, *Hell's Fringe,* 305.

17. Ibid., 306.

18. Ray, 31-32.

19. Shirley, *Hell's Fringe,* 306.

20. Ibid., 307.

21. O'Neal, 325.

22. Shirley, *Hell's Fringe,* 306.

23. Ibid., 307.

24. Ibid.

25. O'Neal, 325.

26. Shirley, *Hell's Fringe,* 308.

27. Adams, *Burs under the Saddle,* 382.

28. Shirley, *Belle Starr and Her Times,* 72.

29. Ibid.

30. Ibid., 73.

31. O'Neal, 260-61.

32. Shirley, *Belle Starr and Her Times,* 147.

33. Shirley, *Law West of Fort Smith,* 181, photo and name identification.

34. Ibid., 94.

35. Ibid.

36. Ibid., 95.

37. Ibid.

38. Ibid., 96.

39. Ibid., 97.

40. Smith, *Daltons,* 176, 197.

41. Ibid., 196.

42. Ibid.

43. Ibid.

44. Ibid., 197.

45. Ibid.

46. Shirley, *Heck Thomas,* 187.

47. Smith, *Daltons,* 198.

48. Helmer and Mattix, 181.

49. Steele and Scoma, *Bonnie and Clyde,* 29, 33, 46.

50. Barrow, 40, 73.

51. Yeatman, *Frank and Jesse James,* 27.

52. *The Holden Enterprise,* Johnson County, Missouri, February 2, 1911.

53. Shirley, *Belle Starr and Her Times,* 252.

54. Steele, *Starr Tracks,* 76.

55. Ibid.

56. Ibid.

57. Ibid., 94.

Chapter 7

1. Wallis, *Pretty Boy,* 36.

2. Helmer and Mattix, 5.

3. Mattix, "Bonnie and Clyde in Oklahoma," 4.

4. Helmer and Mattix, 43.

5. Mattix, "Bonnie and Clyde in Oklahoma," 5.

6. Ibid.

7. Ibid.

8. Barrow, 262-63, n 2.

9. Mattix, "Bonnie and Clyde in Oklahoma," 6.

10. Ibid.

11. Ibid., 4-7.

12. Wallis, *Pretty Boy,* 327.

13. Mattix, "Bonnie and Clyde in Oklahoma," 7.

14. Ibid.

15. Wallis, *Pretty Boy,* 31.

16. Ibid., 34.

17. Ibid., 36.

18. Ibid., 113.

19. Ibid.

20. Ibid.

21. Ibid.

22. Morgan, *Bad Boys,* 71-72.

23. Ibid., 65.

24. Ibid.

25. Morgan, *Tri-State Terror,* 204.

26. Morgan, *Bad Boys,* 54.

27. Morgan, *Tri-State Terror,* 200.

28. Morgan, *Bad Boys,* 151.

29. Ibid., 139.

30. Ibid.

31. Helmer and Mattix, 14, 22.

32. Wallis, *Pretty Boy,* 350.

33. Ibid., 325-26.

34. Ibid., 336.

35. Ibid., 338.

36. Newton and Newton, as told to Claude Stanush and David Middleton, 298.

37. Ibid., 1.

38. Ibid., 26-27.

39. Ibid., 311.

40. Ibid., 190.

41. Ibid., 281.

42. Ibid., 190.

43. Ibid., 321.

44. Ibid.

45. Ibid., 325.

46. Ibid., 321.

47. Ibid.

Chapter 8

1. Shirley, *The Fourth Guardsman,* 61-63.

2. Ibid.
3. O'Neal, 91.
4. Shirley, *The Fourth Guardsman,* 61-63.
5. Shirley, *Hell's Fringe,* 406.
6. Ibid., 391.
7. Ibid., 392.
8. Ibid., 391-92.
9. Ibid., 392.
10. Ibid.
11. Ibid., 393.
12. Ibid.
13. Ibid., 394.
14. Ibid.
15. Ibid., 397.
16. Ibid.
17. Ibid., 399.
18. Ibid., 406-7.
19. Ibid., 408.
20. Ibid., 409.
21. Ibid., 410.
22. Ibid.
23. Ibid., 411.
24. Adams, *More Burs under the Saddle,* 105, 112.
25. Ibid., 112.
26. Cordry, *Alive If Possible,* 27.
27. Ibid.
28. Morgan, *Desperadoes,* 134.
29. Cordry, *Alive If Possible,* 27.
30. Ibid., 28.
31. Drago, 294.
32. Cordry, *Alive If Possible,* 28.
33. Morgan, *Desperadoes,,* 134.
34. Cordry, *Alive If Possible,* 30.
35. Ibid.
36. Ibid, 30-31.
37. Ibid., 30.
38. Ibid., 32.
39. Smith, *Daltons,* 55.

40. Hanes, 7-9.
41. Farris, 105-10.
42. Ibid.
43. Whitehead, "Sideshow Outlaw."
44. Svenvold, 127.
45. Ibid., 136.
46. Ibid., 208-11.
47. Ibid., 252.
48. Ibid.
49. Morgan, *Bad Boys,* 147.
50. Winter, 10, 11.

Chapter 9

1. Morgan, *Desperadoes,* 26.
2. Ibid., 15.
3. Ibid., 17.
4. Ibid., 50.
5. Cordry, *Alive If Possible,* 20.
6. Cordry, *Outlaws and Lawmen,* 1998.
7. Cordry, *Alive If Possible,* 18.
8. Ibid.
9. O'Neal, 298.
10. Ibid.
11. Helmer and Mattix, 24.
12. O'Neal, 298.
13. Ibid.
14. Smith, *Daltons,* 165.
15. Ibid.
16. O'Neal, 89.
17. Shirley, *Hell's Fringe,* 428.
18. Ibid., 429.
19. Ibid.

Chapter 10

1. Hanes, 194.
2. Samuelson, *Dalton Gang Story,* 148.

3. Nix, 123.

4. Ibid., 130.

5. Ibid.

6. O'Neal, 56.

7. *Oklahoma Daily Times-Journal,* July 1, 1895.

8. O'Neal, 289.

9. *Oklahoma Daily Times-Journal,* July 1, 1895.

10. Ibid.

11. Burton, 112.

12. Shirley, *Hell's Fringe,* 289.

13. Ibid.

14. *Oklahoma Daily Times-Journal,* July 1, 1895.

15. O'Neal, 56.

16. Wilson, 56-59.

17. O'Neal, 57.

18. Shirley, *Hell's Fringe,* 301.

19. Tanner and Tanner, 59, 69-74.

20. Shirley, *Hell's Fringe,* 301.

21. Butler, "Outlaw Career of Bob Rogers," 7.

22. Ibid.

23. Ibid.

24. Shirley, *Law West of Fort Smith,* 105.

25. Butler, "Outlaw Career of Bob Rogers," 8.

26. O'Neal, 88.

27. Butler, "Outlaw Career of Bob Rogers," 8

28. Shirley, *Law West of Fort Smith,* 106.

29. Ibid.

30. Butler, "Outlaw Career of Bob Rogers," 9.

31. Ibid., 10.

32. Shirley, *Law West of Fort Smith,* 107.

33. Butler, "Outlaw Career of Bob Rogers," 11.

34. Shirley, *Law West of Fort Smith,* 108.

35. Butler, "Outlaw Career of Bob Rogers," 11.

36. Ibid., 12.

37. Shirley, *Law West of Fort Smith,* 113.

38. O'Neal, 120.

39. Ibid.

40. Drago, 167.
41. Shirley, *Marauders,* 48.
42. Ibid., 64, 78.
43. Drago, 167-68.
44. Ibid., 169.
45. Shirley, *Marauders,* 150.
46. Shirk, 107.
47. Ibid., 166.
48. Shirley, *Outrobbed Them All,* 1-2.
49. Ibid., 2.
50. Ibid., 3.
51. Ibid., 9.
52. Ibid., 14.
53. Ibid., 22-23.
54. Shirk, 113.
55. Shirley, *Outrobbed Them All,* 32.
56. Haines, "Osage Lawman," 6.
57. Shirley, *Outrobbed Them All,* 76.
58. Ibid.
59. Ibid., 101.

Chapter 11

1. Burton, 10.
2. Ibid.
3. Ibid., 11.
4. Ibid.
5. Ibid.
6. Shirk, 179.
7. Ibid.
8. Keen, "Blue Duck."
9. Ibid.
10. Shirley, *Belle Starr and Her Times,* page not specified.
11. Harrington, 99.
12. Bill O'Neal in *Encyclopedia of Western Gunfighters,* page 335, has the year as 1889.
13. Shirley, *Hell's Fringe,* 139.

14. Ibid.

15. Wellman, 205, 208.

16. O'Neal, 242-43.

17. Wellman, 206.

18. Ibid., 205.

19. Ibid., 218.

20. O'Neal, 336.

21. Wellman, 219.

22. O'Neal, 336.

23. Wellman, 220.

24. Shirley, *Hell's Fringe,* 341.

25. Ibid., 343.

26. Sergeant W. J. L. Sullivan, *Twelve Years in the Saddle for Law and Order on the Frontiers of Texas,* as cited in Shirley, *Hell's Fringe,* 347.

27. Shirley, *Hell's Fringe,* 350; Wellman, 227; O'Neal, 336.

28. Sullivan, as cited in Shirley, *Hell's Fringe,* 349.

29. Ibid., 350.

30. Shirley, *Hell's Fringe,* 350.

31. Ibid., 351.

32. Shirk, 100.

33. Fugate and Fugate, 26.

34. Ibid., 27.

35. Speer, *Ned Christie,* 78.

36. Burton, 29.

37. Ibid., 30.

38. *Northwest Arkansas Times,* November 16, 1964.

39. Burton, 32.

40. O'Neal, 59.

41. Burton, 29, 32.

42. Ibid., 33.

43. Elman, 151, 161.

44. Burton, 33.

45. Farris, 42-43.

46. O'Neal, 59.

47. Elman, 151, 161.

48. Burton, 36.

49. O'Neal, 60.

50. Burton, 37.
51. Ibid.
52. Farris, 47.
53. Burton, 38.
54. Farris, 47.
55. Ibid., 48.
56. Ibid., 39.
57. Ibid., 48.
58. Burton, 39.

Chapter 12

1. Burrough, 68.
2. Ibid., 73.
3. Ibid., 72.
4. Ibid., 80.
5. Ibid., 80, 82-83.
6. Ibid.
7. Ibid., 117.
8. Oklahoma City Police report, UKF # 732.
9. Burrough, 93.
10. Hamilton, *Machine Gun Kelly's Last Stand,* 105.
11. Ibid., 126.
12. Burrough, 134.

Chapter 13

1. Karpis, 235-50.
2. Ibid., 26-31.
3. Burrough, 34.
4. Ibid., 33.
5. Ibid., 34.
6. Ibid., 509.
7. Ibid., 516.
8. Ibid., 35.
9. Ibid., 172.
10. Karpis, 116.

11. Smith, *Literature of the American Gangster,* 3.
12. Burrough, 550.

Chapter 14

1. O'Neal, 100-101.
2. Metz, *The Shooters,* 271.
3. O'Neal, 138.
4. Ibid., 217.
5. Ibid., 127.
6. Metz, *The Shooters,* 256.
7. O'Neal, 127.
8. Metz, *The Shooters,* 256.
9. Ibid.
10. O'Neal, 130.
11. Ibid.
12. Metz, *The Shooters,* 263.
13. O'Neal, 148-50.
14. Ahlquist, "Tom Horn's Indian Territory Manhunt," 16-18.
15. Poulsen, 75-76.
16. Burrough, 548.
17. Helmer and Mattix, 21.
18. Phillips, Glen A. Jr., 182.
19. Helmer and Mattix, 9.

Bibliography
Books

Adams, Ramon. *Burs Under the Saddle: A Second Look at Books and Histories of the West*. Norman: University of Oklahoma Press, 1964.
———*More Burs Under the Saddle*. Norman: University of Oklahoma Press, 1979.
Darrow, Blanche Caldwell, edited by John Neal Phillips. *My Life With Bonnie and Clyde*. Norman: University of Oklahoma Press, 2004.
Bartholomew, Ed. *Biographical Album of Western Gunfighters*. Houston: Frontier Press, 1958.
Brant, Marley. *The Outlaw Youngers*. Lanham, MD: Madison Books, 1992.
Burke, Bob. *From Oklahoma to Eternity: The Life of Wiley Post and the Winnie May*. Oklahoma City: Oklahoma Heritage Association, 1998.
Burrough, Bryan. *Public Enemies, America's Greatest Crime Wave and the Birth of the FBI, 1933-1934*. New York: Penguin Press, 2004.
Burton, Art. *Black, Red and Deadly: Black and Indian Gunfighters of the Indian Territory, 1870-1907*. Austin, TX: Eakin Press, 1991.
Butler, Ken. *Oklahoma Renegades*. Gretna, LA: Pelican Publishing, 1997.
Carter, Robert. *Buffalo Bill Cody: The Man Behind the Legend*. New York: John Wiley & Sons, 2000.
Colcord, Charles Francis. *The Autobiography of Charles Francis Colcord, 1859-1934*. Tulsa: Privately Published, 1970.
Cordry, Dee. *Alive If Possible, Dead If Necessary*. Mustang, OK: Tate Publishing, LLC, 2005.
DeArment, Robert K. *Deadly Dozen*. Norman: University of Oklahoma Press, 2003.
Debo, Angie. *The Rise and Fall of the Choctaw Republic*. Norman: University of Oklahoma Press, 1961.
———*Tulsa, From Creek Town to Oil Capital*. Norman: University of Oklahoma Press, 1943.

Drago, Harry Sinclair. *Outlaws on Horseback.* New York: Dodd, Mead and Co., 1964.

Edge, L. L. *Run the Cat Roads.* New York: Debner Books, 1981.

Elman, Robert. *Badmen of the West: The First Complete Book of the American Outlaw, the Lives and Times of Renegades, Bandits, Rustlers, and Gunfighters, Who Made the West Wild.* Secaucus, NJ: The Ridge Press, 1974.

Ernst, Robert. *Deadly Affrays: The Violent Deaths of the United States Marshals 1789-2004.* Phoenix, AZ: Scarlet Mask Enterprises, 2005.

Farris, David A. *Oklahoma Outlaw Tales.* Edmond, OK: Little Bruce, 1999.

Faust, Patricia L. (editor). *The Historical Times Illustrated Encyclopedia of the Civil War.* New York: Harper Collins Publishing, 1991.

Franks, Clyda R. *Tulsa: Where the Streets Were Paved With Gold.* Charleston, SC: Arcadia Publishing, 2004.

Fugate, Francis L. and Roberta B. *Roadside History of Oklahoma.* Missoula, MT: Mountain Press, 1991.

Fulton, Maurice G. *History of the Lincoln County War.* Tucson: University of Arizona Press, 1968.

Girardin, G. Russell with William J. Helmer. *Dillinger, The Untold Story.* Bloomington and Indianapolis: Indiana University Press, 1994.

Haines, J. D. *Wiley G. Haines: Frontier U.S. Deputy Marshal.* Austin, TX: Eakin Press, 2002.

Hall, James M. *The Beginning of Tulsa: First Men, First Events.* Tulsa: Tulsa Tribune, 1928.

Hamilton, Stanley. *Machine Gun Kelly's Last Stand.* Lawrence: University of Kansas Press, 2003.

Hanes, Col. Bailey C. *Bill Doolin, Outlaw O.T.* Norman: University of Oklahoma Press, 1968.

Harman, S. W. *Hell on the Border.* Muskogee, OK: Indian Heritage Association, 1971.

Harrington, Fred Harvey. *Hanging Judge.* Norman: University of Oklahoma Press, 1996.

Helmer, William J. and Rick Mattix. *Public Enemies: America's Criminal Past, 1919-1940.* New York: Facts on File, Inc., 1998.

Hogan, Lawrence J. *The Osage Indian Murders.* Frederick, MD: Amlex, Inc., 1998.

Johnson, Curt. *The Outlaws of Cooweescoowee (District of the Cherokee Nation)*. Privately Published, 2004.

Karpis, Alvin with Bill Trent. *The Alvin Karpis Story*. New York: Coward, McCann and Geoghegan, Inc., 1971.

Katz, William Loren. *Black Indians*. New York: Atheneum, 1986.

King, Jeffrey S. *The Life and Death of Pretty Boy Floyd*. Kent, OH: Kent State University Press, 1998.

Klasner, Lily. *My Girlhood Among Outlaws*. Tucson: University of Arizona Press, 1972.

Knight, James R. with Jonathan Davis. *Bonnie and Clyde: A Twenty First Century Update*. Austin, TX: Eakin Press, 2003.

Koch, Michael. *The Kimes Gang*. Bloomington, IN: Author House, 2005.

Kohn, George C. *Dictionary of Culprits and Criminals*. Metuchin, NJ: Scarecrow Press, 1986.

Lamb, Arthur. *Tragedies of the Osage Hills*. Pawhuska, OK: Raymond Red Corn, 1964 (reprint).

McCullough, Harrell. *Seldon Lindsey, U.S. Deputy Marshal Also Gunslinger, Cowboy, Outlaw, Indian Fighter*. Oklahoma City: Paragon Publishing, 1990.

McLoughlin, Denis. *Wild and Wooly: An Encyclopedia of the Old West*. New York: Barnes and Noble, 1975.

Matera, Dary. *John Dillinger: The Life and Death of America's First Celebrity Criminal*. New York: Carroll and Graf Publishers, 2004.

Metz, Leon Claire. *Encyclopedia of Lawmen, Outlaws and Gunfighters*. New York: Checkmark Books, 2003.

———*Pat Garrett, The Story of a Western Lawman*. Norman: University of Oklahoma Press, 1974.

———*The Shooters, A Gallery of Notorious Gunmen from the American West*. El Paso, TX: Managean Books, 1976.

Miller, Nyle H. and Snell, Joseph W. *Great Gunfighters of the Kansas Cowtowns 1867-1886*. Lincoln: University of Nebraska Press, 1963.

Milligan, James C. *The Choctaw of Oklahoma*. Durant, OK: Choctaw Nation, 2003.

Milner, E. R. *The Lives and Times of Bonnie and Clyde*. Carbondale, IL: Southern Illinois University Press, 1996.

Morgan, R. D. *The Bad Boys of the Cookson Hills*. Stillwater, OK: New Forums Press, 2002.

———*The Bandit Kings of the Cookson Hills*. Stillwater, OK: New Forums Press, 2003.

———*Desperadoes: Rise and Fall of the Poe-Hart Gang*. Stillwater, OK: New Forums Press, 2003.

———*The Tri-State Terror: The Life and Crimes of Wilbur Underhill*. Stillwater, OK: New Forums Press, 2005.

Nash, Jay Robert. *Encyclopedia of Western Lawmen and Outlaws*. New York: DeCapo Press, 1994.

———*Blood Letters and Badmen*. New York: M. Evans and Company, 1973.

Newton, Willis and Joe. *The Newton Boys: Portrait of an Outlaw Gang*. Austin, TX: State House Press, 1994.

Nix, Evett Dumas. *Oklahombres: Particularly the Wilder Ones*. St. Louis, MO: Eden Publishing House, 1929.

Nolan, Frederick. *The West of Billy the Kid*. Norman: University of Oklahoma Press, 1998.

O'Neal, Bill. *Encyclopedia of Western Gunfighters*. Norman: University of Oklahoma Press, 1979.

Owens, Ron. *Oklahoma Justice, The Oklahoma City Police: A Century of Gunfighters, Gangsters and Tourists*. Paducah, KY: Turner Publishing Co., 1995.

Padgett, Ron. *Oklahoma Tough: My Father, King of the Tulsa Bootleggers*. Norman: University of Oklahoma Press, 2003.

Phillips, John Neal. *Running with Bonnie and Clyde: The Fast Years of Ralph Fults*. Norman: University of Oklahoma Press, 1996.

Poulsen, Ellen. *Don't Call Us Molls: Women of the John Dillinger Gang*. Little Neck, NY: Clinton Cook Publishing Corp., 2002.

Rasch, Phillip J. *Trailing Billy the Kid*. Stillwater, OK: Western Publications, 1995.

Ray, Grace Ernestine. *Wily Women of the West*. San Antonio, TX: The Naylor Company, 1972.

Reed, Nathaniel. *Life of Texas Jack*. Tulsa: Privately Published, 1936.

Rogers, Will. *The Papers of Will Rogers Vol. I*. Norman: University of Oklahoma Press, 1996.

Samuelson, Nancy B. *The Dalton Gang Story*. Dexter, MI: Thomson-Shore, 1992.

————*Shoot from the Lip.* Eastford, CT: Shooting Star Press, 1998.

Settle, William A., Jr. *Jesse James Was His Name.* Columbia, MO: University of Missouri Press, 1966.

Shirley, Glenn. *Belle Starr and Her Times: The Literature, The Facts, and The Legends.* Norman: University of Oklahoma Press, 1990.

————*Gunfight at Ingalls.* Stillwater, OK: Barbed Wire Press, 1990.

————*Guardian of the Law: The Life and Times of William Matthew Tilghman (1854-1924).* Austin, TX: Eakin Press, 1988.

————*Heck Thomas, Frontier Marshal.* Norman: University of Oklahoma Press, 1981.

————*Henry Starr: Last of the Real Badmen.* New York: David McKay Company, 1965.

————*Law West of Fort Smith.* Lincoln: University of Nebraska Press, 1971.

————*Marauders of the Indian Nations: The Bill Cook Gang and Cherokee Bill.* Stillwater, OK: Barbed Wire Press, 1994.

————*Shotgun for Hire.* Norman: University of Oklahoma Press, 1970.

————*Six-Gun and Silver Star.* Albuquerque: University of New Mexico Press, 1955.

————*Temple Houston: Lawyer with a Gun.* Norman: University of Oklahoma Press, 1980.

————*The Fourth Guardsman.* Austin, TX: Eakin Press, 1997.

————*They Outrobbed Them All: The Rise and Fall of the Viscious Martins.* Stillwater, OK: Barbed Wire Press, 1992.

————*Thirteen Days of Terror.* Stillwater, OK: Barbed Wire Press, 1996.

————*Toughest of Them All.* Albuquerque: University of New Mexico Press, 1953.

————*West of Hell's Fringe.* Norman: University of Oklahoma Press, 1978.

Shirk, George with a foreword by Muriel H. Wright. *Oklahoma Place Names.* Norman: University of Oklahoma Press, 1965.

Smith, Patterson. *Literature of the American Gangster.* Clifton, NJ: A. B. Bookman Publications, 1986.

Smith, Robert Barr. *Daltons! The Raid on Coffeyville, Kansas.* Norman: University of Oklahoma Press, 1996.

————*Last Hurrah of the James-Younger Gang.* Norman: University of Oklahoma Press, 2001.

Speer, Bonnie Stahlman. *Portrait of a Lawman: U.S. Deputy Marshal Heck Thomas.* Norman: Reliance Press, 1996.

————*The Killing of Ned Christie.* Norman, OK: Reliance Press, 1990.

Stansberry, Lon. *Passing of the 3-D Ranch.* Tulsa, OK: Privately Published, 1930.

Steele, Phillip and Cottrell, Steve. *Civil War in the Ozarks.* Gretna, LA: Pelican Publishing, 1993.

Steele, Phillip and Scoma, Marie Barrow. *The Family Story of Bonnie and Clyde.* Gretna, LA: Pelican Publishing, 2000.

Steele, Phillip. *Jesse and Frank James: The Family Story.* Gretna, LA: Pelican Publishing, 1987.

————*The Last Cherokee Warrior.* Gretna, LA: Pelican Publishing, 1987.

————*Starr Tracks: Belle and Pearl Starr.* Gretna, LA: Pelican Publishing, 1989.

Stiles, T. J. *Jesse James: Last Rebel of the Civil War.* New York: Vintage, 2002.

Svenvold, Mark. *Elmer McCurdy: The Misadventures in Life and Afterlife of an American Outlaw.* New York: Basic Books, 2003.

Tanner, Karen Holliday and Tanner, John D., Sr. *Last of the Old-Time Outlaws: The George Musgrave Story.* Fallbrook, CA: Runnin' Iron, 2003.

Trekell, Ronald L. *History of the Tulsa Police Department 1882-1990, Tulsa: The Department, 1989.* Tulsa: Privately Published, 1990.

Utley, Robert M. *High Noon in Lincoln: Violence on the Western Frontier.* Albuquerque: University of New Mexico Press, 1987.

————*Billy the Kid: A Short and Violent Life.* Lincoln: University of Nebraska Press, 1989.

Wallis, Michael. *Pretty Boy: The Life and Times of Charles Arthur Floyd.* New York: St. Martin's Press, 1992.

————*Oil Man: The Story of Frank Phillips and the Birth of Phillips Petroleum.* New York: St. Martin's Press, 1988.

Wellman, Paul I. *A Dynasty of Western Outlaws.* Lincoln: University of Nebraska Press, 1961.

Wilson, Edward. *An Unwritten History. A Record From the Early Days of Arizona.* Santa Fe: Stagecoach Press, 1966.

Winter, Robert. *Mean Men: Sons of Ma Barker.* Danbury, CT: Rutledge Books, 2000.

Witteringer, Clyde M. *Starting of Tulsa.* Tulsa: Winteringers, 1991.
Yeatman, Ted P. *Frank and Jesse James: The Story Behind the Legend.* Nashville, TN: Cumberland House, 2000.

Articles

Ahlquist, Diron Lacina. "On the Run in the Spavinaw Hills." *Oklahombres,* Vol. XVI, No. 3, Spring 2005.
————"Tom Horn's Indian Territory Manhunt." 16-17, *Oklahombres,* Vol. III, No. 3, Spring 1997.
Bartholomew, Ed. "Uncovering Myths of the Lincoln County War." *Wild West Magazine,* December 2004.
Bell, Roger L. "Mose Miller, Outlaw of the Greenleaf Hills." *Oklahombres,* Vol. VII, No. 1, Fall 1995.
Bunch, Steve. "Cattle Annie." *OKOLHA Journal,* Vol. 1, No. 1, Spring 2004.
Butler, Ken. "Outlaw Tom Slaughter—Even His Name Spelled Death." *Oklahombres,* Vol. VII, No. 1, Fall 1995.
————"Kansas Blood Spilled in Oklahoma." *OKOLHA Journal,* Vol. II, No. 1, Spring 2005
————"Bank Robber: George Birdwell, Blunder at Boley." Shawnee, OK: Privately Published.
————"The Devious Outlaw Career of Bob Rogers." *OKOLHA Journal,* Vol. 1, No. 3, Fall 2004.
Cloud, Jim. "DEAD: The Man Who Killed the Man Who Killed Jesse James." *Oklahombres,* Vol. III, No. 3, Spring 1992.
Cordry, H. D. (Dee). "Outlaws and Lawmen of the Cherokee Nation." *Oklahombres,* Vol. V, No. 1, Fall 1993.
————"Deadly Business, the Early Years of the Crime Bureau." *Chronicles of Oklahoma,* 63, No. 3, Fall 1985.
Ernst, Robert. "When Heck Thomas Was Charged With Murder!" *Oklahombres,* Vol. XVI, No. 3, Spring 2005.
Gibson, Wayne D. "More Like Comets Than Starrs, The Story of Tom Starr." *Oklahombres,* Vol. X, No. 1, Fall 1998.
Graham Leader Online. "An Outlaw Life." September 8, 2006.
Gumprecht, Blake. "A Saloon on Every Corner: Whiskey Towns of Oklahoma Territory, 1889-1907."*Chronicles of Oklahoma,* 74, No.

2, Summer 1996.

Haines, Joe D., Jr. "Life of an Osage Lawman." *Oklahombres,* Vol. VI, No. 4, Summer 1995.

————"The Log of a Frontier Marshall." *Chronicles of Oklahoma,* 59, No. 3, Fall 1981.

Keen, Patrick. "Bluford Blue Duck, Indian Territory Outlaw." *Oklahombres,* Vol. VIII, No. 1, Fall 1996.

Kirkwood, Herman. "Dr. Zeno Beem Blossom." *OKOLHA Journal,* Vol. 1, No. 1, Spring 2004.

Kirkwood, Kevin. "Corner Saloon." *Oklahombres,* Vol. XI, No. 4, Summer 2000.

Lockwood, Patricia W. "The Legacy of Caleb Starr." *Chronicles of Oklahoma,* 61, No. 3, Fall 1983.

Mattix, Rick. "Bob Brady: Forgotten Depression Outlaw." *Oklahombres,* Vol. III, No. 2, Winter 1992.

————"Bonnie and Clyde in Oklahoma." *Oklahombres,* Vol. II, No. 2, Winter 1991.

————"Southwestern Lawman Slew Dillinger." *Oklahombres,* Vol. VI, No. 1, Fall 1994.

May, John D. "The Most Ferocious of Monsters: The Story of Outlaw Crawford Goldsby, Alias Cherokee Bill." *Chronicles of Oklahoma,* Vol. 77, No. 3, Fall 1999.

Milligan, James C. and Norris, David, L. "The Last Choctaw Execution: A Case of Law and Disorder." *Chronicles of Oklahoma,* 73, No. 4, Winter 1995.

Morgan, R. D. "Severs Hotel Murder Mystery." Privately Published.

Perrin, Tony. "A Trail of Slain Officers," *Oklahombres,* Vol. III, No. 2, Winter, 1992.

Phillips, Glen A., Jr. "From Rackets to Ranches, Al Capone and the 101 Ranch." *Chronicles of Oklahoma,* 75, No. 2, Summer 1997.

Rucker, Alvin. "Newly Opened Pott County: Story of Keokuk Falls and Dripping Springs." *OKOLHA:* excerpted from *The Oklahoman,* November 20, 1932.

Samuelson, Nancy. "Flora Quick aka Mrs. Mundis aka Tom King aka China Dot." *OKOLHA Journal,* Vol. 1, No. 2, Summer 2005.

Shirley, Glenn. "What Price the Brain, An Unusual Case in Indian Territory." *Oklahombres,* Vol. II, No. 1, Fall 1990.

Smith, Robert Barr. "Badman in No Man's Land." *Wild West*

Magazine, February 1999.

————"Murder by Moonlight at Wild Horse Lake." *Wild West Magazine,* June 2003.

Tower, Michael. "Fred Tecumseh Waite: The Outlaw Statesman." *Chronicles of Oklahoma,* 76, No. 2, Summer 1998.

————"The French Family, Indian Territory Outlaws." *Oklahombres,* Vol. XVI, No. 1, Fall 2005.

Whitehead, Terry. "Sideshow Outlaw Elmer McCurdy," *Oklahombres,* Vol. X, No. 3, Spring 1999.

Williams, Nudie E. "United States vs. Bass Reeves: Black Lawman on Trial." *Chronicles of Oklahoma,* Vol. 68, No. 2, 1990.

————"Black Men Who Wore the Star." *Chronicles of Oklahoma,* Vol. 59, No. 1, 1981.

Interviews

Jones, W. F. "Memories of a Marshal: W. F. Jones—Former Territorial U.S. Deputy Marshal," April 19, 1937.

Newspapers

Cherokee Advocate
Chicago Sun Times
Daily Oklahoman
Holden Enterprise
Northwest Arkansas Times
Oklahoma Daily Times-Journal
Oklahoma Leader

Acknowledgments

A number of organizations assisted the authors in the development and preparation of this book over a period of three years. These included, but were not limited to: City-County Library, Tulsa, Oklahoma; Oklahoma Historical Society; Western History Collection, University of Oklahoma Library; Oklahoma Heritage Association; Oklahoma Centennial Commission; Woolaroc Museum, Bartlesville, Oklahoma; Dallas Public Library; Texas Jack Association; Oklahombres, Inc.; Oklahoma Outlaws, Lawmen History Association; Tulsa Police Department; Tulsa Beryl Ford Collection; Oklahoma Publishing Company; Lenapah Historical Society; the University of Tulsa; Kansas State Historical Society; Will Rogers Museum; National Cowboy Hall of Fame; Gilcrease Museum; The Haley Library; Enid Public Library; Boone County Heritage Museum, Harrison, Arkansas; and the Lincoln Heritage Trust, Lincoln, New Mexico.

Individuals who assisted us included Bill O'Neal, Nancy Samuelson, Bob Ernst, Ron Trekell, Armand DeGregoris, John R. Lovett, Mike Tower, Michael and Suzanne Wallis, Terry Zinn, Michael Koch, Diron Ahlquist, Willie Jones, Clyda Franks, Emily Lovick, Lisa Keys, Danielle Williams, Irene and Larry Chance, Glendon Floyd, Curt Johnson, Dee Cordry, Rik Helmerich, and Herman Kirkwood. Thanks are also due to Helen J. Gaines, Jim Bradshaw, Adrienne Grimmett, Beth Andreson, Dana Harrison MacMoy, Mary Phillips, Stacy M. Rogers, Rand McKinney, Jana Swartwood, Gini Moore Campbell, Phillip W. Steele, Colin Kelley, Mary Harris, Charles Harris, and Casey Duncan, reference librarian at the University of Texas at Austin Tarlton Law Library.

Last, without the patient guidance of our consulting editor, Robert Barr Smith, and the support of our respective spouses, Julia Anderson and Martha Yadon, this book would not have been possible.

Index